GREAT GLASGOW CHARACTERS

ACKNOWLEDGEMENTS

Because of the nature of the stories in *Great Glasgow Characters*, considerably more help from a wide variety of people was required in its research than the preceding edition. Most of those involved were either relatives or close friends of the subjects featured in this book. My sincere thanks goes out to each and every one of them, for without their help this book would most certainly not have been possible. In particular, I would like to express my personal gratitude to the following, listed in the order of the chapters in the book:

The Sure and Stedfast Man: John Neill, OBE, Battalion Secretary (retd), Boys' Brigade, Glasgow; Eric Woodburn, of the World Conference youth movement and Battalion Secretary, Boys' Brigade.

The Greatest-Ever Scoop: Mrs Kari Fair, Waterfoot; Robert Anderson, Rutherglen, ex-Anti-Aircraft Division, Royal Signals, Eaglesham; Gordon Stewart, Gargunnock, Stirling, ex-Home Guard, Eaglesham; Lex Watson, former PoW and ex-Scoutmaster, 28th Group, Giffnock; Max McAuslane, Newington, Edinburgh, journalist and former newspaper executive.

The Second Benny Lynch: Tommy Gilmour, manager and promoter; Frank O'Donnell, President, Scottish ex-Boxers Association; Brian Donald, boxing historian; Charlie Kerr, ex-champion boxer.

The Shocking Murder of a McFlannel: Gordon Irving, showbusiness writer and historian; Rikki Fulton; Elizabeth Watson, Scottish Theatre Archives.

Sweets Smell of Success: Lady Thomson, Inverleith, Edinburgh, the daughter of 'R.S.'; Dr Donald McColl, Newton Mearns, Glasgow; Mr J.C. Stokes, Whitecraigs; Paul Joannou, official historian to Newcastle United FC; Jed O'Brien and Anthony McReavie, Scottish National Soccer Museum; Robert McIlroy, Rangers historian; Shelley Hyams, Hyams Editorial Services, Chigwell, Essex.

Celtic's Saddest Day: Jimmy Laing, Leven; Tom Kirk, Cardenden; Jim Ferguson, Aberdour; Pat Woods, Celtic historian.

The Peterhead Papillon: William (Sonny) Leitch, Deans, Livingston; and Edith.

Guys and Dolls and Sammy Docherty: Norman Miller, Scottish Bookmakers Protection Association; James I. Wilson, Drummond Miller W.S., Edinburgh.

Axed for the Pope: Monsignor Tom Connelly; Monsignor Dan Hart; Hugh Farmer; Paddy and Kathleen at the Catholic Media Office.

He Was For the High Jump: Alan Paterson's sister, Professor Johanna Peters, London (who sadly died in May 2000); Mrs Anne Brown, Hutchesons Grammar; Colin Shields, Scottish Association of Track Statisticians; Wallace Crawford, secretary, Victoria Park AAC; Harry Ewing; Alan Heath; Walter G. Fyfe.

And, of course, no book about Glasgow could ever be completed without the willingness and competence of the staff at The Glasgow Room, Mitchell Library, together with those equally helpful researchers at the *Daily Record* and *Sunday Mail* Library; Fife Central Library; the Cardenden Public Library; the Catholic Press Office, Glasgow; and the Army Records Office, Hayes, Middlesex.

GREAT GLASGOW CHARACTERS

JOHN BURROWES

MAINSTREAM
PUBLISHING

EDINBURGH AND LONDON

This edition 2010

Copyright © John Burrowes, 2000
All rights reserved
The moral right of the author has been asserted

First published in Great Britain in 2000 by
MAINSTREAM PUBLISHING COMPANY (EDINBURGH) LTD
7 Albany Street
Edinburgh EH1 3UG

ISBN 9781845966799

A catalogue record for this book is available from the British Library

Typeset in Bembo and Ellington
Printed in Great Britain by
CPI Cox and Wyman, Reading, Berkshire RG1 8EX

CONTENTS

PREFACE

In the Preface to *Great Glasgow Stories*, I remarked that few cities in the world abound with greater stories than Scotland's greatest city. And it's because of the truth of that statement that *Great Glasgow Characters* has come about, for the further I researched into the annals of the city in my quest for these great stories, the more unpublished and unknown details of the most significant and colourful events of our times I discovered. I found not only new and amazing aspects of some of our greatest and best-known stories, but other events, which had never been so fully recorded as here. For instance, when inquiring into the life story of one of Glasgow's greatest ever athletes, I discovered a great human drama of love and bigotry in a family, and how this has affected them and so many other families in recent decades.

It was vividly illustrated in the research for this book that so many of the great stories which have happened in Glasgow, or are about the incredible achievements of the colourful characters who lived in the city, have really only been partially told. For the first time amazing new facts have been uncovered about some of the greatest of these great stories. For instance, one of the most sensational incidents of the Second World War was when a German Messerschmitt plane crash-landed in a field just over the Glasgow boundary. The pilot who came down by parachute was none other than Hitler's second in command. Despite the sensational arrival of Rudolf Hess being the subject of numerous investigations, books, magazine serialisations and TV documentaries, much of that remarkable story of those days in and around Glasgow, the chaotic and hilarious incidents which occurred that summer's night between a cow pasture near Eaglesham and Maryhill Barracks in Glasgow, has not been fully told before.

This truly incredible story of what really happened that night in and around Glasgow in the early years of the war is just one of the highlights of *Great Glasgow Characters*.

The most colourful member of Scotland's criminal community in the twentieth century was the man they called 'Gentle Johnny' . . . the famous cat-burglar and safe-blower Johnny Ramensky, who came to live in Glasgow's East End and latterly the Gorbals. He was such an expert in the art – he had mastered getting into obscure offices and premises and opening strongrooms and safes – that he was parachuted into enemy territory in order to rob Hitler's top officials' safes. But secret Government papers, unseen for 40 years, are now uncovered in full for the first time and reveal a whole new, and most revealing, story about Johnny Ramensky.

Everyone knows about Ally McCoist, Jim Baxter, Kenny Dalglish and all the other great stars of the Scottish soccer scene. But just who was our very first Scottish football star? Surprisingly, he was a Glasgow man whose very name is known today in every household in Scotland . . . yet that same name has nothing to do with his sensational sporting achievements for Rangers and Scotland and for one of England's top clubs. For, as well as being our first-ever soccer star, he was one of Scotland's greatest business entrepreneurs, his name living on above hundreds of shops throughout Britain.

The grim discovery of a dead man in a Govan flat was one of the most sensational murders Glasgow has known, for that man happened to be one of the BBC's best-known personalities, while one of the leading witnesses to give evidence in the High Court was a man who has now been named one of the most outstanding Scots of the twentieth century. Just one of the surprising details to emerge in 'The Shocking Murder of a McFlannel'.

And the full story of Celtic's saddest day; of the man who was Scotland's second Benny Lynch; and those most colourful *Guys and Dolls* of days of the Glasgow street bookie are just some of the other captivating and intriguing tales included in *Great Glasgow Characters*.

John Burrowes,
Glasgow, 2000

THE SURE AND STEDFAST MAN

There were only around 30 of them who turned up on that first historic night. All were young lads, some being described as a bit on the disorderly side, others bent on mischief. But most were curious. They wanted to know just what this new venture at the North Woodside Mission Hall in North Woodside Road, in the West End of Glasgow, was all about. The locals lads had never heard of anything like it before and their numbers were bolstered on the following two nights when even more lads appeared. When the second week came around, however, many had already decided that one night had been enough for them. Nevertheless, that still left more than half of those who originally turned up to return and enjoy the novel idea from the incomer to Glasgow who had been searching for an effective cure for young lads who got bored and became disruptive during their Sunday School lessons. That idea was to be so successful it was to sweep the world. They called it . . . the Boys' Brigade. It was not only the first-ever youth organisation, but the one to which almost every other movement for the young owes its existence.

It's not the kind of new idea that one might associate with registering, let alone taking off in the new millennium. And yet the Boys' Brigade, the illustrious BB, lives on. And how! There are over 108 companies of them in Glasgow with more than 6,000 members . . . more than 40,000 in Scotland . . . more than 104,000 in the UK . . . and more than half a million young people throughout the world in youth organisations inspired by and affiliated to the movement. And all because of the far-sightedness and perspicacity into the behaviour of young people by a good-living Christian who had come to live in Glasgow and was called William Alexander Smith.

That it is remarkable that such success was to emanate from a movement with such amazing and consuming popularity throughout the world is to an extent an adjunct of the many other happenings in the Glasgow of the turn of the century. For at that period in its eventful history, a basic fact is that in this particular period Glasgow was an altogether remarkable place.

It was the Mecca of Scotland, countless thousands flocking to what had become the country's biggest city in order to be part of the revolution in industry that had the world knocking on its door for the goods it was inventing, creating and producing. There were ships, the like of which no one had made before, whether they be faster, bigger or better designed. It was the same with locomotives that were to haul the passenger and goods trains of the world, as well as all kinds of engines and machinery, bathroom equipment, textiles, chemicals and carpets, hydraulics and prismatics, and all things engineering. Glasgow made more of them than anyone else. And it made them better, too.

The city throbbed with innovation and improvisation. It bristled, too, with pioneers of other sorts, such as doctors, nurses and missionaries and that special breed of people who cared about social deprivation and how life could be improved for the underprivileged masses. Many were to go out to the furthest-flung corners of the world carrying with them the zeal that had been spawned in Glasgow. The city had considerably more than 300 buildings and meeting places for the 30 denominations of the Church, and thousands devoted their free time to the various forms of outgoing work that was instigated and carried on by them.

As well as out there in the world, there was plenty to do right here at home, with souls to be saved, the spirit to be salved in the city that teemed with the incomers who had flocked to its boundaries seeking some share in its prosperity. That the scale of that prosperity was of the scantiest of proportions is as much a comment on the wretched life and times in the villages and glens from where they had come as it is on the factory owners and masters of the day. Housing standards were so dire that more than 30 per cent of the city's households consisted of peope who lived, ate and slept in just one shared room, and yet even that was better than the life they had left to come here, whether that had been in the remote areas of the Highlands or Lowlands, or else escaping from the famines or religious intolerances of a multitude of countries.

Zeal and passion abounded among those fortunates whose social strata amounted to more than that one-room abode. To help in some way, albeit if that was merely to gain recruits for the denomination among which they spent their Sunday devotions, was a way of life for thousands.

It was with William Alexander Smith, an earnest young man with the fashionable walrus moustache of the day, and who, like the majority at the time, was one of those incomers to the city. Unlike most who came, Smith's arrived in Glasgow to grasp opportunities, rather than out of necessity. He was a young lad of 15 when he had travelled south from his remote, but rather handsome and commodious, home at Pennyland, in Caithness, which overlooked Dunnet Head, that unique headland which thumbs out into the wild winds of the Pentland Firth and is the most northerly point on the British mainland. His uncle Fraser had a soft goods business in Glasgow and work as a clerk had been secured for him there.

Smith came from a breed of Scot that gets the appellation 'solid stock'. Father had been an officer in the army. So had grand-dad. They worked hard for six days of the week and on a Sunday the Bible was in their hands, their place was in the family pews of the local church. Later generations were to take different views of that acceptance of life, but around the turn of the century it was the plain Mr Smiths of Scotland who were the rock foundation of the country, the base material of the onward-Christian-soldiers people who, with God in their hearts, were ready and prepared to march and lay down their lives to defend that way of life. In the name of their country, this fearless and courageous breed would wander in unknown deserts, trek across uncharted snowlands, penetrate the most impenetrable of jungles and sail to places where no one had ever ventured before.

The young Master Smith looked like following in the footsteps of his forebears' militaristic ways, and shortly after arriving in Glasgow was to enrol in the 1st Lanarkshire Rifle Volunteers, a precursor of the Territorial Army.

It was in the days long before the drip-feed of telecommunications, or discos and voguish lounge bars into which entry depended on passing scrutineers who imposed some unspecified label-and-looks trend test. Giving your free time to some form of community service was as much a part of routine life as being a sports fan was to be in later years, and there was as much prestige and cachet about being in the ranks of certain volunteer army groupings as later years were to have in being a member of certain socially celebrated golf, sports and country clubs.

Between work, the Volunteers and his activities with the Free

College Church, the life of the young Mr Smith was well and truly occupied. He especially loved his time with the Volunteers, with its blend of camaraderie and social discourse. His Sunday work as a Sabbath School teacher among the local youth in Woodside he had found more challenging, more perplexing. Why, he would often ask, is it that so many of the younger lads at his Mission Sunday School in North Woodside Road, just off Great Western Road, didn't share his enthusiasm? Just what is happening to the youth of today, he would often ask and discuss among his colleagues in the Volunteers and the church. They could be so inattentive, often disobedient, sometimes downright unruly, and apparently the only reason they were there at all on a Sunday was because their parents were practising Christians and insisted on their attendance.

In contrast, the lads in the Volunteers were never like that. They were genuine and willing volunteers and all that drilling and discipline was obviously enjoyed by each and every one of them. Drilling and discipline, orders and obedience! Could that be it, Smith wondered? Was this the vital ingredient which instilled the *esprit de corps* in the Volunteers and which was lacking in their Sabbath Schools? Was it also because Sunday School was so much like ordinary day school, where they sat in class and they had to pay attention to the person standing at the front of the room and who was called teacher? Was it because they had enough of that kind of school during the week that they showed their boredom with it on a Sunday? Could it not be that drill and discipline might be somehow combined or intermingled with their Sabbath classes so that it might possibly alleviate the tedium?

Maybe even add some games and gymnastics to go along with the psalms and scriptures. Drill and discipline, orders and obedience, games and gymnastics! Of course, that was just the very thing that his Sunday School boys needed. At least that was the conclusion he was to put to some friends who were also Volunteers and Sabbath teachers, and, like-wise convinced, they were to formulate the scheme which they considered would be the answer to those bored and reluctant boys they faced every week.

Smith's own words on the subject were that their aim was to devise something that would appeal to a boy on the heroic side of his nature; something that would let him see that in the service of God there was as much scope for all that is brave and true and manly as in the service of King and Country.

The incredible success of the movement which was to be the world's first successful voluntary uniformed youth organisation is not reflected in its first few outings. Smith and his friends had told the pupils of the mission Sunday School about the new venture which it would be fun and enjoyable to join and allocated three nights of that week in October 1883 for recruiting purposes. The 28 who came along on the first night had been from the Sunday School and the further 31 who were to appear the following two nights were local lads from the North Woodside area. That made a total of 59, but the prospect of being brave and true and manly, even in those most conscientious of days, was obviously too much for almost half of them, only 35 showing up for that second historic meeting of the Boys' Brigade in that little hall in North Woodside Road. But that was to be enough to encourage Smith and his friends that not only was there merit in their idea, there also was enthusiasm on the part of the boys.

It was in an era for new movements of varying sorts. The new sport called soccer was becoming firmly established, and not all that many years previously they had formed a club they called Rangers.

And within a few years of the humble birth of that small group of lads in North Woodside Road they were to call the Boys' Brigade, yet another soccer club, to be as equally famous as the one called Rangers, appeared on the scene. It was called Celtic.

The fact that so many boys had returned for further participation in the novel youth meeting was to confirm to Smith and his friends that there would be no question of them having to surrender their founding principle of discipline, one of the first rules being that the Thursday evening parade would be at eight o'clock . . . on the dot. This meant that if a boy was as much as a minute late, he would not be allowed to 'fall in'. Neither would they be allowed to miss two consecutive drills.

The initial shock of the seemingly strict discipline might have been hard to take, but it was to prove quickly and easily acceptable by those who enjoyed the other activities that went with the weekly parades. This was a novel way of getting the Bible without the boredom, of making the hymnal something less than dismal. And word spread round the high-density Woodside area, boundaried by Garscube and Great Western roads, that here was a way of spending evenings in the company of pals where, despite what might be the lofty sentiments of the founding officers, you really could have fun in the games and competition amidst the drilling and discipline. And on Sundays it put a whole new meaning too into those Sabbath-day lessons.

After just three months, the group which was to be called the 1st Glasgow Company of the Boys' Brigade had become established enough to be divided into six squads, each with their own non-commissioned officer, all being promoted from those first recruits, two of them being made sergeants, four sharing the ranks of corporal and lance-corporal. They had also completed their first examinations from the work they had been given, which involved tests on conduct and character as well as the bedrock of drill and discipline.

And they had their own BB badge, that being an anchor, with the motto 'Sure and Stedfast'. And it is spelt 'stedfast', not 'steadfast', the spelling coming straight from the Bible itself (chapter six, Epistle to the Hebrews: 'Which hope we have as an anchor of the soul, both sure and stedfast').

The news was quickly to be picked up by other districts about how lucky the boys in Woodside were to have this great new activity. At the start of its second year, there was still only that 1st Company, but by the end of that year another company had been formed in nearby Charing Cross, followed shortly by a further ten which sprang up in surrounding areas, with another two starting up in Edinburgh.

The Boys' Brigade was on the move. As well as that badge and motto, they also had a uniform, designed strictly along the lines of Smith himself who resisted any attempts to have a full dress uniform, such as he and his fellow officers had when they served with the Lanarkshire Volunteers. The uniform for the BB, it was decreed, should merely be the semblance of regimentality but, more important, it would be economical. And, at a total cost of just 7½p, that indeed it was to be. It consisted of a belt, a cloth haversack, initially meant to carry rations but redesigned to become purely decorative, and a plain pillbox cap, similar to the type worn by many army regiments of the day (the two white stripes, chinstrap and white button being added some time later).

Because of the military background of Smith and his fellow founding officers, they saw their young Christian soldiers as almost real, junior troops, and what's a soldier without a gun? On a tour of the States, to where the Brigade spread within four years of its foundation in Glasgow, the movement's great propagandist, Professor Henry Drummond, of the Free Church College, had addressed students at Harvard University. Naturally, he was to include the Boys' Brigade in part of his address, telling the collegians that while no power on earth would make boys sit up in class on a Sunday, 'put a fivepenny cap on them and call them "soldiers", which they are not, and you can order them about till midnight'.

The wise professor may have spoken the disagreeable truth boldly, but the embellishment of these young soldiers with dummy rifles, which most companies now displayed, was to involve the Brigade in its first real controversy. On drill nights and weekly parades, the young boy members sloped, ordered and presented their arms with all the military slickness of the best of army regiments. But in the years following the Great War, an era concerned with peace rather than parades, more than eyebrows were raised. Such was the reaction from an otherwise admiring public to the movement that many companies were forced to renounce the use of their imitation guns and by 1926 they were abandoned by the Brigade.

In the age of the Game Boy, Playstation, video, disco and the packaged sunshine holiday, perhaps nothing better highlights how times have changed than the regime of the summer camps in those early days of the Boys' Brigade. The camps were the most treasured days of a season's service with the Brigade. They would spend most of the year planning, preparing, training, saving and anticipating them. The annual camp had come about as an answer to the question asked by founder Smith and his senior commanders of how they could keep in touch with members during the summer months' recess. And that answer had been – summer camp. Again it was a military response, but unlike the use of rifles, this was to be a most acceptable and unquestioned one.

Various companies began their preparation, all with soldierly efficiency, of course, detailing how much overall equipment the company would require: tents, bales of straw (for makeshift mattresses), games and sports gear, food per camper, and each boy being detailed what equipment they must bring (to include Bible and hymnal), their clothing (including one blanket, a towel and, if they possessed them, a change of clothing) as well as working out the cost, which included train fare, food and tent hire, which for those first camps came to 45p per week, per boy, payable by 1½p weekly instalments to be handed over at parade nights.

The boys of the 1st Company in Woodside went to Tighnabruaich

– and still go to that area – for their early camps where the daily routine, as it was in other companies' camps, was set out to the minute and invariably went along such lines: 6 a.m. reveille; 7 a.m. swimming followed by biscuits; 9 a.m. the bugle call, 'Come to the cookhouse door, boys', announcing breakfast; 9.45 a.m. morning prayers; 10.45 a.m. dress bugle; 11 a.m. camp inspection and full-dress parade; 1.45 p.m. dinner bugle; 5.45 p.m. tea bugle; 7 p.m. to the boats for fishing in the loch; 9.30 p.m. evening prayers; 9.45 p.m. evening tattoo (return to quarters); 10 p.m. lights out.

As you can see, those early holiday outings were more like boot camp than Benidorm, but the cold routine statistics don't tell all the story. There was lots of fun, frolics and football in between those parades and bugle calls, one Paisley company even arranging to take with them a full-sized piano from their church to Kilchattan Bay on the island of Bute and later reporting it was one of the best innovations at their annual camp. The camps, too, represented for many of the lads their first-ever holiday, the first time they had seen mountains and lochs, real sheep and cows, running wild and carefree in heather and grass, and who would ever forget the appetites which all that expended energy in the fresh air gave them.

As a result of sponsorship from some of Glasgow's leading and wealthiest businessmen, a trust was formed to administer the burgeoning Brigade's funds, and improved headquarters accommodation, which had initially been in Bath Street, was secured in Buchanan Street, where founder Smith took up office as the first full-time secretary of the movement. His creation by now had grown beyond his wildest expectations, there being companies in every town in Scotland, and by its tenth birthday there was already a small army of them throughout the rest of the country, the membership figure amounting to 26,000.

Overseas it had spread like wildfire, sweeping through the United States, across colonial Africa, down to South Africa, out to Australia, to New Zealand and Polynesia, 75,000 of them all within those first ten years.

For the most obvious of reasons, only in Northern Ireland had there been problems in establishing Boys' Brigade companies. When they were first mooted for Belfast, the city magistrates threw up their hands in horror. What, they asked? Someone trying to form a religious youth movement, who would be out on the streets marching like soldiers and even shouldering what had every appearance of real rifles! In the Belfast of more than 100 years ago, as understandable a reaction as it would be now.

In their objections, the magistrates were to make reference to the Whiteboys Act, which sounds more like something out of Alabama than Antrim. The Whiteboys were, in fact, out of Ireland, being a secret society which dated back to the second half of the eighteenth century and which had exercised a powerful and often ruthless sway in the countryside, originally offering protection to the peasantry from the worst excesses of grasping landlords. One of their practices was to carry out their exercises at night wearing white sheets with blackened faces, the mere prospect of which has a particularly chilling connotation. The Whiteboys' activities in later years also targeted Orangemen and authority in general, so much so that less than 20 years prior to that first attempt to establish the BB in Belfast they had been proscribed under legislation known as the Whiteboys Act. All of which makes the early reactions of those Belfast magistrates to the prospect of the Boys' Brigade in their midst more than comprehensible. After talks in Glasgow with Smith, however, the Belfast pioneers were to persist and a company was formed within five years of the birth of the Brigade in Glasgow. Nevertheless, in a society wracked with the intolerances which it has, care had to be taken over the years – as it still does – over the flaunting of the fact that you belong to a particular religious movement.

Despite such obvious problems, there are companies of Boys' Brigade in Ulster as, perhaps surprisingly, there are in Dublin where there are still 16 active companies.

The formation of the hugely popular youth movement was to inspire the beginnings of other similar organisations, although many have since ceased to exist. These included the Church Lads' Brigade, the Jewish Lads' Brigade, the Catholic Boys' Brigade, Catholic Boys' Guilds, the Cadet Corps and the Boys' Life Brigade, the latter amalgamating with the BB. There were also parallel organisations for girls, such as the Girls' Guildry, the Girls' Life Brigade and the Girl Guides.

By far the most successful of all such youth organisations prompted into existence by the BB is the Boy Scout movement. Its beginnings were a result of a visit by General Baden-Powell, on his return from the Boer War in South Africa, to the Albert Hall Display of the BB, a sell-out occasion at the prestigious London venue. It was to prove something of an inspiring evening for the man being hailed as the great war hero, for afterwards, when his party had gone to the home of Lady Robertson, mother of the London BB battalion's president, after many hours of deep discussion into the great need for other suchlike youth organisations, he had conceived the idea for the scouting movement. A plaque in that London house commemorates the eventful meeting and how it inspired the creation of the Boy Scouts Association which, because it was not to be affiliated with the Protestant or any other specific church, was to spread to many more countries than the BB and to eclipse all other youth movements.

In 1933, the BB was to reach a pinnacle of its own with its golden jubilee celebrations in the city of its birth, held in and around Hampden Park and which takes its place in Glasgow's history as being at that time the biggest-ever gathering of people ever seen in the city. A review was conducted at the Queen's Park Recreation Ground on Saturday, 10 September of that year, with a parade of 32,520 officers and boys, inspected by Prince George, later to be King.

The following day a convention of Hollywood dimensions was held at Hampden Park, attracting the greatest crowd ever gathered there . . . 130,000 inside the ground and, unable to hold any more, a further 100,000 outside.

Sadly, founder Smith, who was knighted for his outstanding contribution to the youth of the country, did not live to see that greatest day in the movement's history, having died of a cerebral haemorrhage at the age of 59 while on a visit to London in early 1914. His funeral, following a memorable service in St Paul's Cathedral, was one of the greatest burial services to be witnessed in Glasgow, some 170,000 lining the route as the cortège made its way from Kelvingrove Church to the Western Necropolis where boys from the 1st Company, the one he had begun that night more than 30 years previously in the North Woodside hall, touchingly paid a final tribute to their founder by each dropping a white lily on his coffin.

While having no bearing whatsoever on the impressive and memorable funeral rites of the great boys' leader, there was to be another noteworthy event in that very same area of the city on that cold winter's morning. It was to be the major story of the day. A bomb had rocked the West End of the city and because Irish terrorists had previously targeted the Dawsholm gasworks, the gasworks were at first thought to be the objective once more. But those first reports were to be wrong on both counts. For, although the bombers' purpose had been to create some form of terror, their target was probably the most innocuous objective in the city, unless you were a tropical plant, that is. It had been the splendid Kibble Palace at the Botanic Gardens and in the journalese of the time, 'evidence indicates that the dastardly attempt to blow up the Kibble Palace was the work of militant Suffragettes whose plans had been well laid'.

An alert fire watchman had noticed the burning fuse of a bomb attached to the foundations of the building. He had bravely put his foot on the smouldering string only to be shocked with the discovery that it had continued to burn and, just as it was about to reach the bomb itself, he had opened his pocket knife and cut off the glowing fuse. It was when he was carrying this bomb out of the glassed gardens' structure that a second device had gone off, causing considerable damage to the fabric of the building.

And how did they know that these had been the dastardly activities of the Suffragettes? Again, the morning papers had the answer, and note how, in the language of the day, those involved were referred to not as females, women or girls – they were ladies! Reported the *Daily Record*: 'Superintendent James Muir of the Maryhill Division was early on the scene along with a number of detective officers and constables . . . Near to the spot where the explosion occurred were found together a lady's black silk veil and a piece of white cotton cloth and a newspaper in which it is thought the bombs had been carried. Police discovered that the visitors had partaken of refreshments during their vigil. Pieces of cake and an empty champagne bottle were recovered from the shrubbery . . . The marks on the soft ground bore the impression of high-heels of ladies' shoes. The ladies appear to have made their escape over the wall at Windsor Terrace before the police arrived.'

Silk veils, cake and champagne! These subversives came with some style!

And elsewhere in the newspapers of that day in 1914 another unrelated but just as noteworthy story was the one which detailed that there had been 'an encouraging report with regard to the progress made during the past year by the movement in favour of self-government'. The report was that of the Scottish Home Rule Council.

Following the death of Sir William, his son Stanley followed him into the post as the leader of the Boys' Brigade, the family connection with the great youth organisation dying out with his death. A plaque in the crypt of Westminster Cathedral commemorates the outstanding achievement of Sir William Smith and a contingent, usually of boys from the London battalion, attends a brief commemorative service held there each year on the 4 October anniversary date of the founding of the worldwide movement.

Glasgow has its own heritage trail of historic Boys' Brigade sites, mainly in the Hillhead area. There are the various houses where the founder lived, namely at 38 Hamilton Park Terrace, where he first stayed when he came to Glasgow as a boy of 14; a house in the block at Nos. 9 to 11 Kersland Street; 4 Southpark Avenue; 12 Bower Street and 13 Belmont Crescent. The North Woodside Mission Hall in North Woodside Road, birthplace of the 1st Glasgow Company and the very movement itself, is still there, although now in commercial and private use.

Sir William Smith or any of the other early pioneers of the BB would find it hard to recognise the movement which now exists as a descendant of their creation, the Boys' Brigade. The actual title of the movement is one of the few items in its make-up that has gone unchanged. But, then, changing and adapting have been part of its survival and its continuing success. Those controversial drill rifles which were dispensed with back in the '20s were perhaps the first sign that the BB wasn't to be over-steadfast about its role as a youth movement. All that's left of these rifles are the two which were kept for historical purposes and which are on display in glass cases in the organisation's museum, which occupies part of the ground-floor foyer at Boys' Brigade House, a spruce and modern upmarket office building in Bath Street, Glasgow, premises owned by the movement for nearly 70 years.

Gone, too, are many of the other accessories and adjuncts which had been so long a part of the image of the BB, not the least of these the uniforms. The old pillbox hat has long since gone, replaced in the early '70s with a forage cap, and more recently all headgear was dropped completely. Even the emblematic white haversack has been dispensed with, and the officers have dropped their Glengarry caps. And their modern uniforms of recent years are being changed yet again to what they term as their uniform for the millennium. For most sections, this will consist of sweatshirts and polo shirts, only the colour varying to denote the varying sections, all worn with plain-coloured trousers. Even the officers will be dressed in a similar turnout.

While the BB still believes that discipline is one of its key codes, it is administered in what it terms 'a much more user-friendly' way in the '90s. Boys no longer have to wait outside if they are a minute or so late for evening parade. Parades and drilling, too, have been toned down and there's an ongoing pulling away from anything militaristic, some even seeing the day when words like 'companies' and 'battalion' may disappear from Brigade terminology.

There have also been vast changes in the way the BB relates to its members and affiliates throughout the world. It was fully cognisant of the loosening of colonial ties by scores of countries who at one time were part of the British empire. And in the post-war years, just as that had been dismantled, so too were appropriate adjustments made to the relationship between outposts and the home of the Brigade. Each country member became fully autonomous and instead of having a UK headquarters, a link authority was established. This is known as the World Conference, designed to share resources and co-ordinate the work of Christian Youth Organisations descended from or inspired by the BB and which now exist in more than 70 countries around the world, involving more than half a million young people, a third of its members now being girls. The World Conference is based in Helensburgh and acts as that focal point for those scores of nations' youth movements.

'We're still here because we are prepared to change,' says the Glasgow battalion secretary John Neil. 'Everything changes and we are conditioned by developments in society.'

And that keynote in their attitude towards modern society should keep the movement steadfast, no matter how they spell it, for a long time to come.

To ensure their future, in the summer of 2000 the movement saw the opening of a new £1 million sports and conference centre at Carronvale House, the organisation's Scottish headquarters in Larbert. Wishing it well, Sir Alex Ferguson, the Manchester United manager, said he had a lot for which to thank the Boys' Brigade as included in his B.B. experience had been his introduction to soccer. And many, many more than Sir Alex, who have made their mark in life in a variety of ways, would no doubt echo his sentiments about the benefits the B.B. gave them in their formative years. Some who spring to mind are sportsmen Allan Wells, Cameron Sharp, Kenny Dalglish, Ally McCoist, Danny McGrain, Dave McPherson, Ian Ferguson, personalities Ross King, James Prime (Deacon Blue), Alistair McDonald, Archie MacPherson, Ken Bruce, Rikki Fulton, Andy Cameron, Cliff Richard, Ian McCaskill, the late Roy Castle, former Metropolitan Chief Constable Sir David McNee, and the Scottish Parliament's presiding officer Sir David Steel.

THE GREATEST-EVER SCOOP

The man who was to come to Maryhill in Glasgow in 1941 was to be the key figure in one of the most bizarre episodes in the history of two great wars. They still speculate as to why he came and such is the sensitivity of just why he did, that many of the documents, which have the full details of the amazing behind-the-scenes activities of the politicians of several nations sparked off by the incident, are still classified by the Government as top-secret papers and will continue to be so until their release date in 2017.

Nevertheless, what is known about these sensational days in and around Maryhill in Glasgow is that the man being held there was the sole focal point of judgements which would affect the outcome of the Second World War. Decisions made about him and why he was in Glasgow could cost millions of lives, and could even alter the entire course of world history. For that man who came to Glasgow in 1941 was Rudolf Hess, the 47-year-old deputy to the greatest and most loathsome dictator ever, Adolf Hitler. His flight from Germany and subsequent imprisonment in Maryhill, albeit for only a few days, make it one of the most amazing stories ever connected with Scotland's greatest city. And in researching for this account of his arrival here, I was to discover from various sources, including two of the remaining actual eyewitnesses to Hess's landing, a very different and amusing aspect of his arrival here. An aspect which includes the story of a boy on his bike with a gun, an officer who had been somewhat, as it were, 'well refreshed', a special constable who, it appeared, was anxious to be that way, and the commotion at a Home Guard base when Hess arrived amidst a fish-and-chips supper. And I was to discover too the most logical explanation of just why Hess mistakenly landed in that field at Eaglesham. And more. But first, let's look at those times in our city more than half a century ago.

Despite it being the dark days of the war, many aspects of Glasgow life in 1941 continued just as they had been for decades before. Although normal football was suspended for the duration, games were played, although contested before restricted crowds because of the fear of air attacks, the teams themselves being reduced in stature by reason of most of their star players, being the fit men they were, serving with the armed forces. Yet, some soccer matters were as normal as they had known them up to that time – and were to know for many years to come – as the *Glasgow Herald* had reported following yet another major riot at a football ground. Little need to detail on whose behalf the riot erupted. Rangers. Yes, and Celtic. 'Times were back to normal at Ibrox last night,' said the newspaper, 'at least so far as football as played between Rangers and Celtic is concerned.'

The inimitable Rex, one of the greatest Scottish football writers of all time, was to remark that while many had commented on what these two clubs had done for the game, not enough had been said about what they had done *to* the game. And Alan Breck, another sports writing legend, was to say that you didn't have to go to France to see the fighting. 'If the appeal of these two teams was to be based on what had happened at Ibrox, the future of the game is a dismal one indeed,' intoned Breck, whose real name happened to be Archie Wilson.

What, perhaps, has changed much less in soccer terms since those wartime days is the performance of the Scottish national team. Despite it being wartime, there was an international with England at Hampden Park and despite, too, the fact there were crowd restrictions, somehow 75,000 managed to turn out just days before Hess's arrival to watch this Scotland versus England match, although in the case of the Scots many would have wished they hadn't bothered. Our national team was to play with all the lack of lustre which, sadly, seems to characterise so many of its vital international matches.

As if to demonstrate that there's nothing new in football writing, the great Rex was to describe the meeting as 'a game of two halves'! Although, Rex being Rex, he put it in slightly more colourful terms, writing, 'It was a game of two haufs', and comparing it to having a couple of small whiskies. The first 'hauf', he wrote, went down a treat, that meaning they had been level at one goal each and our boys had done not too badly, although they had been starting to fade as the half wore on, or, more precisely, the English had by then warmed up! And the second 'hauf', said Rex, was a right mess, as bad as dribbling your whisky down your shirt. In other words, the Scottish team gave up after having taken an early lead and got trounced 3–1 for their lack of effort, or talent, or both. For *aficionados* the team was: Dawson (Rangers); Carabine (Third Lanark), Shaw (Rangers); Shankly (captain, Preston North End), Dykes (Hearts), T. Brown (Hearts); Gillick (Rangers), Walker (Hearts), Smith (Rangers), Venters (Rangers) and Caskie (St Mirren).

Elsewhere in Glasgow, there was a valiant effort to keep as much of routine as normal as possible, it being most vital that in what were our most desperate days everything was done to maintain public morale. Most cinemas and dance halls were still open and even premises which suffered bomb damage would do their utmost to keep running, the great and proud slogan of the day being pronounced through the posting of 'business as usual' notices.

The bustling theatre scene offered considerably more live entertainment than the present day. At the King's there was the customary *Half-Past Eight Show* – funny thing, though, it started at 7.45 p.m.! – starring such big names of the day as Jewel and Warriss, an earlier decade's Morecambe and Wise; the Metropole had *Suicide Sal*, with that much-loved Glasgow duo, Frank and Doris Droy; while others had much more long-forgotten names, such as the 'all-star' variety show at the Pavilion with Hal Swain and his Swing Sisters and the Two Rascals; and at the Empress the Ringle Brothers and Renee. And if you didn't fancy any of them you could dance the night away for 10p before Sydney Kyte and his band at Green's Playhouse.

The incredible mission by Rudolf Hess from Germany to Scotland that year was made in the belief that a meeting with the Duke of Hamilton would be the starting point in negotiating a form of peace deal between the two countries. It is still a matter of speculation whether or not Hitler and others in the German High Command had sanctioned the flight and the terms he proposed to put to the British Government. Those secret papers, classified until 2017, may even reveal some duplicity involving Churchill and his awareness of the attempted peace manoeuvre. There is evidence that there was some cognisance, even the suggestion that his flight had been accompanied by marauding RAF fighter-bomber planes. Close friends of Hess were convinced by their conversations with him that he had in fact discussed his proposals with Hitler who had given them his complete blessing, as had Goering, their obese head of the Luftwaffe, the German air force, and the next most senior in the dictatorship. All of which was possible and more than likely to be true, but nevertheless most strenuously denied by the Nazis as soon as Hess had made his landing, and they were aware he was being held in Maryhill on the orders of Churchill himself, not as a peace-bearing negotiator but as a detested enemy and a prisoner.

There was conjecture, too, over just why he had chosen the Duke of Hamilton, Scotland's premier peer and Keeper of the Palace of Holyroodhouse. His family was steeped in the bluest of blue Scottish blood, a family that had always strived to live up to their motto 'Never Behind', just as his great ancestor, the first duke, had done back in the seventeenth century when he had led the Scottish army at the Battle of Preston, only to have been defeated then beheaded.

The Duke had been at Eton and Oxford (Balliol) and all that, but this was no pampered peer, Hamilton being much more than the conventional blueblood. As a sportsman he had been the Scottish amateur middleweight boxing champion and toured a variety of countries giving exhibition bouts to raise money for charity. Which, for a start, identifies him as someone boundlessly different from the average aristocrat. Going into politics as a young man, a Conservative, naturally, he was the choice of the voters of East Renfrewshire, traditionally ultra-Tory country, who returned him their Member of Parliament, the second youngest MP in Westminster at the time.

But it was as an outstanding flier that he was perhaps better known, until Hess wanted to see him, that is. He was a wing commander in the RAF and the commanding officer of the renowned 602 (City of Glasgow) Squadron, one of the most illustrious units in the airforce and which had performed so outstandingly in the Battle of Britain, many of the pilots being household names in the city. Perhaps Hamilton's greatest flying feat had been in 1933 when, as chief pilot in an expedition to the unmapped areas of the Himalayas, he was the first man to fly over Mount Everest. Little of which explains why Hess should have chosen this nobleman Scot in order to present his amazing plan for 'peace for all time' with Germany.

He would, of course, have been influenced by Hamilton having been an MP and a member of the Conservative Party, but had he really known his politics he would have realised there were other dukes, such as Buccleuch, who were much more important political figures and, unlike Hamilton, known to have favoured peace. Hamilton was now a senior RAF officer, being the wing commander in charge of an active flying squadron — he was the commanding officer at Edinburgh Turnhouse — and obviously more consumed with fighting off the enemy than sitting down to peace talks.

There was one link to Hamilton, however. He and Hess had a mutual friend, a German intellectual who did favour peace. Also, the Duke had been to Germany at the Olympic Games in 1936 and, although confessing no knowledge of it, he may well have fleetingly met Hess, who claimed to remember it. As a flier himself, Hess would have been impressed at meeting such an outstanding airman as the young Scottish aristocrat, much more so than Hamilton would have been meeting yet another German officer. Perhaps more important to the Germanic mind was the fact that Hamilton had been made Lord Steward of the Royal Household and would therefore have access to the King who might have a fonder ear to peace proposals than the tough old warrior who was Churchill and who would have no truck with anything Nazi. But the truth of Hamilton's high-sounding title was that it was merely a ceremonial one. In twentieth-century Britain, kings and their cohorts were thankfully kept in their place and that place was far removed from that which had anything to do with either ruling or influencing the ruling of the country.

Nevertheless, and whatever the real reason why this dashing RAF officer who happened to be the Duke of Hamilton should be the one person in all Britain whom the Deputy Führer of Germany was so anxious to meet and to have words with, flying all the way here on his own was the sole purpose of what was to be one of the most historic of flights and which was to end with its author being incarcerated in the grim old barrack buildings of the Highland Light Infantry at Maryhill.

Flying from wartime Germany to an ever-alert Great Britain was not without its problems, especially now that the island nation had increased its defences with the use of radar, on which John Logie Baird, the genius Scot who invented television, had done so much pioneering work. However, as a solo flier of a plane which at the time was one of the fastest of its kind, Hess had more than reasonable odds that his flight would be successful.

Although not as experienced as the Scottish duke he was hoping to meet, Hess too had been an accomplished flier, having as a young man been accepted into the German Flying Corps in the latter stages of the First World War and serving in Belgium and France in a Jagdstaffel (fighter squadron), taking part in some of the last aerial combats of the war. He had tried, but failed, to get backing to be the first to fly the Atlantic, east to west, and won the famous Round the Zugspitze air race. He would fly whenever he could and his house in southern Germany was just 40 miles from the Messerschmitt works at Augsburg.

There was obvious collusion of some kind with other officers or officials in the months prior to his planned flight, it being a regular routine of Hess's to drive to the Messerschmitt plant once, sometimes twice, a week, to practise on one specific plane, a twin-engined, two-seater Me-110D fighter-bomber which, as well as being faster than anything being flown by the RAF, was one of the most advanced planes in existence. It would have had little difficulty outspeeding any British Hurricane or Spitfire, the most likely interceptors it would be liable to meet.

Flying from Germany to Scotland in the sophisticated days of the millennium is, of course, a mere routine journey of just over an hour's duration. A local trip, as it were. It most certainly wasn't that way in the early '40s and what lay ahead of this ageing flier – he was 47 at the time – was a formidable flight, one of which, in the latter stages, there could be no second thoughts, no change of mind, no reflection on the wisdom of the momentous step he had taken. For all its high-technical performance, his Me-110D would be unable to carry sufficient fuel for a return leg of such a long and arduous flight of nearly five hours and over one thousand miles, bearing in mind it was no mere hop across the Channel, coming all the way from southern Germany and overflying two other continental countries en route.

It had been a beautiful spring morning that Saturday, 10 May 1941, and Hess had awakened early, the brilliant sunshine filtering through the shutters of his sumptuous villa home at Harlaching in the southern environs of Munich. Every detail had been finalised, now there were just the farewells . . . well, sort of farewells, for the family was unaware of the great venture which lay ahead for him. Only he would know the implications of that final goodbye.

Just after breakfast he had called on his young son, Wolf Rudiger, who they nicknamed Buz, and suggested they go for a walk together. They strolled out through the French doors and went down the slope of the big garden for their favourite ramble along the banks of the fast-flowing River Isar, which tumbles down from the wondrous backdrop of the Bavarian Alps on its way to its own destiny in the Danube. It was a regular routine for them whenever Hess was at home, the little blond boy jumping and running and cavorting merrily with his devoted father, the enjoyment of those treasured moments doubtlessly heightened by the breathtaking aspect of those nearby *Sound of Music* mountains, still heavily clad in spring snow.

Around 2.30 p.m., dressed in the blue-grey uniform of a captain in the German Luftwaffe, that particular uniform and the rank being part of his game plan, he had bidden farewell to his wife Ilse, saying he would be back by Monday, after which he had gone to little Buz's room and kissed him goodbye. Ilse, of course, would have considered this nothing particularly out of the routine of an active deputy leader of a country engrossed in a war which was to escalate to one of world proportions. He was regularly away from his home, visiting troops, attending rallies, meetings at the Reichstag and the like.

His adjutant and bodyguard accompanying him, they sped off in the big Mercedes to pick up the E52 Autobahn for the journey to Augsburg which would take them just under an hour. One can only contemplate what feelings he would have had as they passed the first route off the motorway just west of Munich. Could it be he was reflecting on the splendid roadways, their adored Autobahn, that were the finest of their kind in all Europe and were one of the great visible achievements of their master race? Or, perhaps, was he having other thoughts as they passed that first slipway sign to the north, the one which indicated it was the road to . . . Dachau, part of their great unspeakable achievement. But then, places like that particular hell were best not to be thought about, especially if you were one of the masters in their master race.

He had arrived at the Messerschmitt works late in the afternoon, that time perhaps being part of his overall planning, there being few workers around at those hours on a Saturday, surprising though it may seem for a nation in an all-out war and needing every plane it could get. But that's the way it was and what few were there naturally paid little attention to the group of people accompanying the tall man in the officer's uniform who, after entering an administrative building, emerged again some time later dressed in the full flying gear of the day, the legs of his leather suit tucked into his fur-lined airman's boots with map and navigation details strapped to his right thigh in a large transparent wallet. Men dressed like that, some of them test pilots, others visiting Luftwaffe officers accompanied by groups of works officials, were obviously a common sight around the Messerschmitt plant.

He had then shaken hands with the party who had accompanied him to the grey-green camouflaged Messerschmitt, a plane normally heavily armed with armour-piercing cannon, but on this occasion unarmed. A mechanic had been warming the engines and as he saw the pilot officer approach, jumped from the plane, Hess returning the raised-arm Nazi salute. The Deputy Führer then climbed into the Me-110D and as he revved the twin engines, turned to the group he had just left to give them a final wave before pulling forward the cockpit cover then taxiing to the end of the runway and roaring off in a northerly direction.

His course would initially take him north over the main industrial belt of Germany, over cities such as Mannheim, Frankfurt and Cologne, towards a location which, like much of the Hess saga, varies in detail, in this case between the Frisian Islands of Holland and a point much further north in western Denmark. It is thought that once he had reached the Dutch coast, instead of then proceeding directly over the North Sea, he veered on a north-easterly course to the west coast of Denmark before turning west for Scotland. He was not to reveal the full details of this unusual and indirect route during initial questioning, the likely reason being that, as he had been flying by the Germans' new and highly secret radio-beam navigation, should the mission fail, such information would have been more than useful to senior RAF navigation plotters.

Whatever route, it was exactly 5.45 in the early evening when he took off and, despite the tedium of the long journey, he had reflected while crossing over the North Sea on the beauty of solo flying, it being 'supremely grand and lonely, the evening light magically beautiful', as he was to put it in a letter to his wife Ilse when he was undergoing the war-crimes trials in Nuremberg.

He had flown most of the way at a height of 10,000 feet, putting him above what cloud there had been that late spring night, a series of small white puffs many feet below his craft offering the comfort of some cover. As he approached the landmass of the British Isles he could clearly see that his navigation, so far, had been as planned, that being confirmed with the scattering of the Farne Islands off the Northumberland coast in a direct line with his plane. Unlike the earlier part of his flight, this latter stage was to be precisely logged, for, unknown to Hess, he was now being plotted by RAF radar detection crews who had given the lone intruder the tag of 'Raid 42'.

They had first observed him just after ten o'clock that night on their early radar screens from an RAF station just north of Newcastle-upon-Tyne. At that time he was some 70 miles off the coast and heading in a north-westerly direction. Thereafter a series of Royal Observer Corps posts would log the solo enemy aircraft, each passing details on to the next as it roared low over the border counties.

Passing over the Farnes, he had eased forward his control stick which put the nose of the powerful plane forward into the kind of steep dive that only an experienced pilot such as himself would have contemplated. His heart raced as he carefully monitored the control dials, the speedometer quickly soaring beyond the 225 m.p.h. point on which it had been constantly fixed for the four hours since his take-off. The needle of the altimeter swung just as fast, but in an opposing direction, moving across the dial like a clock in reverse, the reading going down quickly from 10,000 feet to eight, then six, then four, then two, then 1,000 feet, by which time he was easing back on the controls again as he pulled out of the dive over the agricultural landmass of north-eastern Northumberland, the nose of the plane firmly pointed towards the high hills of the border country and his destination – Scotland.

Like so many pilots, he was exhilarated by the power and beauty of flying, particularly at low level where the soaring eagle becomes hedge-hopping sparrowhawk, and such was his elation he was to write later that he found himself happily waving to people he saw looking up at his speeding plane. Little did he know that two British fighter planes had already been despatched to search for 'Raid 42' and one of the many ironical twists to the story is that the man who had ordered the interception of the lone and unusual intruder had been none other than the Duke of Hamilton himself, as the wing commander in charge of the RAF station at Turnhouse, Edinburgh, responsible for guarding the Forth estuary and the North Sea approaches.

In one of the more recent books on the Hess story, it is said that it had been Spitfire fighters which had been sent to search for the mystery plane, but in an interview in the Scottish *Daily Mail* in the early '60s, the Duke himself said that he had sent up two Hurricanes, but because of the great height Hess was at at the time they had missed the Messerschmitt. 'Then another Hurricane was put on his track,' added the Duke, 'but Hess dived down steeply over the border hills then flew at 50 feet towards Lanarkshire.'

Hess had studied the route so meticulously before leaving that he was to find little need to refer to the flight plan strapped tightly to his right thigh. Whatever planes had been searching for him or had attempted to catch him, Hess was blissfully unaware of any interception attempts and with Bamburgh on the Northumberland coast now well behind, he could already see his next bearing, the 2,600-foot peak of the Cheviot, highest point in the rolling border hills.

Following the contours of the countryside below, he roared up the rounded head of the Cheviot then eased the controls forward once more as he descended on a more westerly course into the glories of the beautiful Teviotdale, over Jedburgh, the River Teviot, and on above Ashkirk and the Ettrick Forest, at which point he was able to give a self-satisfied smile at the pinpoint accuracy of his navigation as he observed ahead his next route markers, to his left the 2,723-foot summit of Broad Law, and to the right that of 2,418-foot Pykestone Hill. All that was left now were the remaining hills and glens of Peeblesshire merging with those of Lanarkshire, where he began slowing his airspeed, passing over Thankerton, then Lesmahagow and finally, to his right, the little village of Sandford, from where, just ahead, he could see the splendid old mansion they called Dungavel House, the home of the Duke of Hamilton, and the final point in his route plan.

That brought another smile, broader this time, one of pride at the achievement at having reached his target. But then he never had any doubts about that, for wasn't he one of that breed who proclaimed they were the master race, that there were no others to equal them and that anything they set out to do, they would do, whatever the means, no matter the cost, and do it with an efficiency no others could match? Such was his ingrained and calculated efficiency, he decided on making a final loop before attempting his landing in order to do a double check on his navigation.

The low-flying and speeding intruder had by now been picked up by the Royal Observer Corps No. 34 Group Centre based at Pitt Street in Glasgow, and commands rang out as the flight proceeded west, the identity tag of 'Raid 42' being moved on the bit plotting chart as each observation was logged. From Strathaven the pointers moved the coded tag over the lonely stretches of the Fenwick moor, then over Stewarton, Auchentiber, then on to West Kilbride, which had them puzzled, for why should a lonely fighter of this calibre, which they knew would be soon running out of fuel, carry on towards the sea?

The RAF base at Prestwick was alerted and a Defiant fighter plane did an emergency scramble, quickly roaring aloft to search for what by now was being considered something of a mystery plane and heading for the Ayrshire coast. The Defiant was never to get within shooting range of the lone Luftwaffe flier.

Soaring over the peaceful waters of the Firth of Clyde, shimmering in the light of what was now a beautiful, full moonlit sky, the Messerschmitt banked sharply to the left, its pilot looking down over his right shoulder on the southern tip of Wee Cumbrae. There had only been the faintest glow from the sun that had set some time ago way out on the Atlantic horizon towards the New World when he had made that penultimate circuit over the Clyde and as he had headed east once more into a darkening sky lit by the brilliant full moon. The loop completed, he headed inland for another pass over the north Ayrshire and Renfrewshire moors, making yet another circuit to his right just south of the little agricultural village they called East Kilbride, the new town it was to become not even a pipe dream.

He had looked down to check the landmarks once more and there again was his target . . . the small town, the smoke from its cottage chimneys cosily wafting into the evening air, and, just as it was on his chart, the big house surrounded by gardens and parkland and whose occupant would that night be receiving the most sensational proposition of the war.

But the sighting of that little town and its nearby big house was to be the one sole error in what so far had been Hess's impeccable navigation. For he was precisely 11 miles – or a mere two minutes' flying time – short of his charted destination. The town he was looking at wasn't Strathaven. The big house wasn't Dungavel. What he had sighted was, in fact, the village of Eaglesham and the big house to its west was Eaglesham House, known locally as the Castle, it being big enough to pass for one. And he was unaware of that when he began the preparations for the final act of his long journey, by parting company with his plane and descending by parachute to as near as possible to that big house.

He opened the throttle for more engine power and pulled the

control column towards him in order to gain sufficient height for the parachute descent. By now he was just over the highest peak on the moor past that point, the 1,084-foot Ballygeoch, one of the dominating points of Glasgow's surrounding hills, and was completing the final checks before baling out. Slowing all the time, by which time he considered himself at the desired height and speed, then sliding open the cockpit hatch, he turned the plane over in order to facilitate his departure, but not having parachuted before he found that, even upside down, extricating himself from the cockpit was much more difficult than anticipated. It was only when he had gone into a sort of half roll that he had been able to fall free from the plane, the big canopy of his 'chute opening with that loud cracking sound which comforts and thrills every parachutist.

Rudolf Hess was on his way to make one of the most sensational entrances any man had ever made into Scotland. It was just a few minutes after 11 o'clock at night when the eagle landed in a field just a couple of hundred yards or so from the big house he thought was the Duke of Hamilton's home. And the amazing story of Hitler's man who had come to Glasgow was about to begin.

It was to contain all the elements of high drama, including the most intense secret political intrigue and the most astute journalistic enterprise in the pursuit of the story of a lifetime. It was to be a story too which was to demonstrate how, amidst all the crises of the day, there could still be comedy. And so the story that was to become a legend was to be copiously laced with the finest of British burlesque, stuff that would have done credit to Captain Mainwaring, Sergeant Arthur Wilson, Private James Frazer and all the others in the hilarious *Dad's Army* platoon.

The first details of the story that was to develop into one of the greatest ever scoops in British journalism was to begin with the routine call from a local correspondent to the *Sunday Mail*'s office in Glasgow in the early hours of that Sunday morning, 11 May. His information was that a German aeroplane had crashed somewhere near Eaglesham. In today's terms, such a call would be a sensation on its own, and teams from the various media would be in an all-out charge to be first at the scene. However, as stories went in wartime Scotland, the crashing of a German aeroplane, provided no locals were injured, didn't really mean all that much as a newsworthy happening.

But it was a man called Eric Schofield who was the first to recognise that this might just be no ordinary story. He had picked up some local rumours about the crash and, if true, there could be sufficient consequences to make this a significant newspaper tale. Schofield lived in the Mearns area, a small scattering of pleasant rural dwellings untouched by the suburban sprawl that was to later link continuously with Glasgow. His house was a mere two and a half miles away from where the plane had crashed into the pasture just by the junction of the Eaglesham road at the Bonnyton Moor road end.

As it so happened, Schofield's business was newspapers, for he was the general manager of the *Daily Record*, *Sunday Mail* and *Evening News* newspapers, printed at Kemsley House in Hope Street, Glasgow, and while in that capacity was not a journalist, he did recognise that the gossip he had heard was a newsworthy event and should be passed to the journalists of his company. Being a Sunday, he was at home, but had been quick to make note of local chat about the plane crashing just along the road near Eaglesham. But it was no ordinary German plane, according to the neighbourhood talk. For, as the story went, it had mysteriously come all this way without sufficient fuel to return again. Also, it had come all that distance on its own. Why, they were asking? And what's more, went the chat, neither did it have an ordinary pilot. In fact, as the gossip went, its pilot was even asking to see the Duke of Hamilton! That's the truth, they swore, for had the story not come from one of the locals who had been in the Home Guard and who had heard it himself and had told his neighbours who had told other neighbours who had told Schofield?

The newspaper executive immediately contacted the news department of the *Daily Record*. Being around lunchtime, the news editor was at the Press Club at the time . . . well, being a Sunday and the pubs all closed, where better for a news editor to be than this city hub of the buzz of the business? Schofield spoke to reporter Max McAuslane at the news desk. He immediately contacted his boss, John Simpson, who told him he knew about the story, having been left a memo about it by the *Sunday Mail* news team from the previous night. They hadn't time to check out the story and get a clearance from the Government's news censor and therefore passed on what information they had for the *Record*. Simpson quickly downed the remainder of his drink and headed back to the office to arrive in the midst of a heated argument between the news and photo desks of the paper. Reporter McAuslane had a car standing by to head for Eaglesham but couldn't get the agreement of the picture editor for an accompanying photographer.

When Simpson arrived the pictures boss was arguing, in the customary strong language of such newspaper situations, that some 300 German planes had crashed in Britain that week and a picture of one more wouldn't make news and, anyway, the photographic plates they used were strictly rationed and, bloody hell . . . 'Don't you know there's a war on?'

If only the picture editor had known all the details that had been enacted out in the preceding few hours in and around the southern edges of Glasgow!

Davie McLean, the ploughman at Floors, a mixed dairy and agricultural farm, had been in his bed that evening at his little cottage near the farm steading, as had his mother and brother. In wartime Scotland you paid attention to aircraft, all overflying aircraft, for the first thing you wanted to know was, is it one of ours . . . or one of theirs? Davie could hear the plane at first in the distance, then its engine noise becoming louder as it came closer and closer until it seemed to be almost overhead. Then, he sat up with a startle as he heard the engines spluttering, starting again, then spluttering. And then there was silence.

He jumped from bed, ran to the cottage window, but there was no sign of any plane. Instead, he got the shock of his life to see gently floating down from a bright, moonlit sky the figure of a man swinging at the end of a parachute. Davie dressed quickly and ran from the cottage in the direction of where he had last seen the descending parachute.

There was smoke and flames coming from what was obviously the crashed plane which was in the field of neighbouring Bonnyton Farm over on the western side of the main Mearns to Eaglesham road. Before he had got that far, however, he was more than surprised to come across the tall figure of a man unfastening himself from his parachute harness in the middle of the gently rising slope of the field. Startled at the sight before him, Davie was to get an even bigger surprise when approaching the man and asking him the question everyone had on their lips in those days: are you one of us, or one of 'them'?

The reply had been in almost perfect English that he was one of them, explaining, 'I am Hauptmann [Captain] Alfred Horn and I have an important message for the Duke of Hamilton.'

Being the gentle and civilised sort of man he was, Davie helped the stranger, who had badly injured an ankle on landing, towards his cottage, but after only a few paces the German had asked if he could also bring his parachute as 'it has saved my life'. Davie returned for it then the pair of them headed for the cottage where the others in the house had also been awakened by the noise of the plane.

Davie's mum inquired, just as any decent Scottish housewife would, if the man with Davie would like a cup of tea. He was to politely decline, asking if he could have a glass of water instead.

Meanwhile, just a few hundred yards away, there had been pandemonium among the soldiers stationed at the big local mansion called Eaglesham House, now the site of an upmarket recording equipment manufacturer. They were a unit of about 100 men serving with No. 3 Company, Anti-Aircraft Division of the Royal Corps of Signals. Glasgow man Robert Anderson, who had been a designer with the famous Templeton's carpet factory in the city, was the orderly sergeant on duty. His version of the events of that night is told here for the first time.

'You have got to bear in mind it was the early days of the war and we were anything but prepared. For instance, there was a secret password which meant that the German invaders had arrived. It was "Cromwell" and, as I said, a secret. But everyone knew it! They knew it down at the village in Eaglesham. They knew it in the Eglinton Arms pub there. It was all a big joke. So were we soldiers, I guess. We were a bit like Fred Karno's army, I suppose. We would go out for keep-fit runs from our base then as soon as we got to Eaglesham we would all nip into the Eglinton Arms for a refreshment. And as for being defenders of the local community, well, if that word "Cromwell" had been used in earnest there was little we could have done about it for we had only a few rifles between the entire company. And what guns we did have had been taken from us. That was because when they had issued them a soldier had accidentally set one off, nearly killing one of his colleagues. So we were issued with pikes and clubs to defend the nation.

'I was duty sergeant that night Hess's plane came over and remember seeing it so low overhead, then the man dangling on the end of his parachute just up the road a little past Floors farm. As I had to stay on duty in the camp, I sent two of my men, unarmed of course, up the road to see what was happening. They were Signalmen Emyr Morris and Danny McBride and they were the first two army personnel to meet the newly arrived pilot, who said his name was Horn. And together with the man from the farm who had first met Hess, they all ended up having a cosy chat with each other, Hess presenting Danny McBride with an inscribed cigarette case which he kept until senior officers heard about it, when it was confiscated.

'Anyway, while my two men were chatting away to Hess just up the road, the panic had set in at the camp, one of the senior officers having seen the plane reckoned it had been a pathfinder flight for an invasion force. There was shouting and confusion and the duty officer had guns issued to myself and Signalman Sanny McLauchlan, who was an ex-Cameronian, and ordered us to climb to the top of a heap of telegraph poles which had been stored nearby from where he said we were to "await the enemy and hold off the attack". Others were issued with their pikes and sticks and ordered to be ready for the worst. I'm telling you, when you look back on it all you wonder how on earth we survived and eventually won the war.'

If it was Fred Karno's army at the soldiers' base, it was *Dad's Army* at another point just along the road at Eaglesham. There, having been alerted about the possibility of the crashed plane being German, a local detachment of the Home Guard had been mustered and began arriving by car. Their Captain Mainwaring, apparently, had been enjoying his Saturday night in a fairly traditional Scottish way, which would doubtless have had him bemoaning the fact that the price of whisky had just gone up to a record high, being 88p (the old 17s 6d) a bottle, or at the local Swan and Eglinton Arms bars it would now be 5½p for a 'half', or 9p for what the locals called 'a loud yin'.

Fortified by the whisky and waving a large-calibre First World War officer's pistol which was more howitzer than sidearm, he was to lead his squad of Home Guardsmen together with a couple of regular soldiers who had joined them, as well as a reserve police constable, into action. Well, dammit, wasn't that what they had trained so much for in their nights together in various local community halls? Battle plans, emergency drills, targeting areas where the invader might land, where they might hide, how to capture them. Or, if necessary, how to dispose of them. And now, for the first time locally after nearly two years at war, they were about to be confronted with the real thing, if the news about the crashed plane and the parachuting pilot was true, that is. The word had been that the crash had been out towards Bonnyton, and that's where they headed.

They had practised converging manoeuvres before and knew precisely what to do when the captain in charge gave that order. After seeing the smouldering wreck of the Messerschmitt, its big black German crosses unmistakably identifying just whose plane it was, they were to converge on Floors farm, the nearest buildings to where the parachutist had been seen to fall.

The ensuing scene is not difficult to imagine, the motley semi-military, semi-police, semi-trained and, in at least one case, semi-sober squad covering each other with a variety of weapons, the officer with his cannon of a revolver stealthily hunching forward to surround the farm buildings, then searching the byres and barns. And meanwhile, the Hauptmann from the heavens is serenely ensconced fifty or so yards away in the ploughman's little cottage, being offered kindness and tea and chatting away to his newfound Scottish hosts.

Gordon Stewart was one of the Home Guard men there that night. He had been up at the head of the village of Eaglesham when the plane came over and seeing it crash in the distance he and some comrades had gone by car by the little track over Bonnyton Moor to the scene. By the time he arrived some soldiers from a nearby anti-aircraft unit were also out searching for the parachutist. Gordon too was to tell me his story.

'Then some cars arrived with Home Guard officers, one of whom obviously had been having a good drink. He hadn't been on duty that night and therefore there was no need for him to be there. But he turned up anyway. And as for one of the drivers, well, I knew him, and the only reason he would have been there would have been to get a drink. That was the usual reward for turning out like that.'

The *Dad's Army* men had then converged at the cottage where all was peaceful and quiet, the German inside, relaxed and at ease with these sociable Scots. And that was to be the end of this cottar's extraordinary Saturday night.

As Davie's mother was later to tell local reporters about what happened from then on after the assorted detachments arrived, 'There was considerable excitement', not the least of that excitement coming from the direction of the man with the big revolver who, Hess was later to write, was 'staggering and smelling of whisky' and who, according to Gordon Stewart, had at first wanted to shoot the prisoner but had been restrained by another officer.

As Sergeant Robert Anderson and the other soldiers at Eaglesham

House awaited the invasion their officer had fearfully predicted, Hess was being ordered from ploughman McLean's little cottage by the pistol-packing officer who by now, again according to Hess, was 'belching merrily and continuously stumbling', so much so he was fearful that his mission was going to end right there and then. 'God's finger was truly between his unsteady finger and the trigger,' he was to put it later in a letter to his wife. And, as Davie's mother was to tell it, 'The big German was the coolest man of the whole lot.'

God's finger, thankfully for the Nazi, was to stay there and the newly arrived German prisoner was taken by car to the 3rd Battalion (Renfrewshire) Home Guard headquarters, a local Girls' Institute hall in the nearby town of Busby, about two miles down the road towards Glasgow. It was while heading there that the car in which Gordon Stewart was travelling had to swerve to avoid a strange cyclist . . . strange because he only looked like a lad yet he was in uniform and had a rifle slung over his shoulder. It turned out he was a schoolboy much younger than the *Dad's Army* Private Pike and had got into the ranks by adding three years to his age. He had seen the plane crash more than two miles off and, being the dutiful Home Guardsman he was, had grabbed his rifle and was speeding for the scene on his pushbike!

There had been some debate between the police and the Home Guard about where to take the prisoner, *Dad's Army* winning out by taking him to their Busby HQ because there would be a night guard there on duty.

Just how much guarding they were doing, however, was to be quickly ascertained on their arrival at the hall.

When they got there, they marched up the path to the building in single file, the man with the revolver still covering Hess in the kind of fashion that let it be known to the German that he would be ready to blast him should he make any attempt to escape. Arriving at the door, there was no response to their first knocks and they had to hammer loudly in order to be heard by the men inside who were supposed to be on guard! Eventually, they were able to get a response, a voice from within demanding, 'Who's there?'

There was an immediate scramble from inside as they were informed that it was the police and the Home Guard – and a German prisoner. After another delay the door opened, and an invisible malodorous cloud erupted from the interior of the room. The great

Scottish feast of fish and chips can be the most succulent of dishes, but in its wake and in confined conditions can leave a stale and unwholesome stench. And combined with the fumes of countless cigarettes and flavoured with some pipe tobacco smoke, stewed together in the locked and poorly ventilated hall, this was clearly a place for only the strongest of stomachs. As well as having enjoyed their late-night supper, many of the guard, as they were called, were in a state of undress and getting ready to settle down in makeshift beds for the night. They were in for the rudest of awakenings, an officer yelling at them as soon as the door had been opened, 'Turn out the guard!' The call didn't exactly create a state of panic, perhaps utter confusion as fish and chip papers were screwed up and boots and uniforms were hastily located, some arguing about whose boots and whose uniforms were whose, while the police and Eaglesham Home Guardsmen together with Hess, by this time with a strange smile on his face, waited for the Busby men to be readied. Home Guardsman Gordon Stewart had been one of the escorts with Hess to the hall in Busby and his words to me were, 'I'm telling you, Hess was the sanest man there that night.'

Apparently there had been some more pistol prodding when they eventually gained entry and Hess was ordered into a small side-room and the door securely locked, whereupon he was to calmly lie flat on his back, yoga-like, on the bare floor, completely relaxed and detached from the excitement he could hear going on in the hall outside. There were more shouts and more orders issued, followed by a debate on who should and who should not be informed about this one-man invasion which had come their way. That little room, incidentally, is the members' bar of what is now a Masonic Lodge.

After about half an hour or so, a decision had been reached and Hess was roused from his resting position and was being marched and escorted once more. This time he was taken to another Home Guard base in commandeered Boy Scout premises, the 28th Troop's hall, which sits today, just as it did then, amidst a row of pleasant suburban bungalows in Arthurlie Drive, in the outer Glasgow suburb, although not within the city boundary, of Giffnock. If only the troop's scoutmaster could have realised the irony of that situation at the time. But it was to be some years before he was to hear the news about the unlikely visitor to his scout hall, for scoutmaster Lex Watson had been serving with the HLI and had been taken prisoner in France.

It was now just after midnight and news of the prisoner and his repeated request to meet the Duke of Hamilton had by now been conveyed to proper military authorities, whereupon there had been some debate between them and the Home Guard officers over whether or not he should be held in a police station or taken into military custody, the Home Guardsmen advocating the latter, insisting that their prisoner was an 'officer of some importance' as well as one who required some medical attention for a badly injured ankle. However, before a decision had been made where to send their prisoner, an interpreter had arrived at the Arthurlie Drive hall along with a group officer from the Royal Observer Corps, a Major Graham Donald, together with some RAF officers.

Questioned by Major Donald, the German was to insist he was Captain Alfred Horn and to reiterate his desire to see the Duke of Hamilton. He was to do so repeatedly, so much so that it had become a bit of a joke with the collection of police, Home Guardsmen and the other soldiers who had by now all crowded into the little hall.

Major Donald was to note how the German looked 'plain fed up' by all that was going on. Donald was an astute man and after some conversation with the airman and closely studying him, he was then to put the surprise question which was to shock not only him but all those who heard it.

'Is your name not Rudolf Hess?' he queried.

It was Hess's turn for the jollity now, briskly standing up to answer the question by smilingly ridiculing the officer's suggestion and, between bouts of forced laughter replied that he had often been mistaken for the deputy leader. But he insisted yet again that he was Captain Horn and that he did have a most important message for the Duke of Hamilton and therefore could a meeting be arranged? By now, more senior army officers at the headquarters of Clyde Command had decided on the overnight location for their unusual prisoner with the strange request. He was then moved on once more, this time across the city to Maryhill Barracks.

The huge barracks, now a much more pleasant housing estate, was a grim collection of buildings. The sort of place that could make even Barlinnie Prison look attractive. Nevertheless, the barracks had figured considerably in the history of Glasgow, it not generally being appreciated that the reason for their existence had been as part of a general plan to keep order in the city and other areas of central Scotland, if required, should the immigrant situation get out of hand.

The main group of immigrants they had in mind was the Irish. The city magistrates had been worried about the possibility of rioting and general disorder among the huge number of inadequately housed immigrants who had poured into Glasgow, mainly but not exclusively from Ireland, and who supplied the vast labour force required for the industrial revolution, the heartbeat of which had been in the city. The old barracks in the Gallowgate, which had been there since the days of Bonnie Prince Charlie, had become unsuitable, so new ones were ordered to house even more soldiers as well as cavalry and to be built on part of the old Garrioch estate at Maryhill. Building work had begun in 1869, but even in those days there were disputes with contractors and because of these the project, consisting of four huge barrack blocks, officers' quarters, offices and other buildings, were not to be completed and occupied until 1876. Thereafter, the barracks were to become something of an institution in Glasgow, becoming the depot of the Highland Light Infantry, once described as the British Army's 'most dreaded regiment' and the 'boot camp' of countless thousands of young Glasgow men called up for the services.

The great dictator's not-so-great deputy must have been wondering at this point about some aspects of the wisdom of his flight to Scotland. In the morning and afternoon of one day he had been one of the most powerful men on earth, used to all the trappings of a nation which had the world quivering, strutting in prestigious chancelleries, delivering hectoring speeches to the masses, the recipient of countless banquets, and living in the most luxurious of homes amidst the mountains and rivers of one of the most beautiful parts of central Europe. And a few hours later there he had been, one minute being huckled around by a whisky-reeking Scotsman of the Home Guard, then enduring the stinking aftermath of a fish supper feast while lying on his back on the dusty floor of a Girls' Institute hall in Busby, and finally a prisoner in the guard block of the HLI's barracks at Maryhill. Then again, perhaps he also considered his fate had he been a Jew and back in his beloved Germany, where his destiny would most certainly not have included the pleasantries of boy scout and girls' group halls and a hospital bed at Maryhill Barracks.

Hess's insistence on meeting with the Duke of Hamilton was to pay off, senior RAF men who had been called by the army being aware that the Duke was one of their senior officer colleagues and stationed just 40 miles away at Turnhouse, Edinburgh. With Hess securely locked up in Maryhill, they were to call him during the night, and he, bewildered at the news, was to respond that he would be at the barracks first thing in the morning.

The Duke had motored through early that Sunday morning, 11 May, arriving just before ten o'clock, reporting to the guardroom at the Maryhill Road entrance to the barracks, the orderly officer being made aware to expect him. Before being ushered in to meet the mystery man calling himself Captain Horn, the Duke was given a briefing about his arrival. They told him his only possessions appeared to be a Leica camera, maps, medicines, some family photographs and the visiting cards of a Professor Haushofer and his son, Dr Albrecht Haushofer, the latter name being that of the mutual friend of Hess and the Duke, who met him at the 1936 Olympic Games in Berlin.

The Duke and the small party of officers headed off for the medical block at the far side of the barracks, circumventing the vast barracks square, sacrosanct ground not to be trespassed and where countless recruits – including myself – received those first and never-to-be-forgotten sharp shocks from dreaded drill sergeants, those maestros of the yell from hell whose intimidating bawls and bellows mark the first stages of conversion from callow civilian to smart soldier.

Accompanied by two other officers, the Duke entered the room in which the imprisoned airman had been undergoing treatment for his injured ankle and, after closely studying him, was to say that he did not know or have any recollection of having previously met the man.

Hess then asked if he could speak to the Duke alone. The other officers looked at each other, the senior one of the two giving an imperceptible nod before they turned briskly and left the room. Hess was then to reveal the shock news to the Duke about who he really was and why he had come all the way to Glasgow on his own. His message was that he was on a mission of humanity, that the Führer didn't want to defeat 'England' and wished to stop the fighting and have a meeting in order to stop the war . . . with honour. At the same time Hitler had convinced them they would win the war within three years but wanted to end the slaughter.

Hess was also to explain why he had chosen the Duke as an intermediary. It was because the Duke had been in contact some time in the past with the son of one of his close friends, Professor Haushofer, and he had been told that the Duke of Hamilton was 'an Englishman' who might understand and help.

He was also to reveal that this had been the fourth time he had planned to make this trip to Scotland, the previous ones having been set back either because of the weather or because the British were beginning to win vital battles in North Africa, and he had not wished to come at such a time for fear such a mission might be interpreted as a sign of weakness.

But now that he was here, perhaps the Duke could get together members of his party, the Conservatives that is, in order to talk over his peace proposals.

Hess was obviously assuming that Churchill was in charge, so too were the Conservatives, the Duke having to remind him that because of the war the political parties were united and ruling the country with a coalition government.

After submitting his many proposals, Hess was then to ask the Duke to grant him four requests: that the King be asked to give him parole as he had come on his own free will; that his identity would not be revealed to the press; that a telegram be sent to an address in Switzerland (to the family name of Rothacker, 17 Hertzog Str, Zurich with the message that Alfred Horn was in good health); and finally, and with some passion – could he be moved out of Glasgow? His reason for this special request was: 'I am anxious not to be killed by a German bomb.'

There was little wonder he had asked that last favour, obviously being aware that the city had just had its worst ever attack the week before when for five successive nights there were German bombers over Glasgow as well as over a variety of Clydeside towns and there had been considerable casualties. On three nights alone these had totalled 1,083 killed and 1,602 seriously injured, all in Glasgow and the Clydeside area. And countless thousands of homes had been destroyed or damaged.

While the Duke had been at Maryhill Barracks that Sunday morning meeting with the man who was now saying he was Rudolf Hess, journalists at the various newspaper offices in Glasgow were at work trying to piece together more details about what was now generally regarded as a genuine mystery plane and pilot at Eaglesham. The authorities were saying very little about the incident, which meant only one thing to the inquisitive pressmen – that there was something to hide. So – just what was it?

At the *Record* office in Hope Street, the dispute over sending a photographer had been resolved, the chief photographer himself being ordered to accompany news editor Simpson and reporter McAuslane to Eaglesham. The three men sped south through the city to the field at Floors farm where the crashed Messerschmitt was being guarded by armed RAF personnel who told them about the pilot having gone to the Floors farm cottage after landing by parachute. Their opinion, however, was that the plane had been merely a fighter escort accompanying bombers on a raid and had been caught by a Spitfire. A fairly routine incident and not really much of a story, the chief photographer almost visibly breathing 'Bloody told you so'. The reporter McAuslane, however, thought he should persist with his inquiries as there was that intriguing report of the pilot wanting to meet the Duke and he headed on his own down the little road to look for the man who had first met the pilot.

Davie McLean's cottage at Floors farm was the first house he came to, and there he met the slenderly built ploughman dressed *de rigueur* for a man in his job – hodden grey suit, collarless shirt, the generous bunnet, the Johnny Soutar boots, aye, and the nicky tams as well. And, as they chatted together, ploughman McLean was to confirm everything they had heard about the plane crash and its parachuting pilot. 'Aye, he was with us last night in the house for three-quarters of an hour, chatting away in the kitchen with my mother and brother,' said McLean.

'Did he mention anything about wanting to meet somebody?'

'Aye,' said Davie candidly. 'He asked how far it was to the Duke of Hamilton's house at Strathaven for he wanted to meet him.'

After that he had relaxed in the best chair of their little parlour and began speaking about his family. He showed them photographs of his little son whom he had farewelled that morning.

He then told them that he was 47 years of age, coincidentally the same age as Davie McLean, and how he had fought in the First World War with the infantry and had been wounded, McLean telling him that he too had been a soldier then, the pair then discovering they had been fighting in the same sector of the Western Front, probably shooting at each other.

McLean told McAuslane he had been puzzled by some aspects of the German, the fact he was 47 and still a relatively junior officer and also why he was flying operationally at such an age. And why did he keep stressing the importance of his meeting the Duke of Hamilton?

McAuslane, more than convinced there was a major story behind it all, then headed back to his office to make more inquiries about the mysterious German, only to find the official portcullis had already fallen on the story, the police and other authorities only revealing that the pilot of the plane had been injured and was 'somewhere in hospital'.

Still unaware of the full ramifications of what was to emerge, McAuslane had sufficient material for what he considered something of a scoop, 'Mystery German Comes to Meet Duke', which seemed the most likely heading for the story which was sure to be a page-one splash for the next day's paper.

But the censor's office (based in the War Room for the West of Scotland) in Bothwell Street had other ideas. Any stories involving enemy action or the movement of troops had to be submitted to this office for approval. Usually the journalists' copy would be taken to them by one of their young copy-boy messengers, but McAuslane, in view of the importance of the story, decided to take it to them himself.

'I sat on the high stool by the counter at the office and in due course a middle-aged man appeared and I handed him my story,' McAuslane remembers. 'He was gone for only minutes when he reappeared with my copy marked with the letter C which meant it could not be used at all. Sometimes they would cut out details of a story, such as the precise location of an incident or even a reference to the weather. But this marking C meant we could not publish any of it at all. I asked the censor for an explanation to pass on to my editor. He replied by saying the story was "rubbish". I pointed out that it was not the censor's job to prevent a paper printing "rubbish" provided it didn't breach security. His answer to that was the story was speculative and it made no difference to him when I argued that I had been to Eaglesham and seen the plane myself.'

McAuslane returned once more to the censors with another version of the story which he thought they might pass, but once more it was given a 'C' marking. That, it seemed, was the newspaper stumped. Well, nearly. Like McAuslane, editor Clem Livingstone was now aware of the immensity of the story so far, even though they were without the real name of the most important of the *dramatis personae* involved. Livingstone cogitated on the prospect of perhaps some radio news coming out of Germany about the incident and as his company maintained a radio-monitoring service run by a staff of linguists, many of them Polish refugees, they were alerted about the story. The radio station was based near the Glasgow police's own communications station on the heights of Cathkin Braes, the Glasgow park on the southern rim of the city, and at Livingstone's request the shortwave monitors were to pay particular attention to any broadcast mentioning anything connected with a German plane or senior pilot being missing or anything that mentioned Scotland.

Hess, by now, had been in the country for just over 24 hours and the Duke of Hamilton, now convinced that he was in fact Hitler's deputy, wanted to immediately alert the Government about the man in custody at Maryhill Barracks. Despite the fact that he was the senior earl of Scotland, that he was a senior officer in the Royal Air Force and the commander of the important base at Turnhouse, getting in touch with someone high up in government proved at first to be no easy task.

He immediately thought that the person best to be informed should be the Foreign Secretary, at the time Sir Alexander Cadogan. But all his efforts to do that were to prove a failure, his office informing the Duke that Cadogan was 'an extremely busy man'.

Hamilton insisted that he had to see the Foreign Secretary on the most important of matters and apparently what ensued was the most heated of exchanges. With some disdain, the civil servant handling the call suggested that perhaps he should try the following morning when there might be the possibility that Sir Alexander would be able to see him between engagements. The Duke's frustration can be imagined, being in possession of the biggest story of the war and the sole link in what appeared to be a deal that could affect the lives of millions.

As fortune would have it, however, the Prime Minister's own secretary was in the Foreign Office at the time and he took over the call, undoubtedly remembering the Duke from his time as a Member of Parliament. It transpired that Churchill himself was to be easier to meet than his Foreign Secretary, Hamilton being told that in view of what he said was the urgency of the matter, he should fly south immediately to meet the Prime Minister.

With all haste late that Sunday afternoon of 11 May, Hamilton returned to Turnhouse where a Hurricane fighter had been readied for him, and he immediately took off for Oxfordshire, landing at the nearest RAF base to his destination, the handsome and ancient sixteenth-century mansion of Ditchley Hall, between Oxford and

Chipping Norton and where Churchill was spending the weekend with some friends.

The assembled guests had just finished dinner and, as was their way, the ladies were with the ladies and the gents were with their brandy and cigars when the Duke was shown into a room where Churchill and a group were obviously hugely enjoying the kind of jaw that only a fine repast and its post-indulgences can induce. Churchill and the Duke were no strangers, having known each other since the latter's days in the House of Commons. In fact, Churchill had been by his side when Hamilton was fêted with a celebration dinner given by the House of Commons for his daring feat over Mount Everest. Although they shared widely similar Conservative views, it couldn't be said that the pair were political pals, the two having parted close company because of what Hamilton had considered the legendary Winston's 'English attitude' to Scottish affairs, which must have given the daring Duke a few plus points in Scottish eyes.

Hamilton rightly thought that the after-dinner brandy and cigars crowd wasn't the most appropriate of audiences for the incredible story he had to impart and when he suggested that what he had to say should be between himself and the Prime Minister alone, Churchill insisted that the Duke should have dinner first. He had been in full flow at the time, entertaining his guests with some samples of the remarkable experiences that had been his life, and, as the good and genial host, would wait till the Duke had enjoyed some of his weekend home's hospitality before hearing his tale.

Only one other person, Sir Archibald Sinclair, the Secretary of State for Air, was with the two men when they eventually did get together in the sanctuary of a smaller room away from the conviviality of the other guests. The Duke then gave a graphic account of his meeting that morning in Maryhill with the man in the Luftwaffe officer's uniform. Churchill had glowered through a big puff of cigar smoke when he took in the details of what had occurred between the Duke and the German.

After hearing all of Hamilton's story and what the German had told him, Churchill's eyes fixed on the Scottish peer and in that distinctive way of his, the rumbling, unmistakable tones, pausing with staccato emphasis between each word as he queried, 'Do you mean to tell me that the deputy Führer is in our hands?'

He was given the assurance that this was indeed the case. What was to come next was to shock the Duke, although with Churchill he realised he was the kind of man from whom you never knew what to expect. It was 1941 and there was no nightly TV, but if you were privileged enough to live in the style of the mansion-house people, there were such luxuries as having your own cinema theatre. And Churchill, an avid fan of certain movies, had that in his plan for the evening entertainment that night at Ditchley Hall. Despite the momentous impact of the news he had just been given, that they were at the epicentre of a moment in history, nothing was to deter the great man from his favourite hobby. And that was watching old films of Harpo, Groucho, Chico and Zeppo.

'Well, Hess or no Hess,' he was then to tell the Duke and his senior cabinet minister, 'I am going to see the Marx brothers!' And at that, he turned and shuffled out of the room for a date with his favourite film show.

Meanwhile, back in Glasgow, with Hess safely locked up and under guard at Maryhill Barracks, the world still waited to be told the sensational news that Hitler's very own right-hand man had fled and was in Scotland. One newspaper had all the details but couldn't print a word. There could be no appeal to the censor's office, their verdict being final. So strict were they that for the past three months these same censors had been incising all details of locations and casualties in every story submitted to them about the heavy air raids in and around Glasgow.

Newspaper reports instead would merely state that there had been enemy activity over a particular region and that casualties were either light or heavy. Pictures, too, had to be submitted to the censor, lest they reveal a location which could in some way help the enemy.

The story of the German pilot and the plane crash at Eaglesham was by now taking a sensational turn. Editor Clem Livingstone's instructions that their radio listening service should be on special guard was to pay off. Early on the Monday evening, 12 May, news editor Johnny Simpson was to receive a message from the radio men up on Cathkin Braes that a strange broadcast from Berlin had just been picked up and its message had been that Rudolf Hess had gone missing. There had been no other details. He went straight to Livingstone with the broadcast flash as well as his newsman's hunch. 'That's our boyfriend.'

Livingstone nodded in reply, the pair of them not revealing the excitement they felt at being on to what might be the biggest story of the war. Despite the earlier knockback from the censor, there was no bar on them making more inquiries into the mystery airman who had landed in the field in front of the McLeans' cottage. The McLeans! Of course, Davie, his brother and mother were the very people. They would be the ones to know whether or not that was Hess who was in their cottage on Saturday night. He had been there long enough before the *Dad's Army* squad had arrived. They had chatted to him, they had said.

Quickly, a buff folder was filled with an assembly of photographs from the paper's picture library. They had just one thing in common, that being they were all head-shots of famous males. Film star Tyrone Power was one. So was Cary Grant. So were the pictures of as many dark-haired sports stars as they could muster. And so, too, in the folder were a couple of pictures of the man himself – Rudolf Hess.

News editor Simpson sped south across the city for Floors farm to meet the ploughman McLean with a prearranged code message with his boss which would let him know the news but mean nothing to any other listening ear. Mobile phones were only the stuff of science fiction in 1941, communications being strictly limited to public telephones. The arrangement was that if one of the McLeans recognised the man as Hess, the call would be 'Thumbs up – once'. And so on, depending on how many pointed him out.

Editor Livingstone could hardly stifle the tension when his secretary announced Simpson was on the line from a public phone somewhere. Without as much as a hello, Simpson was to announce simply, 'It's thumbs up, Clem. Three times!'

When Simpson had shown the folder of photos to the three McLeans, they had studiously gone over them, stopping at the first one of Hess, being not too sure. But when they saw the second one they were unanimous: 'That's the man!'

Back in Hope Street, reporter McAuslane had been given the go-ahead to proceed with the sensational story and when he had it completed and given it to the editor he suggested that once more he should personally take a carbon copy of it to the censor's office.

'No you won't!' Livingstone shouted. 'The censor has had his chance. He isn't getting another. We are going ahead with this story. Nobody would dare take action against us. The story is accurate in every detail – isn't it?' he added, glowering at McAuslane, who was to reply, 'See you in jail.' The editor laughed at the joke then said they would hold the story from the first edition of the paper so that rival wouldn't lift it from them.

The production staff then proceeded setting the story in type with the heading 'Rudolf Hess in Glasgow Hospital'. Despite his bravado outburst about the censor not being given the story, editor Livingstone was, in fact, making the biggest decision of his newspaper career. Flouting the censor could mean grave charges leading to the heftiest of fines or imprisonment, or even both. If ever a newspaperman was living up to the maxim of publish and be damned, this was it. But fate was to be on his side, for a few hours after taking his bold decision to publish, German radio was to broadcast a more detailed story about the missing Hess which was included as a lead item on the BBC's main radio news at nine o'clock. The story was much more explicit, stating that Hitler had expressly forbidden Hess to use an aeroplane 'because of a disease which has been becoming worse for years'. Despite that, said the Germans, he had gone on a flight from Augsburg from which he had not returned. And he had left behind a letter 'which showed traces of mental disturbance justifying the fear that Hess was a victim of hallucinations'.

The broadcast had gone on to say that Hitler had now ordered the arrest of Hess's adjutants who knew of the flight. It was now assumed that 'Party Comrade Hess' had crashed or met with a similar accident.

Now everyone knew about Hess, except for one vital detail. Just where was he? Only one newspaper in Glasgow knew that and they were busy getting ready to tell the world.

Like other editors, Livingstone knew full well that one of the main sources of story leaks from a newspaper office comes from somewhere among its own staff. Therefore he had to ensure that the sensational details of what they were about to publish would be kept as secure as possible, bearing in mind the large number of varied staff who, in the course of making a newspaper in those days, had access to its contents as it went from reporter to sub-editor to typesetter to proof-reader to compositor to process worker to printer to machine-room minder to dispatch bundler. He therefore put out the order that all entrance doors to the office were to be firmly locked and that no staff from any department in the building would be allowed to leave, nor would anyone be allowed to enter.

The command was accepted with rather more sang-froid than it would have been in peacetime, similar instructions having been issued regularly for the safety of the staff during air raids when workers would descend to the building's basements for cover, as they had done again that night on the assumption that raisers were on their way.

All that remained to be done now was to wait until the time when Livingstone decreed the presses should run with the story that would shock the nation. Just before nine o'clock they let the first edition, the one they call the 'streets edition', run with no mention of Hess. It's this edition that goes to the night street vendors and within minutes of it appearing it would also be examined by rival news teams in the other newspaper offices for stories they may have missed.

Just after ten o'clock Livingstone gave the orders for the Hess story to run and the sensational news was soon rolling from the presses. It didn't take long to reach the world, a teleprinter message from London around 11.30 p.m. revealing the Ministry of Information had called a press conference at the Savoy Hotel where they gave details of the story running off the presses in Glasgow and correspondents were told they should refer to the *Record* for any further details. Because of the shortage of phone lines, the Ministry set up a special line to Glasgow and correspondents from all over the world lined up to put questions to reporter McAuslane who handled the calls. He was to remain on duty doing this until six o'clock the following morning.

When the Duke of Hamilton returned to Glasgow the following day he was accompanied by Sir Ivor Kirkpatrick, who had been on the staff of the British Embassy in Berlin and had known Hess. They learned that Hess had been moved from Maryhill Barracks to Buchanan Castle at Drymen, being used as a military hospital at the time. Kirkpatrick was to confirm that the man who said he was Hess was in fact just that.

Twenty years later, when Hess was undergoing life imprisonment for his part in the monstrous Nazi war machine, documents released from secret German government archives showed that Hitler had known of his trip to Scotland to make peace overtures. At that same time the Duke of Hamilton was also to reveal that he had been sent a letter by Dr Albrecht Haushofer, the son of Hess's friend, and it too had contained peace gestures. But the letter had been mysteriously held up by British intelligence and when it was eventually received by the Duke the time for any form of negotiations was over.

Haushofer was later executed by the Nazis. Hess, whose mind was to degenerate from a state of confusion to one of insanity, was to remain in captivity for the rest of his life and, 46 years after his dramatic flight to Scotland, he committed suicide, the only inmate left of all the Nazis who had been sentenced at the Nuremberg war-crimes trials in 1946. The Duke of Hamilton died on 30 March 1973.

THE SECOND BENNY LYNCH

He was headline news just as much as the man he had followed, who had been the best ring fighter Scotland had known. And just like Benny Lynch, the newspapers' page-one news about Jackie Paterson was not always to be for his brilliant performances in the ring. For Jackie, like Benny, had his problems, problems of other sorts which were to involve him in a series of sensational controversies. Problems which were to lead to one of the saddest endings of any of our great champions of the ring.

Pugilistic brilliance comes with many imperfections. Benny had them aplenty. And so too did Jackie Paterson, the man from Glasgow who is rated the city's best-ever boxer, after the undisputed holder of that acclaim, Benny Lynch. And had it not been for the Second World War, during which he spent years in the RAF, it might well have been that Paterson could even have eclipsed the little Gorbals man's outstanding record. But then that's only speculation. What isn't is that this man Paterson was one of the hardest hitters of all time. I have known two men who have been on the receiving end of punches from both Benny and Jackie and who have no doubt that it was the latter who hit the hardest. The late Jim Maharg, a Scottish flyweight champion back in the '30s who went 12 rounds with Lynch in 1933, assured me of that when I asked him whose wallop packed the most power. There was not the slightest hesitation in his reply: 'Oh, without a doubt', he said, 'Paterson . . . the wee fella from Anderston.'

The other man to have been both on the giving and receiving end of punches with Benny and Jackie was Charlie Kerr, now in his eighties and one of the rare remnants of those glory days of boxing back in the '30s – he was a Scottish bantamweight champion, which was something then, and was a sparring partner to the two Glasgow superchamps.

Here's his view: 'There was none as clever or as wily as Benny.' Then he squares up to me, the way boxers do when they wish to demonstrate a point, holding up his flint fists, so huge and gnarled it seems like he's wearing mailed gloves. Shaking one, he said, 'Benny would lead you on with this fist – okay? He would have you convinced it was coming for you. Then, when your eyes were off the mark, he would wallop you with the other one.' At that, Charlie connects with a set of knuckles that come from nowhere to my jaw. But lightly, like. 'You see, that was Benny. Nobody as fly as him. But Jackie, on the other hand, what a wallop he had with his right! There was nothing like it. And that's what made him a world champ.'

Jackie Paterson was usually associated with the suburb of Anderston, having lived there and been a member of the famous boxing club which existed there for many years and which bore the district's name. And while he was always known as a Glaswegian, Jackie, like so many who live in the city, was one of our incomers. He came to Glasgow as a youngster from the Ayrshire village of Springside, near Kilmarnock, where he had been born in 1920. The family had emigrated to the United States where they were to spend five years in Scranton, Pennsylvania, before returning home, the young Jackie, a keen sportsman, still with the trace of his American accent when he joined the local Dreghorn Juveniles soccer team, where he was rated one of their ablest centre-forwards.

Not long after their return from the States, the family were on the move again, this time to Glasgow, where Jackie switched sports from soccer to boxing and became a member of the Anderston Boxing Club, one of several clubs for young pugilists in the city at the time and also one the most highly rated for the number of champions it produced.

He was just 15 when he first entered the ring for a serious bout and right from the start he was to demonstrate something different, too. It wasn't just the fact that he was what the boxing trade calls a 'southpaw', a boxer who leads with his right hand and off his right foot, but unlike most southpaws he was not naturally left-handed. But there was something more special about him than that, and that was his devastating punching power, winning seven of his first 11 ring victories by knockouts. He was only two years into the sport when he was considered good enough to challenge Bobby Watson of Leith for the Scottish amateur flyweight championship, but this was to prove a fight too far for the young and inexperienced challenger who lost to Watson, making that the only defeat in his amateur career.

It was not long after this match that Paterson was to be involved in his first controversy, although on this occasion it was not of his making. The trainer of the Anderston club at the time was Pat Collins, one of the most experienced men in the business and who was also a fight promoter. In May 1938, he had a fight show arranged for the Argyll Theatre in Greenock and one of the star performers was the tough and highly experienced Irish champion Joe Kiely, from Limerick. But on the night of the show, Kiely's opponent suddenly pulled out, leaving Collins with the embarrassment of having no replacement. There was the young amateur Paterson, of course, but putting him in against such an experienced man would have not only been a risk but in all probability would have had him in conflict with the boxing authorities.

But it was to be Jackie himself who was to put the proposition to Collins that he should take the place of the absentee fighter. 'What about me?' he asked. There was more than a tinge of the plea in the way he put it to the trainer. Paterson had expected him to laugh off the suggestion but instead Collins had replied, 'You know, I think you've got something, Jack.' Unlike everyone else he always called him plain Jack. 'I'm convinced you can beat Kiely, but we'll have to see your parents first.'

Jackie's mum, a douce wee Ayrshire woman, turned to her young son when the prospect of him taking part in a professional contest was put to her. 'Are you sure this is what you want to be, Jackie? Is this what your heart is in?' she asked. When he answered that it was his one and only ambition, she then turned to Collins and asked if he thought he could be really good at boxing. What he said in turn wasn't meant to sweeten her for he was genuinely convinced of the ability of the young lad he called Jack: 'He'll be a champion one day. Nothing's surer than that.'

Ten years later Jackie was to recall that night when he took part in his first professional fight and the prospect of facing up to Kiely, well known on the circuit at the time as a tough-as-they-come, wily and experienced Irishman. His clear-cut memory of it was to be a graphic insight into just how the boxer feels and what runs through his mind in those raw and sensitive few minutes immediately prior to the first bell of a contest. He was talking to his friend, the journalist Hugh Taylor, at the time.

'"This is it, then," I thought as I sat on the hard stool in my corner

. . . and tried to relax. It wasn't easy. I hoped I looked less nervous than I felt. The buzz of the crowd in the little hall sounded deafening. Under my old dressing-gown I moved my elbows in little circles to loosen my shoulder muscles but otherwise I was still. I could feel my heart thump. I squinted across the ring to where Joe Kiely sat in the other corner. He looked cool and relaxed and tough.

'And just at that moment I wished I were anywhere else than in the Argyll Theatre, Greenock, on that sweet May night of 1938. I wished I had never wanted to be a boxer. I wished I didn't have to meet in my first professional fight an opponent who was as capable as Joe Kiely. I thought: "You and your dreams of being a champion. You're crazy. Why, you've only been an amateur for a few months. You've no chance. Get up and run." Then I felt a tap on my shoulder. I looked round and there was that face, solemn but friendly, which was always to be allied with me in my boxing career. "Okay, Jack," said Pat Collins. "You can do it. Remember, keep your hands up. And don't rush it. Just do your best, son."

'That steadied me and I felt better at once and it made me so determined that no matter what the result of the fight would be I wouldn't let Pat Collins down. For Pat had faith in me and I knew that if I lost that would do Pat more harm than me. Many people had been saying that he was crazy to let a novice like myself fight such an experienced battler as Joe Kiely.'

Because he was the matchmaker of the show that night in the Argyll Theatre, Collins was barred from being in his protégé's corner for the fight. But he was to find the best of replacements, the veteran Johnny MacMillan, a man they had called the 'Prince of Boxers' for his many years in the ring. MacMillan had been one of the champions who had inspired the young Benny Lynch when he had watched him in one of the many demonstration bouts arranged by his mentor Father Fletcher at St John's Boxing Guild club in the Gorbals. There wasn't a better man to have as your supporter in a fight like this.

Paterson was never to forget the help MacMillan was that night. Being the novice he was, all the flaws were to be revealed against his more seasoned and skilful opponent as the fight wore on, although there was to be no sign from either man that it might not last the full distance. MacMillan berated his young charge for his faults, his shortcomings, his bad ring habits and was to do so in a fashion that quickly registered.

'What Johnny said to me about a habit I had to struggle hard to conquer is nobody's business,' Jackie was to say afterwards.

Whatever it was, it worked. For the pupil-professional lasted the distance. Not only that, the referee had no hesitation in raising his hand at the end of the tenth and final round. He had won his first professional fight as a clear points winner. And collected his first purse – £10, which worked out at around 33p a minute. But there were to be much more lucrative days ahead.

Despite the fact he had won his first professional fight against the more seasoned Kiely, the fact that he had gone into the ring with such a highly overrated opponent was to predictably land trainer Collins in trouble with the authorities. Officials at the Anderston club were furious at what they considered not only an ill-matched but unwise bout. Paterson, they maintained, had been far too young, too inexperienced to have taken on such an adversary. So upset were two of the directors of the club they resigned in protest. The remaining officials acted swiftly and ordered Collins to end his association with the Anderston club. It was one of the biggest sporting *causes célèbres* of the day, but did highlight Paterson as a name to be watched.

His amateur days over and buoyed with his victory, albeit with its controversial backwash, Paterson now looked forward to what he thought might be a promising career as a professional boxer, there being every prospect it would reward him better than his job as an apprentice butcher in a shop in Canal Street, just off Dobbie's Loan, Port Dundas.

Another fight was quickly arranged for the young Paterson by Collins, now his manager and trainer. Again it was to be in a stand-in capacity for yet another boxer who had to pull out of a fight, not an uncommon situation in those days with boxers often fighting more than once a month, many even having at least a fight a week in order to make a living. And, by coincidence, it was again to be against an Irishman, this time one who was even more experienced and more competent than Kiely. He was the colourful little flyweight from Belfast called Rinty Monaghan, who was to become a household name in Glasgow for his amusing habit of giving the fans a song at the end of any major contest, most of which he was winning at the time. Once, at the height of a riot in Belfast following a split-decision fight, Rinty had stilled the ringside combatants by belting out one of his well-known Irish ballads.

Despite his scraggy appearance, his shoestring legs, the bony biceps, Monaghan was a tough proposition. He had been a professional fighter since he was 14 years of age and had won his previous 30 professional fights, a record which more than eclipsed pro-novice Paterson. Undaunted, he willingly agreed to take on the man they called the 'Pride of Belfast' . . . and in front of a home Ulster audience. It was to be a new experience for the Belfast crowd for they had never seen their man Monaghan on the floor before. One of Paterson's fierce flatteners had done that before the fight had really got under way. They were even more shocked when the unknown Paterson did it yet again and were to be stunned into silence when in the fifth round Paterson was to hit him with the kind of blow that required a lot more than a count of ten from which to recover.

The Irish crowd knew that night there was a new young master on the scene, for anyone who could do what he did to their very own Rinty Monaghan had to be a champion in the making. But that was no news to trainer Collins or, for that matter, Paterson himself, the pair of them confident they could take on allcomers. And that's just what they did. Who cared what the opponents' records might be, they thought. Sure, Paterson might still be a teenager, and he might not yet have been a professional for a year, but they had the kind of confidence from which world champions are made. The whole boxing world had already sat up with that shock defeat of Rinty Monaghan in front of his own fans in Belfast.

They were to sit up considerably more when he did much the same thing to the Belgian champion Raoul Degryse, the boxer who had made a big name for himself by flooring the redoubtable Englishman and world champion Peter Kane three times in the first round of a non-title fight. Kane, always referred to as the Golborne (just outside Manchester) blacksmith, was one of the real legends of the fight game, especially noted for his punching power and for his celebrated clash with Benny Lynch, a fight that is part of ring lore. To floor a man such as him three times, as Degryse had done, gave you, in boxing terms, an instant reputation. An instant huge reputation.

And Jackie Paterson was to more than double his own fast-growing reputation by doing even more to Degryse than he had, in turn, done to Peter Kane. For Jackie had him down no less than six times before running out a clear points winner. His boxing CV was to grow most impressively month by month after that. Within a year of turning professional, Paterson had taken the Scottish flyweight title from Freddie Tennant of Dundee in the eleventh round. A few months after that it was another title, this time the British empire title, from Kid

Tanner of British Guyana, one of the toughest and most rugged men in the ring at the time and who Paterson said gave him one of the hardest fights of his career. It was the kind of fight that would have been stopped in much later days, such was the injury Paterson received, the nastiest of gashes in a cheek as a result of a head clash in the fourth, the injury described by one boxing writer as looking as if had been caused by a jab from a chisel. He had fought much of the 15 rounds of the contest that way, blood covering his face and chest, demonstrating that as well as being the little man with the biggest of punches, he was also a giant when it came to courage.

But it wasn't till years later that another story about this fight, staged at Belle Vue, Manchester, was to emerge. It was to be the very first of the many tales to be associated with Jackie Paterson and his problems of getting to the appropriate weight for his fights. In the days prior to the contest, Paterson had been in a butcher's shop in Manchester and had asked if he could use the shop's scales to test his weight, difficult as it is to imagine such a scenario occurring in the age still to come when athletes were to have the aid of computers and all sorts of high-tech measuring devices.

When Paterson, his face a picture of dismay and despair, asked the butcher if his scales were really accurate, he was to be given the reply that not only were they precise, they were the most exact ones of their kind in all of Manchester. 'A feather from a duck's back would make 'em shiver,' said the butcher, annoyed at the suggestion that his scales might be out.

Making the normal allowances for shoes and clothing, the scales had registered him as being one and a half pounds overweight and there was less than 24 hours to get the weight off. Paterson and his accompanying party immediately headed for one of the city's suburbs where an aunt of Jackie's lived. Trainer Collins took charge, stoking up the coal fire in the living-room and dressing Jackie in every available sweater he could pull from his trainer's bag. Jackie's brother Robert was there and began belting out music from the piano – fast, foxtrot music to which Jackie skipped. He did eight rounds in that little, oven-hot living-room of his aunt's house, the music going from quickstep to fast quickstep and, at Collins's urging, even faster quickstep. It more than worked. For when he was to finally face the official weigh-in scales, he was pounds underweight. The butcher's scales had been wrong after all! His weight problems were not always so easily and happily resolved.

Despite the concern it had given them and the unnecessary weight loss, it was to make no difference to Paterson's performance against Tanner, the man he was always to say was the greatest boxer he ever met. And boxing writers and commentators unanimously agreed that it was one of the finest and most thrilling boxing matches ever staged at the famous Manchester venue.

Norman Hurst, one of the most famous and respected boxing writers of the day, said that the final round of the contest had been one of the most exciting and hard-fought fights he had ever seen. Like most of the named boxing reporters he had given Paterson little chance of winning against Tanner, rated one of the most formidable flyweights of all time, certainly one of the toughest. 'But Paterson got the last laugh over a lot of the boxing critics, your correspondent among them,' said Hurst. 'Paterson, badly handicapped by that shocking gash on his left cheekbone, must be commended for the way he made a fight of it instead of trying to protect the damaged spot. A magnificent display of courage.' Watching Paterson had clearly demonstrated to him two things: 'that he is a great and worthy champion and that, provided he can continue to make the weight, there is no man at flyweight in the world to beat him'.

The endurance test against Tanner certainly stood him in good stead, for only the best were now being considered to take on the man from Glasgow who the boxing world now acknowledged was one of the hardest punchers they had ever known. And although he had been beaten in that non-title fight by the Belgian Degryse, the best around at that time was the reigning world champion himself, Peter Kane. Paterson was 23 years of age and it was time to go for it.

It was by now wartime and although there were strict Government restrictions on crowds gathering at sporting events – for fear of them being likely targets for marauding German planes – more than 35,000 turned up that night in June 1943 to see Paterson face up to world champ and legend Peter Kane, the man who had been a professional since he was 16 and had been fighting even long before that as a youth in the booths around the market towns of the north of England.

Kane was one of the best-known boxers in Britain, but was to be forever remembered in Glasgow for his legendary battle with their beloved Benny Lynch just six years previously, mentioned earlier as the fight that had become ring lore.

That had been the famous Shawfield Park fight, the ground being capacity packed with more than 40,000 to watch their Benny defend his world title. In boxing terms it was something of an equivalent to what many still say was soccer's greatest game, and that had been in Glasgow too, the one back in 1960 between Eintracht and Real Madrid in their European Cup final. Well, the Lynch–Kane fight had been one of those occasions, the sort of event you would boast about for years . . . 'I was there.'

It had been a night of vintage boxing, the like of which the experts concurred they had not seen before and would be unlikely ever to see again. Some of the greatest legends in and around the fight game had been there, men who had reached out and touched the stars – Jimmy Wilde, the bag-of-bones Welsh wizard they said was the unbeatable man, and the great Tommy Farr, the very man who had gone to America to so nearly beat the greatest of them all, Joe Louis; and Victor McLagen, fighter and now Hollywood film star, who was to jump into the ring after the fight to lift Lynch aloft, telling everyone that he, the man who had seen Louis and the Dempseys and the Tunneys, considered that this had been the greatest fight of them all. It was that kind of night.

Kane had put up the battle of his life that night for the 13 rounds he had lasted with a merciless Lynch at the peak of his fitness and fighting prowess. And here he was, the man who had shaken the hands and taken the punches of the most legendary boxing Scot of all time, once again facing up to a Glasgow man in Glasgow, the venue still in the southside of the city, but at Hampden Park on this occasion.

Paterson's more than impressive fight record showed that he had won 42 of his 50 fights, drawn three and had avenged three of his defeats. However, the big wartime crowd of some 35,000 was not to be given the treat of another Lynch–Kane classic. The local fight fans might have got the result they wanted, but they weren't to get much for their money by way of pugilistic entertainment.

For Paterson was to be at his devastating best . . . too devastating for Kane, who was knocked out almost before the last resonance of the opening bell had died. In fact, he had nearly been disposed of even sooner than that, for just within a blink of the fight being started, Paterson had connected with a vicious left hook which had floored Kane for a count of five and it was evident from that moment which way the fight was going, and it was heading in that direction at speed. When Kane had scrambled to his feet from that initial count of five, he had been so dazed he was facing in the opposite direction from his opponent and looking for all the world like he was saying to himself, 'Where the hell is he?'

The flurry of rat-tat-tat punches that quickly followed soon told him where he was. It required much more concentration for the boxing writers on this night to assess the fight, for Paterson gave them just over a minute, 61 seconds to be precise, to note his ability. It was to be one of the shortest ever world-title fights. It was also the first occasion on which a southpaw had won the world flyweight title.

One of the first men to jump into the ring that night and to be lovingly welcomed by the new world champion, who instantly recognised him, had been a small man of just over five feet, one of the archetypal little Glasgow men of old, the kind that makes you ask today, whatever happened to the Glasgow wee man? He was a nondescript little fellow, perhaps the clothing gave that away, of indeterminate age, maybe around fortyish, and not in the best of physical condition, the puffed face, the awkward way he ducked under the ropes giving that away. And he was to hug and congratulate Jackie in a way that only a man who had been through what the new champ had been in order to get that title really appreciated, really understood. For those who recognised him – and many didn't – knew the little man as the one who had been the greatest legend of them all . . . Benny Lynch.

He was just 30 years of age but looked more than ten years older, even more, and was now in his less-than-happy days, the glory era just a memory, and even some of that was fading. Yet it had been just over three years since he had last been in the ring, having returned to the booths, the small fairground arenas where you challenged allcomers as he had done back in his apprenticeship days when that was the way you graduated, just as they had done way back in the days of the followers of The Fancy. But there was nothing to associate even those last overweight and unfit days of his in the booths to the Benny they saw that night. And before he turned and shuffled from the ring and out into the anonymity of being just one more punter in that wildly cheering crowd, those who had watched those precious nostalgic moments had to do their damnedest to hide their emotions.

Paterson was to explain some time after the fight that Kane had actually lost to him more as a result of events outside the ring. Kane, he said, had been lulled into a totally false impression of his true ability.

This had not, he stressed, been intentional, instancing the famous story of the American challenger for a major title who, when he had met the champion on Broadway the night before the fight, had staggered up to him pretending to be drunk. The champ, then thinking he was facing an out-of-condition walkover when they met in the ring, cockily back-pedalled, only to be clobbered. No, it hadn't been like that, assured Jackie, an honest man who considered such subterfuge as sharp practice. What had happened, he explained, was that while he and Kane were serving together in the RAF they had been friends while stationed at a camp in England. Kane had been a sergeant there and had, in fact, been one of his first friends in the service. They were to box often against each other in exhibition bouts. However, Jackie considered himself the world's worst exhibition boxer.

He just couldn't do 'demo' fights, his reaction when participating in them being that because they weren't the real thing they would make him slow and lethargic. Kane, he reckoned, had completely misjudged him because of these show bouts, had been under the impression he was faced with the easiest of tasks and had dearly paid the consequences for doing so.

The disappointment of not getting the fight entertainment they had expected was at least made up to the fans by witnessing the result they had wanted. They had gone absolutely wild at the victory, hundreds of them storming to the ringside and jumping on to the canvas. Because of the heavy rain there had been before the fight, they had carried Paterson to the ringside from the dressing-rooms, not wanting his feet to get wet in the mud. To keep him warm, Big Bill, an off-duty policeman and close pal of Jackie's, had put his cloth cap on his head and thrown his coat over his shoulders as his seconds lifted him in their arms. Not a piece of that clothing would be returned, the ecstatic fans in their frenzy tearing them to scraps for souvenirs of their new champion. He's our new Benny, they yelled. Aye, that was it. They had another Benny Lynch. And just like that very same Benny, it was to be in more ways than one.

The fight against Kane and the way he had so quickly demolished such a legendary champion was to be the pinnacle of Jackie Paterson's career. It had been hectic, barnstorming, triumphant days of invincibility till that point. Not that it was to be all downhill from the high peak he had reached, there being a summit plateau on which to coast, at least for a while. The downhill bit was still to come, along with all its accompanying headlines . . . headlines for reasons other than what he did with his gloves on.

Being called up for the RAF in the early years of the Second World War wasn't a help, breaking his regular fight and training routine and taking him away from the immediate supervision of Pat Collins, the manager who had been in charge of his career since that first controversial professional fight against the Irish man Kiely in Greenock. He had married his teenage girlfriend Helen and became a doting father to a young baby son who was to so tragically die aged just five weeks. Paterson had longed for a son and had taken the death of his little one badly, noticeably drinking much more than he had ever done, although there was no sign of him being as sorely affected the way Lynch had been by booze. But Jackie had found himself another affliction – betting.

The thrill of the gamble had the little man from Anderston absolutely hooked. Greyhounds were his speciality. Perhaps somewhere in his inner psyche there may have been some confusion over the meanings of bet more and *bête noire*, or that 'going to the dogs' had more than one interpretation. Whatever, he was a regular at all the big Glasgow venues, places like White City, Carntyne and Shawfield, punting with the best of them, often as much as £200 on a single race, the precise equivalent of that in the years of the new millennium being £2,126.

Like so many with the punting penchant, Jackie had a theory. And just like the others, the theory had just one conclusion – winning. His winning, that is. The theory was okay. It was the putting of it into practice in which everything went wrong. The doctrine which Jackie had worked out was basically nothing new, but then are any of them? Nevertheless, he was convinced it would win him a fortune or, more accurately, another fortune, for he was by now grossing big money at the fight game.

His theory about the dogs was that if he backed well-bred racers which were currently out of form, he would get long odds. By doing this often enough, the chances were, he figured, that the dogs' good breeding would always come through in the end.

There was doubtlessly good logic in his canine conjecture, but his gambling downfall was that he was rarely to prove it. And every time he didn't, his dwindling bank balance took another big deficit. And at £2,000 or more a bet, you can figure for yourself just how fast it went.

The fact that he had wisely invested some of his ring winnings in a couple of prosperous fruit shops was to be of little avail, for so heavy were his losses that these had to be sold in order to cover some of the bets for the races those well-bred dogs hadn't won.

Like many flyweight boxers when they reach full physical maturity, Paterson had increasing problems making the eight-stone limit of that division. Perhaps his training routine was part of that problem. He hated road training so much he avoided it as much as possible. To make up for it, he worked extra hard in other departments, even though, for a sportsman, he kept the most bizarre hours, doing much of his indoor routines late at night; even in the hours well past midnight he would still be there in the Anderston gym skipping, shadow-boxing and sparring.

And when he couldn't get sufficient pounds off, there would be hurried visits to do workouts in places where there would be tremendous heat, so that even more sweat, even more pounds, could be wrung from his small body. Pat Collins knew the manager of the Kelvin Cinema in the Anderston end of Argyle Street. It was one of the old picture theatres built in the days of the cinema boom with all the weird architecture which was the hallmark of that era. The architect of the Kelvin had obviously been caught up in the new wave of consumer art deco, the exterior being a mixture of decorative towers, the interior even more bizarre, one side of the stage styled in the fashion of a Turkish mosque, the other side depicting something out of ancient Spain. All to show movies from Hollywood! More important than the architecture, however, was that its central heating system was provided from a good-sized furnace room, where Jackie was to 'wool up' and do concentrated shadow-sparring bouts to peel off even more weight. At other times they would go into the city where Pat had got access to an even bigger and hotter furnace area, provided this time through his boxing-writer friend Euan Wellwood, in the bowels of the office building fronting on Buchanan Street, which at the time housed the *Glasgow Herald*, *Evening Times* and *Bulletin* newspapers.

He tried fighting featherweights (8st 7lb to 9st) but without much success, then concentrated for a while in the bantam division (up to 8st 7lb). That brought more wins than being a featherweight and he was to add two more prestigious titles to his already impressive collection, beating Jim Brady of Dundee for the Empire title and at the same time collecting a purse of £4,500, a record payout of the day, from promoter George P. Grant. In today's terms that sum would be £47,835. After that it was the turn of Theo Medina, the French gypsy and ex-Resistance fighter, which was to give him the European title.

It was one of these bantamweight fighters, Danny O'Sullivan, who had held the British title, who perhaps best described just what it was like being on the receiving end, as he had been, of a Paterson knockout punch. These were no wild haymaker swipes, the kind that take so much momentum there's almost enough time to send a telegram on ahead. Paterson's KOs were more along the lines of the classic Joe Louis dream-maker, a short, nine-inch jab that hit home with all the impact of a slab of concrete.

You didn't see it coming and you hardly knew it when you went. Fans really had to keep their eyes peeled to see that lightning piston in action. Boxer O'Sullivan certainly hadn't seen the one he received, making the memorable comment afterwards: 'It was like walking into a strange room and then someone turned out all the lights. I didn't feel anything.' As well as being an apprentice butcher, Paterson at one point had worked as a hammerman in the shipyards, which might not have given him much pay but had left him plenty of punch.

Although he had by now fought at both feather and bantamweight, he had still held on to his world flyweight title, the war minimising the number of challengers. But by the summer of 1946 there was a serious contender bidding for that coveted world title. The war by now was over and it was to be a great summer with Glasgow and its citizens absolutely determined to forget the horrors of six years of war and get back to the peace and normality of 1939. They didn't even complain about many of the shortcomings of that normality, things like the continued food and petrol rationing.

To get away to most places for the Fair holidays meant queuing for hours at the main railway stations. The two most popular destinations were Aberdeen, where landladies were advertising a full week's board at £4.20, and Blackpool, where the going rate was 63p a day and that included four meals! There were agonisingly long queues for the latter. They began lining up at the Central Station the previous night and by the morning the queue snaked out of the station all the way down Hope Street to Argyle Street, where it turned east under the rail bridges, the Hie'lan' Man's Umbrella, to Union Street.

At the Broomielaw they camped out all night in order to be on board the first sailings to Rothesay and Dunoon. For those who weren't going away there were always plenty of good theatre shows, like Tommy Morgan starring in *Civvy Symphony* at the Pavilion. If you couldn't afford an 8p seat for that there was plenty of free entertainment, including concert parties, pipe and military bands playing at the Springburn, Tollcross, Victoria, Kelvingrove, Linn and Queen's parks.

And, of course, there was the big fight, the very first world championship fight to be held in Britain after the war. And being between a champion fighter from Liverpool called Joe Curran and a man from Glasgow called Jackie Paterson, it had everyone talking.

The fight was scheduled for Hampden Park and tickets were on sale at the Central Halls in Bath Street at 25p, 50p, 75p, £1 and on up to the nearest ringside seats priced in élitist guineas, three of them to be precise, or £3.15. Wartime crowd restrictions had been removed and with a good weather forecast, more than 45,000 packed the two grandstands and all but one of the terraces on a bright and sunny summer's evening for what promised to be one of the greatest fight nights in years.

Curran, 32, was a formidable boxer with an impressive record of some 200 fights, winning 160 of them, drawing eight and losing 32. Paterson at 26 had fought Curran three times previously, Curran leading two bouts to one, a score which Paterson sorely bore, being that he had been disqualified in the fourth round of their first contest.

As well as his world title, Paterson had also put up for stake his British and Empire titles, all enhancing the stature of the promotion which was to receive the biggest press coverage of any sporting event since before the war. Curran boasted that Paterson would not last the distance and that as the more experienced boxer with his 2–1 fight advantage over the Glasgow man, he would easily run out the winner. But only for a few moments during the fight did it ever look like it might go the way Curran predicted, that being when Paterson suffered from the re-opening of an old eye injury. His corner worked wonders, however, and Paterson was to clearly demonstrate that if he couldn't land one of his spectacular short KO jabs, he was still a first-class ringmaster.

Curran barely won a round, boxing writer Elky Clark's score sheet giving him only one out of the 15 in which the points may have gone his way.

Paterson's fight that night against Curran, despite the fact he won and was still the British, Empire and world champion, was to mark the end-point of the pinnacle plateau of his fight career. Sure, he had demonstrated that he was still a copybook pugilist and that Curran had been no match for him, but those in the know were saying this wasn't the slam, wham-bam Paterson of old. That part of him, it seemed, had gone. And the proof of that was to come in ensuing fights that same year, first losing a non-title fight to his old ring opponent Rinty Monaghan, and then the Frenchman Theo Medina came back for another go at him, this time taking back his European bantamweight title by beating him in just four rounds.

Although he was clearly not the man he was in his early twenties, Paterson retained an amazing bounce-back factor and while he was losing some fights, he was still winning others, regaining his lost British bantamweight title while still holding his world flyweight title. Among the several around the world who had their eyes on that was a colourful little Hawaiian named Dado Marino. He had a long and impressive fight record, beating some of the toughest opponents around the Pacific rim, including Filipinos, Japanese and Americans, and although he was on the wrong side of 30, he could still lay claim to being the premier contender for that world title.

The arrival of the exotic Marino and his party from Honolulu was one of the most colourful events in the city after the Second World War. It was a black and white world in Glasgow then. Clothing, severely restricted by rationing for nearly eight years, was drab, styleless, and if it wasn't a grimy grey it was boring brown; the only proviso on colours, it seemed, was that they be dreary, that they be dull. You couldn't notice the beauty of the city's fine buildings being, as they were, hidden from sight by the soot and grime of centuries. Colours only happened in rainbows and what Hollywood supplied via Technicolour in the cinema.

Then this little Hawaiian appeared on the Glasgow scene in the most colourful of floral tropical shirts, together with an equally flamboyantly attired manager with the never-to-be-forgotten name of Sad Sam Ichinose. Their very presence that spring of 1947 cheered up Glasgow no end. Being a friendly and outgoing pair, they were the talk of the city and it was an event on its own just to see them walking around the streets, getting fond and friendly shouts everywhere they went. They were immediately taken to the hearts of Glasgow folk, even though their prime purpose here was to take home with them a sporting title that had almost become a part of the city itself.

Although he was anything but a Sad Sam, manager Ichinose had good reason to be everything his name implied when it came to the prospect of seeing his protégé meet the world champion from Glasgow. For the fight against Paterson, it seemed, was doomed never to take place, Jackie now making headline news for events other than those in the ring. First of all he had an attack of boils and the fight had to be delayed until they had healed. Then he was back on page one once more, this time asking for another postponement, due to another illness, presumed to be a virus of sorts. And then on Monday, 7 July of that year, the biggest sensation of all, when just hours before he was due to fight for a third time at Hampden Park he didn't appear for the weigh-in scheduled to take place at the Astoria Dance Hall. The story was that he had collapsed and was in bed. There were also stories about his having problems with his weight. And they were big problems.

The promoter had astutely made his arrangements for such an event, signing Paterson's old adversary, the Irishman Rinty Monaghan, to deputise for the Glasgow man in a non-title match with Marino should Paterson not appear.

When the story emerged of this third and most dramatic of call-offs, it turned out that the previous night at around eleven o'clock a doctor from the British Boxing Board of Control, as well as his own practitioner, was called to Paterson's bedside after he had taken ill yet again. He received treatment from his own doctor and amazingly revived sufficiently for him to get up from bed and restart training again. He carried on his various routines, sparring and exercising, until three in the morning, the wee small hours having become something of a pattern for Paterson, who still shunned the boxer's vital roadwork.

Having gone to bed after three that morning, he had been up again at ten and was back training hard once more in the gym at Anderston. It was crammed with boxing writers who were more intent on how he appeared at training than they had ever been with any other boxing champion. They eyed him microscopically as he sweated at his gym work, noting that he was wearing several sweaters and doing the most vigorous and intensive of exercises in an obvious attempt to shed more pounds. 'It's like he's boiling himself down to the weight,' observed one of them. The whispers went round that there was no way a man working as hard as this could reduce his weight and at the same time retain his strength. The whispers were right for, as they watched, his body appeared to go limp and the effort went out of his exercising before he dramatically collapsed to the floor.

He had at this point been training till well after midnight, but was still more than three pounds over the eight stone limit. Once again Jackie Paterson was headline news – not for what he could do in the ring but for what he couldn't do in preparation for it. His defence of his titles was off yet again and substitute Rinty Monaghan had to be quickly summoned to Glasgow for the fight scheduled for Monday night, 7 July 1947.

Despite Paterson's non-appearance and it being a particularly miserable night with a constant downpour of heavy rain, the like of which we know all too well in Glasgow around the Fair, more than 25,000 turned out to see the Irishman take on the man from the South Seas in what was now a non-title match. Because of the last-minute stand-in arrangements, an out-of-training Monaghan fought at half a stone heavier than the 7st 12lb Marino and, despite his poor condition, the Irishman put up his customary gutsy stand against the wily Hawaiian. However, he had to be cautioned several times by referee Moss Deyong for holding, eventually being disqualified in the ninth round for his persistence in this ring offence. He said later he hadn't really given it all by that stage and that he was holding back to give the fans a 'real thrill in the last round'. Thrill or no, when he was presented with an orange lei after the fight by Marino, then Monaghan gave the fans his other customary treat by singing 'When Irish Eyes are Smiling'.

The big question now was, just who was the world champion? The controversy was to rage for some time and once more Jackie was back in the headlines. Some were saying the title should go to Marino as Paterson had lost the right to it by not showing up for the fight, London promoter Jack Solomons being of that school of thought. However, Paterson had in his possession the certificate issued to him by the British Boxing Board of Control doctor on the eve of the fight declaring him unfit to fight. When there were moves to strip him of his flyweight titles and promoter Solomons announced he was arranging a rematch with Marino and Monaghan with the British titles at stake, Jackie took a court injunction out against anyone else assuming his titles, other than by doing so with him in the ring. But with the Boxing Board declaring the titles vacant, Solomons pressed on with the match, a fitter and trimmed down Monaghan winning enormous admiration from the Harringay fans in London by defeating the Hawaiian on a big points tally.

Incidentally, three years later, fighting in his home city of Honolulu, Marino, at the age of 34, was to win the undisputed world flyweight title, at the same time becoming the first grandfather in boxing to hold a world crown.

The controversy over the titles continued and could obviously only be settled in the ring, not in the courts, and a match was arranged for Paterson versus Monaghan, the two rival world champions, scheduled for the King's Hall in Belfast on Tuesday, 23 March 1948. And once again it was headline news whether or not Paterson would make the weight and turn up for the fight. Jackie and his family had been living in a fashionable terrace house in Ashton Road, Hillhead, at the time. A week before the fight he was still training hard at the Anderston club and telling boxing reporters that he was not yet up to what he called 'concert pitch'.

'But I will be next Tuesday when I defend my titles against Rinty Monaghan,' he assured them, one cynic among them exclaiming, 'Concert pitch! He's no' even fit enough to play the piano.' The joke being that piano playing was the little sportsman's favourite hobby.

Meanwhile, his precise weight continued to be a mystery. He had promised to have a special weigh-in just for the benefit of the press on the Thursday prior to the fight, which was to give the newsmen yet another Paterson sensation, for when he showed up for this he was four and a half pounds overweight. Try trimming off the weight of a couple of 2lb bags of sugar and some more from your body in a few days!

A few of the boxing reporters had been champion boxers themselves and they knew just how tough it was to lose a few ounces, let alone a few pounds. None knew better than Elky Clark, who covered the sport for the *Daily Record* and was something of a legend in his own time having been a British, Empire and European flyweight champion, a holder of the Lonsdale belt and only narrowly having lost a memorable world title fight in an epic battle at Madison Square Garden with Fidel La Barba. He had not only lost his championship bid that night but also his career, the most ferocious of ring battles having cost him the sight of an eye, it being removed in an operation just after the fight. Commenting on how tough it was to shed weight, Clark was to reveal that he had once gone for three weeks without drinking water in order to make the eight-stone mark for a flyweight fight.

'I was only once in my entire career over the 8st 2lb mark four days before a fight,' he wrote that morning in the *Record*, 'and that was with Fidel La Barba.' Clark said he was more shocked than surprised at Jackie's weight, adding, 'Getting rid of four and a half pounds will weaken him too much.'

The news of Paterson's weight problems was to be continuing front-page news, and bearing in mind that because of Government restrictions on the use of newsprint the daily tabloids were slashed to a mere eight pages, for a story to make page one it had to be really big news. When they heard about it in Belfast, the worried promoter of the Paterson–Monaghan fight immediately signed the promising young continental flyweight Maurice Sandeyron as a stand-in replacement should Paterson either not show up or fail to make the weight limit for his big fight.

There was just one major story for the rest of that week . . . would Jackie Paterson make the weight for the big fight? News reporters were there in force at Renfrew Airport when he had been due to fly out on a scheduled flight on the Monday night, the eve of the fight, which was to put them on to yet another sensational development in the Paterson weight saga. For he didn't show up for the plane and carloads of reporters and photographers set off for the city to try and trace him. Most headed for his house in the handsome terrace just off Byres Road. There they were to find that while the lights might have been on and there was obviously someone in, no one was answering the door.

The pressmen waited and watched. A car drew up at the house and out got Norman Lewis, the Welsh bantamweight champion who had been assisting Paterson in his training. He told them nothing.

One reporter headed for a nearby telephone call-box where he asked the operator to be put through to Paterson's, but the reply was, 'Sorry . . . no calls are being accepted at this number.'

The reporters waited and continued to watch. It was dark by now and as they stared at the house they could see silhouettes behind the drawn linen blinds in the main room of the house. They were those of two men and they could clearly see they were wearing boxing gloves and were sparring with each other. Seeing this, the reporters thought it time to give the Paterson main door another knock, and this time there was an answer, out stepping John Rafferty, now Paterson's trainer.

'Where is Jackie?' the reporters yelled.

'I don't know,' said Rafferty.

'Is he in the house?'

'No.'

'Can we come in then and look for ourselves?'

'Definitely not.'

And that was all he was saying.

Paterson wasn't sighted again until just minutes before the weigh-in at the Ulster Hall, having been able to dodge the pressmen on his trip over to Belfast. By now it seemed there was as much interest in the weigh-in as there was in the fight itself and the hall was packed by eager media people and fight officials anxious to know what the scales would be revealing.

Monaghan, a slender and scrawny little man, had no problem with his reading. Then Paterson stepped on the machine's weighing platform. He looked pale, drawn and tired, so weak he needed assistance to walk across the room, one writer describing his appearance as being 'sunken of eye, hollow of cheek, worried, morose of expression . . . the complete picture of nervous and physical dejection'.

There was absolute silence as the stewards checked then rechecked the stainless steel balance slides of the scales to get the perfect equilibrium reading before one of them loudly made the announcement: 'Paterson . . . seven stones, thirteen and one quarter pounds.' He had amazingly made the weight limit – with 12 ounces to spare.

If the fact that he had made the weight had been something of a surprise, the outcome of the fight wasn't, to those in the know. His strength and fortitude reserves sapped by the savage weight-reducing measures he had undergone, which included liquid reduction and a near-starvation diet, Paterson was anything but the fine, fit and fearsome boxer he really was.

In round one Monaghan, a most game and competent champion, shook Paterson's confidence with a hard right to the jaw. Paterson fought back but his punches lacked their normal power, although his clever boxing was notching up the points. But by round five it had all the appearance of requiring more than points to win this fight, Paterson's legs showing their first wobbly signs. By round six they were shimmying like they were set to do a sashay and Monaghan, knowing it was all going his way, went hard on the attack.

In the following round Paterson rose from a count of nine, visibly dazed, and the Irishman closed in on him for a quick conclusion. It wasn't to be the usual KO with the beaten man flat on his back and out to the world. The final punch had seen Paterson collapse in a sitting position in one corner, his legs having folded up like a sheet of paper, and staring as if from unseeing eyes as the referee fingered and loudly hailed the count.

He never heard the ten, or the nine, the eight, or any of the numbers of the count as he sat there near comatose, pandemonium breaking out in the hall at the realisation they had a new world champion. And he was Irish. The demise of the Glaswegian as a world champion was to be one of the greatest nights in Irish boxing, Rinty winning for his country their first ever world title.

He not only sang 'When Irish Eyes are Smiling' for them after they raised his right hand as champion, but gave them an encore of 'I'm Always Chasing Rainbows'. For Rinty Monaghan that night in the King's Hall, had caught his rainbow and it was to take the force of some 300 policemen to secure the ring from the clamour of the thousands in the hall who wanted to get near and acclaim the man who had made boxing history for them. Glasgow had known all about that some 13 years before when another little man, the one they called Benny Lynch, had brought his country their first world title. Now it was the turn of Belfast.

It was to be all the way downhill for Paterson after that, winning only three of his final 12 fights, one of his famous bounce-backs being to hold world bantamweight champ Vic Toweel to a ten-round decision in Johannesburg. He continued to have the occasional fight up till 1951 when he was outpointed by Willie Myles. His boxing career of 13 years, which had seen an impressive 63 wins, 41 of them inside time, and three draws in 91 fights, was over.

The career that had pinnacled at the greatest heights in his sport and then had roller-coastered for so long had ended in the giant slalom which only knows one direction. Less than two years after that match and after having made around £100,000 – the equivalent of more than a million today – he was in the bankruptcy court. He said he had gambled away £55,000 and had given away £25,000. He was reduced to working in a pub in Largs for around £7 a week in the summer, but with no wages for the rest of the year, apart from free board for himself and family of two sons.

It was a somewhat distressing story the bankruptcy court was to hear of a man and the money he hadn't been savvy enough to hold on to. The court was told that in 1947, his best-earning year, he had made the equivalent of over £128,000. Another year he had made the equivalent of £116,000. He told the court that during his first five years as a professional fighter he had known nothing about income tax.

It was when he had put his affairs into the hands of a chartered accountant that he had to pay back his taxes. It had been while he was serving with the RAF and stationed at Bishopbriggs that he had acquired the betting habit, he said.

'I used to go to the dogs in the evening and had a run of luck,' he told the court. 'I was winning all the time and started to put on heavier bets.' Then, as is the way with so many in the gambling game, the luck ran out, but the heavy betting didn't result in his savings being devastated. He had started a fruit shop business in Byres Road, another in Argyle Street, but these had to be sold.

Just like Benny Lynch before him, Jackie had also been in the habit of giving money away to people who were little more than nodding acquaintances. He would hand out notes to people living in the same street as him, he said, 'because they were friends'.

In 1954 he sold his dearly prized Lonsdale belt to raise cash to take him and his wife Helen with their two sons, Johnny and David, to South Africa, the country which he had taken to on that trip five years previously when he had fought Vic Toweel. It was to be the new life, as it were, for the Patersons and the news of his departure was met with a genuine feeling of wellbeing from the citizens of his city for the plucky fighter who had entertained them so much and had so handsomely added to Glasgow's sporting fame.

But even this new page in his life wasn't to stop Jackie's downhill slalom slide. In South Africa he had got a job as a hotel manager but was sacked for insulting the owner. He began drinking more and, after 23 years of happy marriage, divorced Helen. However, it was Helen who was there to help him financially when he decided to return to the UK. That was only to find him more unsettled, and the drinking continued, losing one job after another, and in London there was the humiliation of being arrested for being drunk in the street, for which he appeared in court and was fined.

In 1965 there was an attempted reconciliation with Helen, Jackie returning once more to South Africa where he got work as a truck driver. But their reunion was to be short-lived and on Saturday, 19 November 1966, there was to be the saddest news of all about Jackie Paterson. After a night's drinking there had been an argument with another man in their digs at Amanzimtoti, near Durban. Like so many such alcohol-fuelled spats, it had been the merest of humdrum debates. They had been arguing over the names of some London streets. If the subject matter had been of little consequence, the outcome most certainly was. For Jackie was to bleed to death after being stabbed with a broken bottle. He was 47 years of age. A man was arrested for his murder, but the charges were later dropped. There are a variety of reports about the incident, some indicating Jackie had died as a result of a bar-room brawl. But in a book published in 2000, on the life of Paterson (*Triumph to Tragedy* by John Morrison), the author confirms that Jackie's death had been accidental, hence the charges being dropped against the man arrested at the time.

A close friend had been the journalist Hugh Taylor who had said of him that he had been the model boxer and was the quietest and most unassuming of men. All of which Jackie Paterson was, yet while all Scotland was genuinely shocked and saddened at his tragic ending, somehow there was no great surprise that their most gallant little warrior would have an ending almost befitting that of a Greek tragedy.

THE SHOCKING MURDER OF A MCFLANNEL

It was by no means a classic murder. But, oh, how they talked about it. First there was all the gossip and tittle-tattle about what might have been going on in the Govan flat of a BBC man who had been found dead there. Then there was all the chat about what was being revealed while the case was being conducted at the High Court in Glasgow. For this trial had all the ingredients of the most intriguing of murders: a well-known showbusiness personality; the involvement of *The McFlannels*, that being a BBC radio programme which happened to be one of the most popular shows ever presented to the Scottish public; the gruesome finding of the victim in a flat right in the heart of Govan; the dramatic flight of the main suspect to a foreign country; the calling of Interpol and revelations that the BBC man from *The McFlannels* had homosexual tendencies. Now there was something! For this was happening in an age when closet doors were firmly shut. If that was your way, then so be it. But it was never mentioned publicly. Goodness, no. Not even the slightest mention of it out of doors, as it were. And here it was about to happen in a court case involving not only the BBC, but the McFlannels! No! For heaven's sake, no! Not the McFlannels! For nothing like that ever, ever, ever happened to the unpretentious, unworldly, unsophisticated, unimpeachable McFlannels who, as a fictional family, were the ultimate in sexual innocence.

The ensuing High Court trial was to see the appearance of nationally recognised figures in what was the most varied assembly of witnesses ever for a major trial in the city. One of them was even to be named among the top ten Scots of the century, ahead of such famous names as the late Labour leader John Smith, the Queen Mother and Jock Stein. All this, together with the sensational revelations that the murder victim, the much-respected personality from that radio show which everyone knew and loved so well, had a dark and sinister side. It had been years since the city had known such a dramatic or fascinating murder. There have been few, if any, like it since.

Albeit that a murder had been perpetrated, putting it into today's terms, what happened in a tenement house at Water Row in Govan that July in 1954 was, in fact, not all that extraordinarily sordid or sinister. However, before it can be appreciated just how shocked Scotland was at the murder of George Ford McNeill, you must cast back your thoughts to the way we were in Glasgow in those days of the mid-'50s. It was just nine years after the war, although in so many ways you would have thought the war was still going on. The danger of bombing and invasion had gone, of course, but food rationing and other shortages lingered on, and housing conditions in the city, where most didn't even have hot water let alone their own toilet, were absolutely abysmal. The pound notes in your wage packet could be counted on the fingers of one hand, and even good jobs, like customs officers, for which there was a big recruiting drive at the time, paid only £8 a week.

But Glaswegians, being Glaswegians, enjoyed themselves in the ways they know best, seeking out whatever there was to cheer. There were laughs galore at the Alhambra Theatre's *Half-Past Eight Show* starring Jack Radcliffe and Stanley Baxter. If you liked a good song there was John Hanson belting it out as the Red Shadow in *The Desert Song* at the King's and Josef Locke was doing the rounds with *Hear My Song, Violetta.* For a simple holiday you could have a week's full board at Rothesay for £4.75 and from the Broomielaw there was the choice of 16 cruises down the Clyde to far-off places like the Mull of Kintyre, Arran and Inveraray, as well as much closer favourites like Dunoon, Rothesay and Millport, for as little as 30p, with toe-tapping live 'Scotch' music thrown in, and for even less there were nightly bus trips to see what the adverts described as 'the wonderful illuminations' in Largs.

Television was in black and white, the picture was scratchy, the programmes even worse, and TV had not yet become a universal household item. In the evenings everyone still listened to the radio, especially on certain nights when a favourite programme might be featured. And when it was a programme called *The McFlannels*, everyone listened. At least, everyone in Scotland, where the characters were as well known as those in the years ahead on TV's *Take the High Road, Coronation Street, EastEnders* and others. However, the only similarity between the ones you see on today's TV and those listened to back in the '50s is their popularity. For the McFlannels were as spectacularly couthy as they were corny, which is not so much a commentary on the show itself but a reflection on the way we were.

Bear in mind we're speaking of the 1950s, when entertainers kept their clothes on, their mouths clean and rock 'n' roll merely meant that your sea voyage to Arran or the Isle of Man had been a bit rough – an almost vanished era when adultery, nudity, rape, sodomy, masturbation, the 'f' word and the 'b' word, or any other dubious words, toilet functions, women behaving like men and men behaving like women were not part of the nightly entertainment scene. Remove that doubtful selection from any broadcast or theatrical show and you are left with other values for your evening's enjoyment. Which is why in those days programmes like *The McFlannels* were listened to and spoken about just as much as the most popular of the TV soaps today.

The history of *The McFlannels* radio show goes back to just before the outbreak of the Second World War. It had been the brainchild of housewife Helen W. Pryde, who lived in the city and who later moved on to Laurencekirk, Kincardineshire and Forfar. Like everyone else at the time, she was an avid radio listener and on hearing a particular programme, a talk on a country flitting, our very own expression for a house removal, she thought it could have been presented in a much funnier vein. She had written to the BBC telling them precisely that, at the same time presenting some ideas on just how that might be done. To his great credit, producer Robin Russell was to reply with the advice that she should put her ideas in the form of a sketch. She did this and producer Russell liked the result so much he put it forward for programming.

The first series, called *The McFlannels Rub Along*, was an immediate hit, listeners being highly amused at this new folksy family who were to become household names despite the fact each of the characters had the surprising, but fitting, surname of a fabric. *The McFlannels* themselves were, just like flannel, warm and durable. The McVelvets and the McSilks were very definitely superior. The McCanvases and the McTweeds – coarser texture, this pair! McCotton, McGauze and McPoplin . . . all popular punters. And so it went on and on. They even had a Frenchman for a while and he was called Michael Valenciennes, his surname being the name of a popular and fashionable scrolled linen lace.

Patriotic to the core, they were there in our time of need and were a much-needed boost to public morale with their long-running series

The McFlannels in Wartime. Their most simplistic of idioms became hilarious national sayings, such as Willie McFlannel's 'Ach, cheer up, ye've never died a winter yet.' The west of Scotland blend of patter and patois obviously became too much for one of the show's directors, an Englishman, who became so demented with the dialect he gave up and headed south.

It was about that point that the McFlannels were given a prime and regular Sunday evening spot, coming under the producership of Howard M. Lockhart, something of a legendary character in BBC Scotland, being one of their top production executives, and who was to be in charge of the programme for eight years.

The stars of the show were to become as much household names as the colourful characters they portrayed. The regulars included those playing the resident McFlannel family: John Morton as Willie; Meg Buchanan as Sarah; Jean Stoddart as Maisie; Arthur Shaw as Peter; and Willie Joss as Uncle Mattha. Others came in and out of the show, going on to do much greater things, such as film-star-to-be Gordon Jackson, who in some episodes played both Peter and Matt; and Rikki Fulton, also a newcomer to showbusiness at the time, who played the Revd David McCrepe, a sort of remote precursor to his legendary Revd I.M. Jolly.

Like The Broons in the *Sunday Post*, whose kailyard philosophy they shared, most situations were built around the principal characters, who included Uncle Mattha, a born scrounger with neglected adenoids, whose feet perpetually suffered agonising corns; Mrs McCotton (Grace McChlery), a genteel and affected soul whose shocking grammar included such sayings as 'If I'd knew I'd nivver have came'; Ivy McTweed, the wee Glesca keelie, and Mrs McCorduroy (Elizabeth Swan), the warm-hearted neighbour who bantered so easily with Peter.

Some of the titles of the episodes reveal much about the homespun kind of humour they served up, some of the memorable being: 'High Tea', 'Sarah Wrangles and Wangles', 'A Quiet Evening at Home', 'Preparing the House', 'On the Plot', 'When the Cat is Away', 'On the Fuel Front', 'Good Resolutions', 'The Len' o' Five Pounds', 'Willie in Hot Water', 'Country Cousin', 'Spring Cleaning', 'Willie in Hospital', 'The Dog Next Door', 'Home Guard Reunion', 'The Unquiet Wedding', 'Sarah at Hampden', 'Things That Go Bump in the Night' and 'Holiday Romance'.

As the titles all so amply demonstrate, they were the ultimate in kailyard and couthiness. It was *Ma and Pa Kettle* or *Little House on the Prairie* taking place in a tenement instead of amongst the tumbleweed. There was never any need to chase the kids from the kitchen for fear of any broadcast causing embarrassment. Maw, Paw, Gran and the weans could all tune in together and enjoy what they heard. *The McFlannels* were strictly wholesome and homely; and often very, very real. They created that rare achievement of providing genuine fun and amusement for the thousands who listened and loved the show. Viewed in today's terms, though, it's not surprising that you may just ask 'why'?

Here's what was likely to happen in a typical episode. The character called Mrs McTweed knocks on the door of Sarah McFlannel's tenement home. Sarah takes ages to answer and Mrs McTweed impatiently and angrily demands, when she finally opens the door, 'Whit di ye mean keeping me standing here? Were ye kidding on ye wirnae in?' Sarah replies that she was cleaning her shelves and had already had to stop that job about a dozen times that morning because of people coming to the door. Mrs McTweed responds with a favourite expression that she couldn't care 'a tuppenny ticket' about that then goes on to ask if it was Sarah who had stolen her doormat. Sarah erupts at that, denying she ever touched the mat, to which McTweed replies, 'Well, what's that at your door?' Sarah says she doesn't know, but 'If you thought ah would stoop to touch your scuddy wee mat . . .'

It was the stuff of the old music halls or bedroom farce on the stairheid. The pair are by now getting worked up at each other and Mrs McTweed responds with, 'It's no' a scuddy wee mat,' telling Sarah that it was as good a mat as her mat, if not better.

'I'm away to the polis office for I'm sick to death with the McFlannel family. The things ah've suffered!'

Sarah then asks where her mat is and if by any chance it's at McTweed's door. Then she points it out at another neighbour's door. It must have been the children, she says. Mrs McTweed announces her disgust with them (the McFlannel weans, that is). 'Ah wish ah had a haud of them. Tying door handles tae doorbells, putting squeebs in keyholes and stuffing the washing-house chimney and setting fire to the ashpits and playing football in the back court, an' dear knows what. The place hasn't been fit to live in since youse McFlannels flittit in. You ca' it playing yersels. They're nothing but a gang of hooligans!'

Sarah says they are no worse than other folk's children and, knowing precisely what will really get her dander up, says, 'They're a sight better than a dog.'

'You leave my dug alane,' says dog-lover Mrs McTweed. 'Never did you any harm.'

At that, the mood of their stairhead summit moderates, Sarah McFlannel going on to talk about getting a house in a scheme because they were easier to keep clean, although you had to know someone in the Corporation before you could get one. But there was hope, perhaps, for Sarah says that one of the neighbours was friendly with a woman whose sister had a daughter who had just got engaged to a chap in the Gas Board. Maybe they should have words with him.

No innuendoes. No undertones, no overtones; no naughty nuances; no curses, oaths, profanities or blasphemes. Not a *double entendre* in hearing; nothing irreligious or sacrilegious; nothing bigoted, nothing racist; nothing suggestive. That was *The McFlannels*. It should therefore come as no great surprise after reading these few samples of this amazingly successful radio programme to know that Helen W. Pryde, its creator, had a very strict and puritanical upbringing.

Intensely religious, she considered anything to do with the theatre as 'sin'. Imagine, then, the shock she, the players, the producers and the huge listening public were to experience with the news that one of the cast had been found murdered. It was a page-one sensation, editors hauling out their biggest type to announce BODY IN CUPBOARD MURDER: McFlannels Actor Dead Three Weeks.

The news broke in the morning papers of Tuesday, 3 August 1954, that George Ford McNeill, who played Mr McZephyr in *The McFlannels*, had been found murdered. His body had been discovered in his flat at No. 1 Water Row, the little street which led down to the old Govan ferry, after his brother had reported him missing for three weeks. Police had broken into the flat to make the gruesome discovery which, because of the victim's McFlannels connection, was to be headlined throughout the country.

The way the *Daily Record* reported it that morning told some of the story: 'Forty-seven-year-old gay, jovial George Ford McNeill, the well-known Scottish broadcaster who played Mr McZephyr in *The McFlannels*, was found murdered yesterday in a cupboard of his four-room bachelor flat overlooking Glasgow's Govan Cross.'

Gay and jovial! Bachelor flat! The appropriate nudges and winks were there right from that first story, even though the word 'gay' at the time had not been totally hijacked for its latter-day meaning.

The story went on to detail how McNeill had been a friend of Dr George F. MacLeod, of the Iona Community, which did considerable welfare and other social work for young people, and that he had been dead for about three weeks. The badly decomposed body had been stuffed into a 6ft x 6ft cupboard just off the flat's main sitting-room; and right away police were saying, 'Yes, it's murder.'

Other details revealed in the first stories were that McNeill was widely known as a youth leader and often gave parties attended by young men connected with the youth movements in which he was interested. It also mentioned that on one or two occasions in recent years he had been threatened by Glasgow teenage gangs 'because of his boys' club activities'.

It didn't take police long to name a suspect, Interpol being called in to help the Glasgow detectives find a man named as John William Gordon, a 24-year-old freelance writer who, they said, they were anxious to speak to in connection with their inquiries. Gordon, it was reported, had lived at several addresses in the city but newspapermen tracked down his most recent, in Scott Street, Garnethill, where they spoke to his landlady. She was most forthcoming and was to tell reporters some considerable detail about her boarder, beginning with the fact that she was under the impression that he had gone to Copenhagen. She said he was a quiet man who 'hated women and didn't drink', although he claimed to be an expert on wine. Gordon knew the murdered man well, said the landlady, and had gone to see him one evening every week and it was often late when he returned.

'He said he went there to act as waiter at all-male bridge parties and that Mr McNeill paid him for that. Often he would come home with a big box containing chocolates and candied fruits.' She was also to say he was interested in religion, especially his work at Community House, the headquarters in Glasgow at the time of the Iona Community, and that he often received letters from a male friend in Sweden and that this man had invited him there for a holiday.

The Copenhagen connection was quick to fizzle out and for the first few days police were baffled by the whereabouts of the 24-year-old Gordon who they were now thinking might still be somewhere in Scotland. However, within a week of the grim discovery of *The*

McFlannels' Mr McZephyr, Glasgow police were to issue a warrant for Gordon's arrest and extradition from Spain. He had been detained by Spanish police on a charge of illegal entry into the country – it was in the days when a visa was required for British subjects to enter General Franco's domain – and he was being held in a police cell in Gerona.

But it was to take a further three months of negotiations, frustrated by antiquated Spanish bureaucracy, before Gordon was finally extradited to Scotland in late November. On his return he appeared in chambers at Glasgow Sheriff Court, where he was charged with the murder of McNeill and remanded in custody for trial.

The summer had gone, so too had autumn and much of that cold winter of 1954–55 – so cold a poor pensioner died queuing in George Square for her travel concession ticket – as the various legal factions went about the lengthy and protracted business of setting up a major court trial. It had been a bleak and nasty winter, with hill farmers searching for thousands of sheep missing in huge snowdrifts. The Chancellor of the Exchequer did his best to make it even more bleak by telling us that we were spending too much money, and he was to announce that no longer could you buy cars, TVs or household items on a no-deposit, hire-purchase basis. Elsewhere in the world the Russians and Americans were rattling their atomic armouries at each other, the Americans boasting their new H-bomb could pulverise the Soviets in a matter of hours. Slightly more cheering was the fact that there was still a little style around when it came to rail travel: for £1.7½p you could book a return to Edinburgh for the rugby international against Ireland, the fare including your lunch at a booked table in the dining-car going out, and another for tea on the way back.

A date for the trial was finally announced, it being scheduled to begin at the High Court in Glasgow on Monday, 22 February. Few trials have been awaited with more anticipation and curiosity than that of John William Gordon, and all because of that McFlannel connection with the victim, George Ford McNeill. Were all these rumours about *The McFlannels* star true? Could he really be gay? Were there really all these happenings going on in his house? And right here in the heart of our very own Govan! Surely not! Not someone from *The McFlannels*. All those who gossiped and speculated – it was the chit-chat of every street corner, every pub – were not to be disappointed as the story dramatically unfolded over the next two weeks.

Gordon faced five charges: that between 12 and 15 July of the previous year he had assaulted George Ford McNeill in his house at 1 Water Row, Govan, by striking him on the head with an axe and 'did murder him'; having stolen a chequebook, a savings-bank book, a passport and clothing and other articles; uttered as genuine a cheque for £45 at St George's Post Office bearing the forged signature of McNeill; and uttered as genuine withdrawal forms bearing the forged signature of McNeill to obtain money.

The court assembled under Lord Sorn and among those defending and prosecuting were some of the most illustrious names in Scottish legal circles. Gordon's solicitor was the famous criminal lawyer Laurence Dowdall, a man who was such a household name throughout Scotland for his outstanding achievements as a defence lawyer that the knee-jerk reaction of anyone arrested at the time was the plea 'Get me Dowdall'. His senior counsel was Sir John Cameron, QC, and the prosecution team was led by advocate-depute R.S. Johnston, both to become famous Law Lords.

The all-star cast conducting the trial was to be more than matched by the eminence and range of the witnesses called to give evidence. Few trials before, or since, have produced such a variety of witnesses, which were to include one of the legendary senior sleuths from Scotland Yard, an inspector from Sûreté in Paris, a murderer, a prominent newspaper editor, second-hand dealers and cleaning ladies, and one of Glasgow's and Scotland's most distinguished and respected ministers of religion.

The first dramatic moment of the trial came with the opening witness, the dead man's 49-year-old brother Robert. He told the court that he was suspicious of a telegram his elderly mother had received on 15 July that previous year. It had read: 'Urgent call to Paris. Back on Saturday.' And it was signed with the single letter 'G'.

'My brother,' said Mr McNeill emphatically, 'never to my knowledge signed himself "G". I was suspicious of it. But I took no action on the telegram. My immediate reaction was to think of my mother who had been an invalid. I had seen her far from well, I thought she was going to die, and the telegram was of such an alarming nature it might have had a bad effect. I decided to wait and see.'

Later, however, out of concern for his brother, he had gone to the police in Govan and together with two detectives they went to the flat in Water Row. There they forced entry and immediately noticed a strange smell in the house, a smell he described as being 'very unpleasant'. The detectives then discovered George McNeill's body.

John Bell of Paisley, a 57-year-old friend and work colleague of McNeill, was to tell the court of a 'tall, suave and mysterious' man with whom he had words at the door of McNeill's flat some two weeks before he had been found dead. Gordon, his hands thrust deep into the pockets of a heavy camel coat, listened intently as Bell said he was a personnel superintendent at Fairfields shipyard where McNeill also worked and explained why he had gone to the flat. McNeill, like most broadcasters in the '50s, subscribed to the old showbiz maxim of it being best not to give up the day job, that being much more of a necessity in those days, their fees for performances, even for starring ones such as in *The McFlannels*, only paying nominal sums. Invariably, there would be long periods between roles, making it essential to have a regular income of sorts. Which was why McNeill had continued his job as a welfare officer at Fairfields shipyard, just along the road from his flat in Water Row.

Bell said he had been concerned when McNeill hadn't turned up for work that Monday, 12 July 1954, so he had gone to the flat, where a man whom he had never seen before answered the door. He was aged between 25 and 28 and when he inquired about his friend George, the man said that he had left the night before for Paris. 'I said that was a very odd thing as he had never told me he was going to do that,' said Bell. 'The man at the door said that McNeill was going to wire Fairfields when he got to his destination.'

Bell, it was said, had been called to an identification parade at Govan police station but had been unable to pick out the man in question.

A second witness, a youth leader at the Pearce Institute in Govan, also said he had called at McNeill's house but had got no reply. He had tried later when 'a young man came to the door'.

'Do you see that man in court?' asked the advocate-depute.

The witness pointed to Gordon.

Two young men who had previously met Gordon in McNeill's flat identified him in court. They said they used to go to McNeill's flat for tea and to have discussions relating to a youth club. When one of these witnesses was cross-examined by Gordon's counsel, Sir John Cameron, about the bond between him and McNeill, he replied that there was the invitation to go to his house for a cup of tea.

QCs like Cameron are the masters of the simple question – simple questions that can so often produce simple but most telling answers. So Cameron was to probe more about that invitation to have tea at McNeill's house.

'And what did you discuss?' queried Cameron.

'Religion and politics.'

Again, a simple reply that demanded more to be asked.

'And were there any older men along with you?'

'No.'

Then he returned to that religion and politics answer he had been given.

'Are you a church member?'

'No.'

'Do you belong to a political party?'

'No.'

Of course, one doesn't have to belong to a church or a political party to discuss such subjects, but by the slant of the questions and the answers they brought about, some seeds of doubt were indubitably being planted and the distinguished QC seemed satisfied with what he and the court had learned from that little piece of cross-examination.

A married couple who lived in the flat beneath McNeill's house were to tell in their evidence of how in the early evening of 12 July of the previous year, when they were having their meal, the wife heard a heavy thud upstairs on the floor of McNeill's kitchen. The thud had been followed by three taps and then, a few minutes later, there was the sound of footsteps crossing McNeill's kitchen. She had asked her husband whether or not she should go up and see if McNeill was all right but it had seemed everything was in order after hearing the footsteps.

The following day a young man had called at her flat in the afternoon and inquired why Mr McNeill had not been at work. When her husband came home they discussed this and around six o'clock that evening she had gone to McNeill's door. It was Gordon. She had asked about Mr McNeill and Gordon had replied that he was all right but had packed a bag and gone away in a hurry. She hadn't asked where he had gone. When she mentioned the thud of the previous night, Gordon had replied that they had been shifting furniture and she accepted this to be the explanation for the noises.

McNeill's housecleaner, a 32-year-old woman from Ibrox, said that she had gone to the house on Monday, 12 July, and had been surprised to find the storm door open, which meant that someone was at home.

She'd gone inside but there was no sign of McNeill. Then she described how she had been startled at the sudden appearance of a young man wearing one of McNeill's silk dressing-gowns. 'He seemed quite at home,' she told the court. 'He said to me that George [McNeill] had said I would be coming to tidy the flat and that I was just to carry on.'

Two days later, on the Wednesday, when she had returned to do more cleaning, Gordon was there again. 'He was the only person in the house and told me that Mr McNeill had been called away in a hurry.'

The house, said the cleaner, had been disarranged, some carpets having been rolled up. McNeill's bed had been stripped of the bedding, furniture had been moved around and a pile of dishes lay on the floor ready for packing. Gordon had told her not to bother tidying the flat as George had been called away in a hurry and that he was waiting on a van to come and take the furniture away for storage.

The cleaning lady was also to note what she described as a 'peculiar smell' in the house. 'I said to Mr Gordon that there was a fusty smell in the sitting-room. I thought he had opened a tin of meat and had forgotten about it. He said he didn't notice the smell and opened one of the windows.'

Asked if she had noticed anything unusual about Gordon's behaviour, she replied, 'No, he was quite chirpy.'

There were more unexpected sensations the following day when a woodyard labourer told a hushed court how 12 years previously he had murdered a girl by strangling her. Following this he had been found insane and went to Perth Institution, from which he had been released more than two years previously. Going into some detail about the murder he had committed, he said he had strangled the girl 'in a temper'.

The court sat in spellbound silence as he gave further details of the incident. 'I was very much in love with her at the time. She returned it for a time but latterly we were always quarrelling.' After being released from Perth Institution, McNeill had been appointed as one of his guardians and he met him regularly every five weeks. He had gone to see McNeill on the night of 12 July, which was on or about the time he had been murdered.

The man tightly gripped the rail of the witness-box when he was then asked, 'Are you connected in any way with the death of George McNeill in his flat at Water Row?'

The reply came in a firm voice. 'No, sir – definitely not.'

He said he had gone to McNeill's house on the night in question in the company of his fiancée, whom he married a month later. They wanted to speak to McNeill about their forthcoming marriage. McNeill had wished them the best of luck and said that he would send a telegram on the night they were married. But at the start of their conversation with him, McNeill had said to them, 'I'll give you five minutes and then chuck you both out.'

The witness had interpreted that as meaning that a friend was coming to the house. The girl, now his wife, corroborated the story, but was to add that while in McNeill's house that night, she thought she heard sounds from another part of the flat. 'It was as if there was a housekeeper moving about the house,' she said.

There was considerable surprise in the court the following day when a witness with the same name as the accused was called to give evidence. He was none other than John Gordon, the distinguished 64-year-old editor-in-chief of the *Sunday Express*. He revealed that he had been given an envelope from the Foreign Office containing a letter dated 30 August 1954 and addressed to him at his offices in Fleet Street, London. He said he had not known John Gordon, the accused, and had therefore handed over the letter to Superintendent Capstick of New Scotland Yard. The advocate-depute then asked editor Gordon to read the letter.

The highly respected newspaperman adjusted his spectacles, cleared his throat and in a clear voice read the letter exhibit which was to detail some of Gordon's adventures after leaving Glasgow that previous summer.

> Dear John Gordon,
> I write as a reader to the only honest journalist in Britain. You are, of course, aware of the rather horrid suggestion that is at present in the air. Need I say I am innocent, that is of murder. I have given a statement to Scotland Yard by letter and I write to you because as the papers carry the suspicions of the police, I give you the opportunity of carrying my refutation as an exclusive . . . I always wanted to be an exclusive journalist but had not the opportunity. But I can still help an honest man and an honest paper. As you are aware I have a record and a man with a record carries a burden. I had made good, as the saying goes, and

then George McNeill offered me the use of a room until I got on my feet again. He made the dining-room into a bedroom for me. On the morning of 12 July he asked me not to disturb him as he was expecting a guest. Naturally, I was careful not to. I left the flat at 11 a.m. and went to town to visit a cinema. I didn't return until the ferry about 2 a.m. across the Clyde. I entered the flat and went to bed. On the morning of 13 July I rose around 10 a.m., bathed, prepared and ate breakfast and started tidying up. In the process I entered George's bedroom and found him shot dead in bed. Remembering the Bentley* fiasco and knowing the boy, do you wonder that I was panicky? My friends were not accessible. I was alone.

Gordon's letter to the newspaper editor then went on to detail his experiences after leaving Glasgow, of how he had gone first to Paris, then on to Germany, to Belgium and to Italy, where in Rome he found 'too many English tourists' which made him return to France. In Marseilles he joined the French Foreign Legion but had then been 'kicked out because my nationality was unsuitable'.

From Marseilles he had then taken a ship to Barcelona and it was in Spain, while trying to secure a visa to go to Brazil, that he had been arrested. His letter ended: 'In innocence and all confidence, I sign myself John William Gordon.'

That same day in court a handwriting expert testified that some documents bearing the signature of George F. McNeill, which included a bank cheque, two Post Office bank withdrawal forms and a receipt, were written not by McNeill but by Gordon.

'There were superficial resemblances,' he said, 'between specimens of the dead man's writing and the alleged forgeries. But there was no doubt that the hand printing on two of the documents was Gordon's.'

There was more damning evidence to come. The sister of a Maryhill furniture shop owner, who assisted in the business, said she had gone to McNeill's flat after a phone call from a man saying he had some furniture for sale.

---

* In 1952, two years before the McNeill murder, Derek Bentley and Christopher Craig, two English youths, were sentenced to death for the killing of a policeman. Despite being under arrest at the actual time his accomplice Craig shot dead the policeman, only Bentley was hanged, his mate being reprieved because he was just 16.

'I rang the bell and a man answered the door and invited me in.' She identified Gordon in the dock as the man in the flat. 'He told me,' she said, 'that his sister was coming home from South Africa and he was getting rid of stuff in the house as she had her own furniture. I saw a rather nice vase and he said I could have it as a gift.' She then bought several articles and agreed to pay £12 for them. There was no haggling over the price, although she agreed it was a bargain for her.

The son of another second-hand dealer said he too had gone to McNeill's house after an inquiry by Gordon about some articles he had for sale. Gordon had come to his father's shop about them on 13 July. At the house Gordon repeated the story about his sister coming home, only this time he had told this dealer that she was returning home from France, and because she was bringing her own furniture he was selling what was in the house. In the kitchen he had showed him some cutlery, asking if it was really silver or not.

The first of Gordon's adventures abroad after he fled from Glasgow was detailed by Inspector Claude Michel Robert, of the Sûreté Nationale in Paris, who was also an officer of Interpol. He said that on 17 July, Gordon had booked into the Mazagran Hotel in Paris, stayed the night, but had left the following morning without paying the bill. The hotel proprietor, however, had been able to seize two suitcases which Gordon had left.

It was then the court heard the first grim details of just how McNeill had died and the state of his body when found by police. It had been Chief Detective Inspector McAulay who had found McNeill's body in a boxroom of his flat in Govan. The battered body had been buried under a pile of bedclothes and boxes and was 'wrapped up like a cocoon'. McAulay told the court that McNeill had severe head injuries, mainly to his left temple. He had obviously been attacked as he lay prone in bed and his body was naked except for a blue-striped pyjama jacket. McAulay had also been the policeman who arrested Gordon in Spain and when he had charged him there, Gordon replied, 'I am not guilty. I thought George was shot.'

Superintendent George McLean, head of the police identification bureau, said he had counted 1, 175 blood spots covering an area of 15ft x 7ft in the bedroom of McNeill's house. From the wide area of the bloodstains he imagined that McNeill had been assaulted violently and repeatedly. He said he had found no signs of a struggle and in his search for the murder weapon he had found an axe lying on papers which had been placed on top of coal in the cellar.

'It struck me that the handle of the axe was unusually clean to be lying in a coal cellar.' When he had examined it for fingerprints, none were found. He was of the opinion that the handle had either been washed or rubbed to remove any marks. He thought the assault was carried out with an axe. In cross-examination, he agreed that McNeill had been hit with repeated blows struck 'with maniacal force'.

A male nurse from what was called at the time Hawkhead Mental Hospital then told the court about a patient who had said to him he wanted to confess to the murder. The nurse had been, as he said, 'rather sceptical', not just because of the man's mental condition but because of the fact the patient had been in hospital on the day McNeill was said to have been killed. The nurse also said that he had discovered a letter to the patient with a London postmark and that he had given him the impression that he knew something of the whereabouts of Gordon, who police were looking for at the time.

There had been some considerable anticipation at the calling of the next witness, a person who was a nationally known figure and one of Scotland's eminent men of the day, even being named as one of the top Scots of the century. He was Dr George F. MacLeod, one of the best-known and most highly respected ministers of his era for his work among the under-privileged and for his founding and leadership of the Iona Community. Often called the Kirk's Crusader, Dr MacLeod had been the minister of Govan Old Parish Church in the 1930s, going on to become, among so many other things, life peer, baronet (Lord MacLeod of Fuinary), Doctor of Divinity, establishment aristocrat and controversial campaigner. An adjunct of the Iona Community he founded had been the Iona Youth Trust, of which McNeill had been an office-bearer, involving considerable work and contact with young people.

Under questioning, Dr MacLeod was to sensationally reveal that after McNeill had decided to leave the Iona Youth Trust, where he had been the secretary, it had come to his knowledge that there had been a case of 'homosexual tendency' concerning him. Later he had spoken to a man who had told him that McNeill had 'made a pass at him'. He had considered this information so serious he had met McNeill for the 'most painful interview of my life'. He had encouraged him to see a therapist as a result of this interview.

Dr MacLeod was also to speak in the highest terms of McNeill. 'He was one of the ablest workers in youth I have ever known. For years he ran a club in Dalry and scores of boys are grateful for him having done so. He ran camps for borstal boys in places like Mull. These boys were always told at the end of the camp that they would be made welcome at Community House so that eventually they could be integrated into decent society. In connection with that work, George McNeill spent an immensity of time being generous to the most uncomely and the most desperate cases from the highest kind of motives. A large number of borstal boys are profoundly grateful for what he has done.'

The questioning then switched to Gordon and he said he had been his guardian when he had come out of prison for a previous offence. He had known him when he was a boy of five living with his mother in a farmhouse near a campsite in Barrhead. 'He had a voracious inquisitiveness for a boy of that age. I have never experienced anything like it for a boy of five.' He was also to say other things about Gordon: 'He has apparently great abilities . . . a man of extraordinary gifts but unable to use them . . . a quite exceptional person with great potentialities . . . unbalanced since he was 12 . . . a sick person . . . a demented person.'

Dr MacLeod said that he had pled in four courts for Gordon; in London, Cardiff and twice in Inverness. As chairman of the Scottish After Care Council he had thought that Gordon had 'turned the corner' and he had discussed with him Gordon's 'great desire' to help other people.

In his summing up for the defence, Sir John Cameron was to claim there was as much circumstantial evidence against the witness who had strangled a girlfriend as there was against Gordon. He pointed out that if Gordon had been the killer, then why hadn't he disposed of the axe which the police maintained was the murder weapon? 'He had disposed of all that was movable in the flat and had ample time for the disposal of the axe.' There had been no sign of any ill will between Gordon and McNeill nor was there any positive motive for the crime, he maintained.

More news coverage was devoted to the trial than any other in years and not until the infamous killer Manuel did a High Court case have such media prominence. On the tenth and final day of the trial, it was the page-one sensation of the day with the news that Gordon had been found guilty and sentenced to hang, that to be carried out in just under three weeks' time.

Gordon was scheduled to walk to the gallows in Barlinnie Prison on Thursday, 24 March 1955. Solicitor Dowdall and counsel Sir John Cameron appealed to the Scottish Secretary on the death sentence and, two days before Gordon was due to hang, Thomas Kerr, the Lord Provost of Glasgow, accompanied by Town Clerk Sir William Kerr, visited the condemned man in his cell at Barlinnie. Their news for him was that he had been reprieved, the death sentence being commuted to one of life imprisonment. After serving this sentence, he was last heard of living in Tangier.

Despite the incredible public interest in the case, mainly because of *The McFlannels* connection, the murder of George Ford McNeill was not a sordid saga, merely the posthumous outing of a popular broadcaster. It was really just another humdrum Glasgow murder, heightened to High Court stardom through the adventures of the accused Gordon in his flight to the continent, the calibre and variety of the witnesses who gave evidence, and the innuendo, such as it was, being aired in much more innocent days.

Rikki Fulton was to tell me his memories of the murder. He had been in *The McFlannels* for about three years in the late '40s, as well has having toured with a stage production of the legendary radio show. The role he played as the Reverend David McCrepe was to bear an amusing similarity to the hilariously dour Reverend I.M. Jolly of much later days on TV.

'We were all shocked by the murder,' Rikki recalled. 'McNeill was a big man, very respectable and the last kind of person you would have expected to end up the way he did. Then again, I suppose we were all rather sheltered back in those days. Most of the people in the show and in broadcasting at the time were semi-pros, having other jobs as well as their ones on radio. I did myself until I became a full-time actor. *The McFlannels* were tremendously popular and everyone would listen to the show. I was certainly thrilled to be in it at the time.'

Lurid murder trial or no, the McFlannels, with their fabled flippancies, carried on as though nothing had happened. They were still there as late as 1963 when the BBC was celebrating its fortieth anniversary, one of the programmes for that evening being the McFlannels in an episode which was more than appropriately entitled 'Time's Up'. Even by that late date, the McFlannels were still having their very own homespun fun in their own wee kailyard, this ultimate episode featuring Uncle Donald making up a bouquet for Aunt Nell's birthday – from cabbage leaves and fish heads. And if you ask why fish heads, his reply was that they represented the flowers in his bizarre bouquet. It was, he said, his way of getting revenge on Nell for her giving him a stick of rock for his birthday which was so hard 'it nearly broke ma fause teeth'. Imagine trying to get laughs out of a line like that today.

When Helen W. Pryde moved to live in Forfar, she would come to Glasgow once a month to discuss future developments in the programme with Howard M. Lockhart and other BBC officials. She would also make a point of being there for the Saturday afternoon rehearsals, much to the disdain of the producers and actors, and showed more than a passing interest in just how they were performing. She would even take the extras aside for a word about the way they were interpreting their roles. Once, when a particular script had been short of dialogue for the time allotted to the programme, Howard M. Lockhart had to add some lines which, as Lockhart recalls in his book, *On My Wavelength*, made Mrs Pryde furious and she accused him of ruining her characters.

As so often happens in long-running shows, whether they be TV, radio or stage productions, working relationships become strained. Tittle-tattle erupts among the cast; petulances spring up between personalities; characters have clashes and attitudes become affected by angst. In the case of *The McFlannels*, the actors became so popular that instead of being cast under their own name, they would often be billed in other shows and in the theatre under their McFlannel name. Helen W. Pryde was furious and wanted the BBC to insert a clause in the actors' contracts forbidding them to appear publicly in any way associated with *The McFlannels*. The BBC refused; so she then produced a document at rehearsals for the cast to sign as an undertaking to comply with her wishes on the matter of billing for public appearances.

Rikki Fulton was in the production at the time and said the last thing any of them wanted to do was be billed in any name but their own. But he pointed out it would be clearly impossible to guarantee this when programming was supplied by the organisers of concerts and shows. No one signed the document.

Producer Lockhart then tells the story of how author Helen tried to write the role of Maisie out of the script. She wanted to marry her off and send her abroad. It was a bit like writing out your favourite barmaid from *Coronation Street* or *EastEnders*. They refused her demands at first but she eventually got her way and disposed of Maisie from the script by packing her off to America. Then, a year later, she brought the character back again, the role being given to a different actress. But then, that's showbusiness!

SWEETS SMELL OF SUCCESS

Scotland's first-ever football star was a quiet, reserved Glasgow man who was to become a household name. His name, in fact, was to become known not only by everyone throughout Scotland, but also in most other parts of the United Kingdom. No British footballer's name has ever been so universally well known. But, ironically, it is not for his soccer prowess and captaining his country in one of its great victories against England that the legendary Bob McColl is remembered. It was in another guise, after his footballing days were over and with another version of his name, that this man became an even greater legend; for that other name was R.S. McColl.

R.S. McColl's was to become the greatest sweetshop chain the country had known. There were hundreds of his shops the length and breadth of the nation. The name was a byword for quality confectionery throughout Scotland, England and Northern Ireland and it is still there above hundreds of newsagent and retail outlets. The story of the man they nicknamed 'Toffee Bob' is not only that of the star footballer, good enough to be capped many times for his country and to play with one of England's leading clubs, but is one of the great success stories of Scottish business enterprise.

Another twist to the remarkable story of Scottish soccer's very first star is that, contrary to the usual tale, it wasn't him that founded one of the biggest sweet empires ever known in the country. The credit for that goes to another McColl, his brother Tom. It was the skill and enterprise of confectioner Tom McColl, younger than brother Bob by eight years, which was to see the beginning of the sweet empire. Bob and Tom McColl, together with another brother and two sisters, grew up in a comfortable home in Mount Florida. Their parents were Donald and Jemima McColl, a hard-working and respectable family, Donald being a superintendent with the Glasgow Cleansing

Department. Like other families in the city, the McColls' antecedents had been incomers from other parts, their particular roots lying in the remote and beautiful wilds of Craignish, in furthest western Argyll, where there are graves of their ancestors.

The McColls enjoyed a much better than average lifestyle, their house being the sort of spacious and attractive home befitting a manager of the day in an important local government department. It was in May Terrace, one of the most handsome terraces of its kind in the south side of Glasgow, cresting the summit of the Prospect Hill and featuring what was probably one of the most stunning and uninterrupted views of the entire city, although when the McColls lived there, for much of the year that view was obliterated by the deadly fug from the forest of tall factory chimneys, forever belching their multi-coloured waste fumes which swirled together with the blue coal smoke of house fires of a quarter of a million homes, forming a ghastly and sinister grey-black blanket. This was the price of being at the heart of the industrial revolution in the sepia city which had once been known as the 'dear, green place'.

Like most lads of their day, the McColl brothers were to leave school at 13 years of age, the normal age for beginning work just before the turn of the century. Both had got themselves good jobs, a good job of the day meaning you worked for a big company and the likelihood was it would be a career for life, and as the years went by and you did your duties well, there would be the prospect of advancement, perhaps even to managerial status. The fact that both had been pupils of Queen's Park School in nearby Battlefield, highly rated academically, would have been a prime factor in their obtaining work quickly, both as junior clerks – Tom in the Royal Insurance offices in the city and Bob with a locomotive engineering company at Polmadie.

Tom was to record his first wage. It was 16s 2d, today's equivalent of 81p. But that wasn't per week; it was his monthly salary! Wages for juniors and apprentices were, as they said, mere sweeties. The average adult weekly wage at the time was £1.19. Well, at least that gave you enough for the occasional glass of beer, that being only 1p a pint. A loaf of bread cost 2p, a new bicycle was £8, it cost 18p to go to Dunoon by rail and boat, and a new pair of men's shoes was 25p.

Tom was an ambitious young man and after some time with the Royal began looking around for other work, eventually getting a superior job with much better prospects in a city stockbroker's office.

Bob had moved, too, to another engineering company, the Sentinel Works in the Polmadie area.

The new sport of soccer was all the rage at the time, it catching on particularly fast in Glasgow and the west of Scotland. Some of the impetus in it gaining such a quick foothold in Glasgow had been the formation of the first football association in 1873, which as well as organising and promoting the new sport, would, it was thought, perhaps go some way to drawing men out of the pubs.

Drink was no new problem to the city, but it was certainly a prevalent and increasing one. It was also one which was causing more than a little concern, which is little wonder when you consider just one statistic connected with it. The year before the football association was inaugurated, on average just under 300 people a week – mainly young men – were arrested in the city for being drunk. Little wonder the Glasgow police required a fleet of special wheelbarrows in order to haul the drunks off to the cells; which makes it all the more appropriate that when that first group of soccer enthusiasts eventually got together to form their very first association for the sport, they did so in Dewar's Temperance Hotel in Bridge Street.

It was just nine years before the young Robert Smyth McColl was born that the very first Scottish football club, Queen's Park, was formed. As it was, its home ground was a mere five-minute stroll from where the McColls lived in Mount Florida. So fast did the sport flourish that within five years of the pioneering Queen's Park formation, they held the country's first international match, obviously there being no better country to conduct that against than England. Because there wasn't a football ground large enough for the occasion, they staged that first international at Hamilton Crescent, the West of Scotland cricket club's home ground. Even it wasn't to be stretched all that much by the crowd which turned up; it numbered 3,500.

But four years later, the year R.S. McColl was born, more than 16,000 were to attend another Scotland versus England international. By that time there were more than 50 new football clubs in Scotland and hardly a month passed without another formation being announced.

The young Bob McColl was quickly caught up in the burgeoning football scene, having been introduced to the game, as was brother Tom, by playing for their school side. The boys couldn't have lived in a better part of the city for that. Hampden Park was less than a five-minute walk away in one direction from their house, and Cathkin Park, home of Third Lanark, the same distance away in the opposite direction, while all around in various parks or unbuilt spaces, landscaping work was going on to create single or groups of football pitches.

Leisure time was curtailed for young men of his age, work occupying so much of their week, or else recuperating from the considerable effort they had to expend in order to make a living wage. Work hours right to the First World War had been a standard 54-hour week, meaning your day began at the office, foundry or factory at six in the morning and didn't end until 20 minutes before six in the evening, except Saturdays, when the finishing time was at midday.

Being a junior clerk meant that, apart from the tedious working hours, the young Bob McColl didn't have to expend all that much physical energy in the pursuit of his meagre wage, the only part of his work involving any muscular output being the two-mile walk from Mount Florida to his workplace in Polmadie and back every day. Like most of his young friends, Bob McColl was soon caught up in the incredible development and growing passion of the new sport, football. He was to spend much of his free time playing and practising with his pals in one of the multiple pitches they had created at the Queen's Park recreation ground or, as he and pals would simply call it, the Rex.

The talent scout for the local juvenile team, Benmore, was quick to spot him and Bob instantly jumped at the chance to join the club. He was just 16 years old when yet another talent scout was to note the abilities of this most promising centre-forward. He was from another local club, one with the most prestigious name in Scotland at the time – Queen's Park, who played at nearby Hampden. The scout called the lad aside after a match to ask some questions and was more than surprised to learn he was somewhat older then he appeared and at 16 had been working for three years. The Queen's Park bosses agreed with the scout's view that his latest discovery would be an asset to the club and signed him up, although he had some problems when he went to play his first game with them, the doorman at Hampden barrng entry, telling him he wasn't even old enough to carry the club hamper.

Bob McColl was an instant success in his new team, scoring a series of spectacular goals that was to make him one of the big favourites of the growing number of fans who were turning out every Saturday afternoon for the sport that was occupying more time, energy and devotion than any other game or pursuit the masses had ever known. Apart from wars, that is.

Two years previously when the young Bob McColl, then aged 14, was playing for Benmore, the newspapers' sports pages, increasingly dominated by soccer news, announced the formation of yet another new club. This time it was over in the East End of Glasgow and was called Celtic. The foundation of a Catholic football team had been the idea of Brother Walfrid of the Marists, the Society of Mary. Like those who had thought the new sport would keep young men away from the evils of the pubs and heavy drinking in their precious few leisure hours, Brother Walfrid saw there could be side benefits from the sport. In his team's case he felt there could be two blessings: they could raise funds to help feed the poor of the East End and it might keep his flock out of the grasp of not so much the pubs, but of Protestantism. Whatever else his aim, it wasn't to deter the new Celtic club from being something of a dramatic force on the Scottish soccer scene, beating Rangers in their very first game – no mean feat considering the club with the light blue colours had been in the sport for some 16 years and were one of the best teams in the country.

Not only did they give Rangers a good trouncing in that historic meeting – the score was 5–2, as any Celtic fan will recall for you – they barnstormed round the country, beating all and sundry and even reaching the final of the Scottish Cup, only to be beaten by that other great team of the day, Third Lanark.

Incidentally, it should be noted that in their first historic encounter, the Celtic versus Rangers game was reported to have been played 'in a spirit of fun and good fellowship'. In ensuing games in those first few years of their rivalry, the two Glasgow clubs were to enjoy a particularly friendly relationship, the *Scottish Sport*, one of the popular sporting newspapers of the day, reporting that Rangers were 'favourites with the Parkhead crowd'. The two clubs even invited each other to watch them play visiting English clubs. Oh, happy days!

Such days weren't to last, however, the atmosphere between the two quickly deteriorating even before the turn of the century. Stories and comments about their degenerating relationship were regularly appearing in the cluster of sporting newspapers catering for the avid interest there now was in all things football, papers such as the *Scottish*

Athletic Journal, the *Scottish Referee, Scottish Umpire and Cycling Mercury* and the *Scottish Sport.* The last was to note that after one disorderly game between the two it was 'all the more regrettable that a handful of fools should have sought to cast reproach upon the proceedings by an outbreak of disorder at the close'. How many times since have such sentiments been expressed in newspaper opinion columns?

The same year the *Sunday Sport* wrote such words, Bob McColl, now 19 years of age, achieved the distinction of getting his first international cap for Scotland, being a member of the team which beat Wales 4–0 at Dundee. Although he masterminded some of the best moves in the game, it wasn't till his next cap shortly afterwards that he was to score his first goal for his country, in a match against Ireland at Belfast which ended in a 3–3 draw.

These were early days in the sport, with considerably less sophistication in the interpretation of the rules, referees and officials being less cultured mortals, as it were. It therefore leaves little to the imagination when contemplating the style of play and the physical involvement of some of the players. If in today's terms you visualise some of the backwoods games around the smaller pitches of Ayrshire, Lanarkshire and Fife, you're getting some of the picture.

Bob McColl, a slightly built 5ft 9in, and weighing 11½ stone, was particularly athletic and noted for his dashing style and quick movements on the ball which, reports said, 'confounded' and 'mesmerised' defenders. Rash tackles were basic antidotes for that style of play and McColl was to miss several further caps due to being the victim of such on-field responses, the words vigorous and robust being more than polite descriptions.

Playing for Queen's Park meant he was still an amateur, although that didn't deprive him of a place in the Scottish national team. But not being able to get leave of absence from work prevented him from enjoying the privileges of the professionals in the team, who would be given time off by their clubs to train together, as well as travel as a party to away games.

In the 1899–1900 season, when Scotland was to play Wales at Wrexham, the team had left Glasgow towards the end of the week, but without McColl, whose work wouldn't release him – to play for his country! On the Friday evening before the game he had to dash home to Mount Florida from his work after six o'clock on the Friday night, change and collect his luggage, then head for the city to get the night train south to Liverpool where he met the others in the squad for breakfast, before travelling on via Birkenhead for the North Wales city and the game on the Saturday afternoon. All that kind of hassle wasn't to put Bob off his game, however, Scotland winning 6–0, McColl collecting a hat-trick.

The Scottish team returned in triumph from their greatest ever victory, and the performance of McColl as their brilliant centre-forward was to capture the sports headlines, not only in Scotland but throughout the rest of Britain. A week later, the crowds packed Celtic Park to cheer on their national team and its new collection of stars, including McColl, in yet another international, this time against Ireland. They weren't to be disappointed, McColl serving them up another of his now legendary brilliant performances, once again delighting them with a hat-trick, Scotland winning the day 9–1.

The following year the Scottish team was back at Celtic Park for a home international against England, that meeting having by now become firmly established as the nation's number one soccer attraction. And it was at Celtic Park yet again where he was to more than delight them, with his third international hat-trick, this one pleasing them more than any other being that it was against England. By now he was being hailed with the same kind of fervour that stars such as Baxter, Law and Dalglish were to get in much later times.

The Scotland versus England meeting of 1900 had been scheduled for Celtic Park, it being the venue for all their meetings in the years between 1894 and 1904, with the exception of just one year. Remembering that the first of this great, but now abandoned, international series had attracted a mere 3,500 to Hamilton Crescent cricket ground less than 30 years previously, note how attendances had soared to their multi-thousands as more and more people were swept up by the enthusiasm for anything and everything soccer. Six years after the first Scotland–England meeting, some 20,000 were there for the first Hampden international in 1878. There was a similar sized crowd for the first one to be held at Ibrox, and by the time McColl was starring as an international centre-forward, grounds were straining to hold the crowds that were turning up.

There had never been such anticipation for any previous big match as for this meeting with England, being as it was that Scotland were on a winning run and there seemed no stopping Bob McColl, their brilliant striker, although they didn't use that term then. When the team came onto the field, led by captain Jacky Robertson of Rangers, they were greeted with a Parkhead version of what came to be known as the Hampden roar. There were no derisory catcalls at the flamboyant strip they were wearing; the Scots' jerseys were coloured primrose – and pink! But there was a good reason for the garish guernseys: they happened to be the racing colours of Lord Rosebery who was the patron of the Scottish Football Association at the time. He was there on the day, silk topper and all, cheering like mad with the rest of the Scots fans.

Celtic Park had never been so tightly packed, some 64,000 having paid to get in, but with estimates of up to another 15,000 having made entry by other means. To the sheer joy of the huge crowd, Scotland's biggest crowd ever at the time, the home team were in fantastic form once more, their jazzy colours most certainly having no deleterious effect on their playing ability. And once more the opposition had no answer to the brilliant attacking, passing, receiving and shooting of the Scottish attack, consisting of Bobby Walker of Hearts and John Campbell of Celtic and centre-forward Bob McColl. Right from the start they were to rip apart a renowned English defence, McColl, the only Queen's Park amateur in the team, scoring in the very first minute of the game and once again being the star of the game. The English keeper was Jack Robinson, said to be the finest they had ever fielded, but he couldn't stop McColl collecting yet another hat-trick – his third – the final score being a memorable 4–1.

McColl's hat-trick that day had been completed in the first 28 minutes of the game, and in the quaint sporting prose of the day the *Athletic News* report of the game was to comment that 'nothing short of a mound of Limburger cheese, which they say is so strong to smell, would keep the Scots out of the English goal'.

There's a great story about the ball that was used in the game that day, a ball which has amazingly survived the years as one of the oldest and most cherished souvenirs in Scottish soccer. During my research for this chapter, I was to come across not only the fascinating story of the amazing wanderings of this football since that 4–1 victory, but the very ball itself.

There were none of today's strict end-of-game procedures back in 1900 and when he blew that final signal at the conclusion of the match, the referee made no move to collect the ball. At least if he did, he was too slow, for it seemed to be a finder's-keeper's doctrine that prevailed at the time, the ball being grabbed by the nearest player to it, the England half-back Ernest Needham. And he refused to give it up.

From Parkhead it was to accompany the Englishman to his home in Sheffield where it was looked after, although it is hard to imagine this being done with all that much pride, it having been in the back of his team's net four times. Maybe that's why when an army friend about to embark for the Boer War in South Africa asked if he could lend him a bladder 'for the boys to kick around', Needham willingly handed over the ball, perhaps even thinking that would hopefully be the last he would see of it. Incredibly, however, years later and having been kicked about in army campsites all over the *veldt*, the focal point in countless knockabouts and matches between cavalry and infantry, the ball returned with the friend and his regiment to England, whereupon it was handed back to Needham – with thanks.

Incredulous that the ball had survived such an adventure, Needham, perhaps in some remorse of conscience, considered that the ball, by now somewhat battered and begrimed, should be given to the man who deserved it more than anyone – Bob McColl. There and then he had it parcelled and dispatched to Glasgow. Albeit that it looks more like something the Romans left behind, this holy grail of Scottish soccer is carefully tended by the McColl family.

Following the great Scots victory at Parkhead, the sporting press everywhere was hailing the new superstar of British soccer. That's right, British soccer, for Bob McColl was no longer a mere Scottish star, his three international hat-tricks and the conclusions of seasoned observers placing him in the category of the best there was anywhere. And he was still an amateur . . . but not for much longer.

The invitations began arriving to May Terrace in Mount Florida for Bob McColl, persuading him to consider quitting his job as a clerk and becoming a full-time professional football player. Had the invites been in today's terms and conditions, he wouldn't have had the slightest hesitation about making that move much sooner. But becoming a professional footballer in 1900 was really no big deal, even though they were sporting idols. For most of them, in terms of the financial rewards, it was just like going to another job. And with the on-field hazards being such as they were, it was the kind of job that came with the prospect of having a much quicker termination than was ever likely to happen plying your trade as a locomotive company clerk or in any similar sedentary occupation.

Blackburn Rovers, Derby County, Liverpool and Newcastle United had all watched him play and were interested in signing the Glasgow man. There was considerable correspondence between McColl and officials at Liverpool FC, who were more than eager to have him on their books. Despite the eagerness, however, they played canny with the coppers. Most of the correspondence McColl had with them was with Tom Watson, who was then the Liverpool club secretary. In one letter Watson was to suggest that if he signed with them, they would offer a guarantee of £2 a week. Then, as an extra bit of bait, he hinted that 'it might even be £4'.

McColl knew his value and while the best-paid players were earning just a few shillings more than the Merseysiders were offering, he reckoned he was worth more than £4 a week. Answering his rejections of the last of the Liverpool offers, secretary Watson was to write saying how sorry the club was not to be getting his services: 'I am sure you would have got a good berth [at Liverpool] which is more to you, I think, than the mere playing of football', the reference to a berth meaning other factors in the package on offer, such as finding the player a good job in order to supplement his income. As McColl had been asking for more than £4, that last letter from Liverpool was to end with a PS stating: 'I might have met the matter [his demand] but £5 was too much.'

Newcastle were every bit as interested and wrote to ask McColl if he would be prepared to meet two of their directors in order to discuss terms, mentioning that they were enjoying the biggest audiences anywhere in England and would be 'delighted to have your assistance'.

The terms were obviously better than the £4-a-week maximum the Anfield side could muster, and with signing-on fees of between £250 and £400, Bob McColl headed for Newcastle in November 1901, where they were to be more than delighted with the assistance, as they put it, he was to offer them.

These were heady, eventful days in British soccer, new as the sport might have been, many remembering the time when there was no such thing as organised football. Never before had a sport burgeoned with such fervent popularity as the game every single working man in the country wanted to see and enjoy in his relatively few, and precious, hours of free time. Football grounds were being inundated by huge crowds the like of which no club had ever anticipated.

Before it received the first of its many ground improvements, St James' Park, Newcastle, had already been the scene of crowd problems – of varying kinds. A 13,000 crowd in one game had overtaxed the facilities to the extent that some railings collapsed and some fans received severe injuries, one young lad having a foot severed. That was to bring about some of the early ground improvements, which included such innovations as a 'bath room' for players and refreshment stands around the ground for the fans, one local newspaper going all high-tech by installing its own direct-line telephone in order to facilitate match reports. And because of some friction between club and local press, a Christmas gift of cigars was sent to the four daily newspaper sports reporters as a PR gesture.

More importantly, the ground capacity at St James' Park was to be increased in stages from 13,000 to 20,000 to 25,000 and on to 30,000, which it could hold by the time Bob McColl arrived. It must have crossed his mind that if things could be hectic or, perhaps more appropriately, 'fiery' in the Scottish soccer scene, they could be even more feisty down in Newcastle. It had only been a few months before his arrival that the club experienced one of its blackest days. The event was a scheduled Good Friday derby game against their greatest rivals, Sunderland; a sort of Rangers v Celtic, if you like, without the nastiness religion inspires, that is. Being the holiday Friday, every working man in the north-east of England, it seemed, wanted to see this game of games, in which there had been unprecedented interest, Sunderland at the time being the First Division leaders, the home side being in seventh position.

With the new terraces and stands now capable of holding 30,000, maybe a few thousand more at a crush, it wasn't anticipated there would be any great problem in coping with the numbers expected. Only thing was, no one had accurately predicted just what these numbers might be. As it was, Newcastle was to be swamped by a multitude, estimates putting it at between 50,000 and 70,000, with only a few club officials and a total of 25 policemen to control them!

Three-quarters of an hour before the kick-off, every part of the ground was packed, and that included the roof of a stand and much of the pitch. The gates were locked, which was to spark off the initial fury which was to culminate in one of the first major football riots in the country. The crowds milling around outside were infuriated by the sight of the locked gates and wanted in . . . and many of those inside witnessing the chaos that was happening wanted out.

Colin Veitch, one of Newcastle's greatest-ever stars, was there to play that day and wrote later about the incredible scenes he was to witness on arriving at St James':

> The gates were closed and thousands of people were outside the ground, hundreds scaling the outer barriers, and a scene of pandemonium in the precincts which had never been seen before and has never occurred since. I managed to get into the ground through a gateman who recognised my voice . . . Inside the ground the scene was almost indescribable. The officials of the club were powerless to deal with the people and the police were little better situated . . . Hundreds were walking about unable to get a glimpse of the playing pitch. The stand was not only full to overflowing, but so were the terraces and hundreds were perched on top of the stand in precarious positions for themselves and for the people underneath . . . The playing pitch was occupied by thousands of people, some standing in groups, utterly bewildered as though to say 'Well, we've got here! What do we do next?' . . . In other corners, 'pitch and toss' schools were in progress in full view of the authorities who were powerless to intervene. Nothing could be done with any hope of getting the people off the pitch, so, as a last resort, the teams made their appearance on the ground.

Perhaps the official ordering the appearance of the players thought that this demonstration of just how impossible it would be to play would bring an endorsement from the crowd concerning the wisdom of abandoning the match and that they would quietly disperse. If he did, it was the biggest mistake of his life, for what ensued at the news of the abandonment was mob madness. After clashing with each other in a huge-scale free-for-all, the crowd then wreaked their revenge on St James' Park itself. The goal posts were demolished and the nets ripped down, but these were no jolly souvenir hunters, should you be reflecting on that day at Wembley when the tartan hordes descended on the pitch. This was an angry, warlike rabble on the rampage and after tearing down the club flag, they uprooted barriers and fencing and undoubtedly would have demolished and carried off the stand had not wagonloads of police reinforcements arrived together with baton-charging mounted men to quell them.

It took them until five o'clock that evening to get the ground completely cleared and Colin Veitch's last words on what he had seen were that the ground was left in a complete shambles and he was never to witness such a scene of devastation till the First World War and he 'landed at the front in France'.

If he had been lucky enough to miss that infamous St James' Park riot of 1901, Bob McColl was to find himself in the midst of another footballing horror story. This time it was being involved in what was the worst ever disaster the sport had known at the time.

He had been at Newcastle for just five months and, as expected, had made his mark as a prolific scorer. Because of his success there and the fact that he was still the best centre-forward available, he was chosen as the Scotland team captain to play against England in the 1902 international to be played in Glasgow. It was to be a game that neither he nor any of the players in both teams would ever forget.

Celtic and Queen's Park as well as Rangers had all competed for the honour of holding the international on their ground that year, but the award went to Ibrox in view of the fact that Rangers had just two years earlier spent £20,000 on a ground-improvement scheme which was on a rather grand scale. That £20,000 would buy merely a few seats at the park today, or go some way to buying one of those chrome hamburger stalls outside it. But at the turn of the nineteenth century it was to convert the old Ibrox ground into one of the most modern in the world, the make-over including two covered stands as well as two magnificently inclined terraces. It was state-of-the-art – 1902 style.

It had been a miserable, wet Saturday morning in early April 1902 and the rain had continued to pour right up to kick-off. The weather was not to deter the crowds, every fan in Scotland, apparently, heading for Govan. The crowds had swamped the ground in such numbers it appeared there had been little control at the entry points, but perhaps there had been no concern about how many got in for, after all, they had been boasting how it could easily cope with 80,000.

Unlike latter-day football grounds where terraces were formed by solid banks of earth, the ones at Ibrox were formed by rows of steel uprights on which there were wooden stagings to hold the fans. Ibrox had never anticipated a crowd such as this, so many having packed into the stadium they overflowed right up to the touchline, and in places onto the actual pitch. It was to be one of those terracings which was pushed over the limits, the enormous crowd standing on it being too much for the structure. There was a crack like a cannon shot as seven rows of the wooden planking snapped under the strain, creating a huge chasm into which 26 fans fell to their death 40 feet below. Hundreds of others who also tumbled into the jagged hole were badly injured.

Fearing the consequences of what might happen should the game be abandoned, the authorities ordered play to continue after an 18-minute hold-up, the players at times having to fight their way round spectators on the pitch as well as opponents to get at the ball.

The great game was to know even more grim disasters, but this first of the worst takes one of the front places in the register of catastrophes.

Scots were all the flavour in English clubs at the time and particularly so at Newcastle. So many scouts had been in and around a variety of Scottish clubs looking for talent that when scouts from Newcastle United were spotted at Leith Athletic's ground one Saturday afternoon they were physically chased from the stadium.

They liked the Scots in England because they played a vastly different game from that played in England. With the game having so much of its roots in the public schools, the style of play that predominated was in the fashion it had been played on the hallowed fields, a style of play such that if you got the ball, no matter what your position, then you headed in a straight line for goal. It didn't matter who got in your way, particularly if you were a prefect and it was a mere fag trying to stop you. You just ran on, pushing all and sundry out of the way, running over the top of them if necessary. A bit like rugby, without picking up the ball, that is. The Scots, on the other hand, had this thing about fine dribbling and passing to others and making a team game of it. And it worked. It beat those heedless charges and straight-for-goal tactics, or lack of them, mainly displayed south of the border. Because of these skills many of these fine Scottish tacticians with the nimble feet, the 'professors', as they were known, were invited south to help the flourishing English club scene. There was hardly any wages in it for them, if any in many cases, but they were helped to get good jobs with better money than they could earn at home and that was as good a reason as any to head south.

One of the reasons for the sizeable number of Scots at Newcastle can be put down to club chairman James Telford, who was virtually manager at the time. He was from north of the border and described in the prose of the day as 'a Scot of sometimes domineering personality'. And the more that is read about the man, the more he appears to be something between a Bill Shankly and a Jock Stein. A formidable cocktail. But then, that's perhaps why he's also described by one prominent star of the day as the man who 'more than any other individual was responsible for putting Newcastle on the football map'.

Telford, as chairman of the club, personally negotiated the transfer of McColl – portrayed as his country's 'number one personality' – from Queen's Park. As described by one commentator of the day, it had been due to Telford's 'persuasive eloquence' that McColl had reluctantly relinquished his amateur status to become a full-time professional footballer. The same commentator was also to note that McColl's capture was the greatest ever achieved by chairman Telford in a record which included many of the great footballers to come to the Tyneside club.

It was to be a whole new way of life for the young Glasgow star, being given the freedom and time to devote all his energies in the sport he loved so much. Daily training sessions in preparation for the rigours of the professional game were already a part of the routine for the Newcastle signings. These would begin at ten o'clock each morning and would consist of a hard three-hour session of weight-training, skipping, ball-punching and sprinting, culminating in an eight-mile walk 'at a brisk pace' followed by a bath and massage. The emphasis was on the fitness side of the player rather than play manoeuvres and work with the ball, that being reserved for some two afternoons a week and the occasional practice match in the evenings when the weather had improved.

McColl, by now always referred to as the 'prince of centre-forwards', was to make a much bigger impact at Newcastle than his record of 67 appearances and 20 goals with the club was to show. The team's superstar, Colin Veitch, in his memoirs wrote in the most glowing terms of the influence McColl brought to the club.

> He was, in my opinion, responsible for moulding the style of Newcastle's game, and he left it in such a condition that the players who remained behind after his departure were able to pursue the pattern laid down, and work it

out in commendable fashion . . . No one could have had a better mentor or one of a more encouraging disposition. I gained more in a few months from the words of Bob McColl than years of experience on the field might have taught me – if ever.

Those words of McColl which Veitch spoke of were those of an articulate and intelligent sportsman who was often to speak and write in the most lucid of terms about his views of the game. And when he did so, he was to reveal this was no mere player who went out there on the field to enjoy his skills and see what that day's play might bring him. There was much more to football than that and he was to reveal some of his philosophy and attitudes about the game in an article he wrote about the 'Duties of a Centre-forward', opinions which at the time would be textbook material for students of the sport – and undoubtedly still are.

The centre-forward, as the pivot of the combination, must have a long eye to the main chance and play for it impartially. On his skill and judgement the players on either side of him depend much, not as wings (for 'wingism' tends to waste), but as members of a forward line working as one man with swift strategy . . . to score.

To pass to the proper man at the proper moment, so that he can accept to advantage, is a great part of centre-forward play. And whenever the pass is made, the centre should keep himself in a clear position that the ball may be sent back again with as little difficulty as possible.

The same applies largely to other positions; likewise, constant watchfulness and complete concentration on the game is necessary. But more than the other forwards, the centre must have the instinct of the leader, think and act as fast as he looks, make and take opportunities, deceive by feint and subtlety – and all in the rapid to and fro movements of the game. And, of course, he must be played to. Having the greatest goal area in front of him, his opportunities for scoring are exceptional. He must be played to not only for his own opportunities, but for the opportunities he can give to others.

Being so well watched, the passes given to him should be judged with the greatest care. A little diplomatic dalliance with the ball is frequently time gained instead of time lost, by enabling the receiver to make the very best of his opportunity. Too rigid a system of play, in which all the moves are known, will not do. There must be flexibility; endless variety and versatility; constant surprises for the other side. System must be inspired by art and innate genius for and love of the game.

He was also to offer his own philosophy on that special factor which constitutes the finest of games and of the elements which make, or break, the best of team-play. The most excellent of games, he said, were the ones where 'on very rare occasions the almost ideal combination is seen – the right union of men and minds and moods, the happy combination of circumstances that makes the great game. This is the harmony we strive for, knowing the futility of the team that works as eleven men instead of one.'

And in his overview of the various positions and individual attitudes to play, he stresses the wastefulness of the selfish player:

> Aimless individualism in any position in the team should always be strongly guarded against. All the more perhaps because of the applause with which the undiscerning section of the spectators is almost sure to greet it. One selfish player is often the ruin of what should be a first-class team. The fleet winger who delights to sprint to the corner flag may get in a rousing shot at the side of the net, or send the ball sailing at an acute angle over the bar, and the crowd will yell with appreciation, not knowing that the chances are all against this method resulting in goals. Equally ineffective, of course, is the midfield dribbler who sticks to the ball as long as ever his opponents or the state of his wind will allow him. Both time and energy must be utilised to the best advantage; the best must be made of every moment and every move. The backs and half-backs must play to the forwards; the forwards be ready to accept and work onwards in swift unison; the play well balanced; each position necessary and filling its part in the harmonious whole.

Then, finally, he lays bare his true passion and zeal for soccer:

> In football, as in other things, there is always something
> to learn. The attitude of the earnest student ensures
> progress. The footballer should always be in perfect form,
> and should neither train too much nor play too often;
> otherwise he may impair his enthusiasm, and enthusiasm
> is the very essence of success. A sound mind in a sound
> body; these are essential to good football and good
> football should help to produce them.

The inspiring words of a man destined to go far in football, to continue in management, where, perhaps, there would be an even greater future for him than as 'prince of centre-forwards'. But that was not to be; another destiny awaited Bob McColl.

With such insight into the game as McColl had, it was little wonder Veitch had said no one had influenced him more. And it was also to be Veitch who was to explain the paucity of goals from McColl during the three seasons he was to play with the club. 'Bob McColl was a much-marked man from the day he entered English football – marked not only on the field in the sense of carrying a "policeman" in attendance, but physically marked into the bargain, such as no other player who had been associated with the club. But Bob never retaliated in kind. The only mark he left was an indelible one in the style and standard which he set for Newcastle United.

Just as it had been club chairman Scot James Telford who was responsible for the consequential move in McColl's career, from amateur to professional, from Queen's Park to Newcastle, it was also Telford, although more indirectly, who was to be the reason for McColl's return to Scotland.

There had been something of a major ruckus among the Newcastle board of directors, a serious division occurring between groupings on the question of the election and re-election of members of the board, as a result of which Telford lost his seat, following which he was to sever all connections with the club. It was the sporting sensation of the day.

The loss of his mentor was to have an impact on McColl, to the extent that he was immediately to consider leaving Newcastle and returning to Scotland. With his more than impressive playing record to date, which included 13 caps for his country in which he had scored three hat-tricks and an overall total of 13 goals, he was snap of the day for the first club to beat it to his door. And the speculation about which club that might be gave the sports headline writers endless stories about where the returning Scottish star would be heading, Rangers apparently being the main contender.

Although he was by now one of the biggest names in the sport, like the rest of his fellow soccer stars, Bob McColl had little to show for it by way of reward. Sure, the sport had given him a good job as a professional with a wage which was better than that of the average working man and there was a few quid in the bank as a result of a couple of transfer fees, but the total of these would be less than half a day's wage for a top Rangers or Celtic player today. Nevertheless, life had been much better for him than it would have been perched on a clerk's stool back in an engineering works in Polmadie. And he had made a name for himself, that in itself being a marketable commodity should he, at the end of his career, follow others and put that name in lettering above the door of something like a pub or a restaurant.

Meanwhile, back in Glasgow, another member of the family had done just that with his name. But the name Tom McColl wasn't to herald a new pub or the like. It was above a little shop at 4 Albert Drive, close by Pollokshaws Road at the point where Pollokshields bordered with Govanhill. His small business sold just one commodity – confectionery.

Such shops had been part of the Glasgow scene for considerably more than a century, being one of the many side-shoots of the substantial sugar trade which had been carried on between the city and the West Indies since its introduction as far back as the mid-1600s. Many of these little shops were, to say the very least, the most doubtful of premises, where it was obvious that the produce had been someone's less than refined handiwork and, if you really fancied consuming the gaudy coloured crudities on display, then you had the kind of sweet tooth that overruled all other judgements. And plenty had. It wasn't only in these little granny's-pastime premises where the dirty tricks in the confectionery trade were going on. While granny's methods might have been raw, others were ruthless and, with efficient hygiene authorities still a thing of the future, some manufacturers were finding more than unwholesome shortcuts to cut costs and boost profits.

There were numerous cases of children suffering various sicknesses, all induced by contaminated confections. One little girl died from peritonitis two days after consuming one of the popular chocolate sweets of the day bought from her local corner shop. The chocolate had been eked out by being liberally adulterated with paraffin wax. One manufacturer hit on the idea of making his fruit drops sparkle more attractively than any rival, who normally used sugar for that purpose. So he coated them with powdered glass, and sure enough they sparkled like no others. No deaths were reported, but many were to regret these extraordinary fruit drops, literally dropping themselves due to the severe pain the sweets caused. And stories abounded, perhaps more apocryphal than accurate, about unscrupulous manufacturers bulking up their brown sugar supplies with sand, about them colouring liquorice with lampblack and using a variety of weird chemicals as substitutes for fruit flavourings.

People, of course, had been chewing sweets for centuries. One of the royals' ancestors, Princess Mary, had five and a half pounds of sugar tablets and more than eight pounds of rose sugar of honey in her baggage when she went on pilgrimage to Canterbury away back in 1317. And, as the Romans, Greeks, Chinese and Egyptians will tell you, their ancestors were having their sweet-tooth needs catered for long before anyone else. But it wasn't all that many years before the McColl brothers went into business that the confectionery trade really happened in a big way in Britain. Chocolate had come into fashion and big manufacturers like Fry's, Cadbury and Mackintosh were already household names.

Tom had taken a great pride in his little shop in Albert Drive, which was to be an instant success due to his insisting on using only the best quality products as ingredients for his confectionery. His theory had been that because of the prevalence of low quality selections from so many of the other small shops, there could be a big market for his category of confectionery. The success of his Albert Drive venture was to prove just that. But there was a lot to learn on the way and he was to spend countless hours in his little back shop mixing syrups and sugars and cocoa powder to make a wide and appealing range of candy, toffee, tablet and sweets which his sisters, working in the front shop, would wrap and sell to customers.

He studied the science of sugar boiling, learning how it would turn to liquid at 100 °C, but waiting till it got even hotter before the syrup would get to the proper working consistency, each product having its own temperature setting. The art of sweet-making lies in knowing and recognising these temperatures, the technicians using gauges, the old hands using a sticky finger as a dipstick, but well wetted first to avoid scalding, although it didn't prevent cracked fingernails. Whatever method, the experts knew that between 107 and 110 degrees the syrup gets tacky, how at 112 degrees you could blow a bubble from the syrupy drips of a dipped skewer, how at three degrees higher than that you would get flossy threads, and by the time it got to 118 degrees the mix in your sugar pan would be ready for making soft ball sweets, at 121 degrees hard ball ones; upping the temperature even more you got to the stage where it would be ready for caramels and butterscotch, and at near peak heat you have the commodity that makes for perfection in boiled sweets, the kind that are as tough and clear as glass and crack with an almighty crunch in your teeth. And there were all those varieties to contend with. One manufacturer alone had a 17-page list with 200 items on offer, which included 38 kinds of boilings, 40 toffees and 15 sticks of rock. And those names! Floral tablet, pear drops, almond rock, hothouse grapes, clove cushions, Trinidad candy, Berlin mixture, lemon sherbets, caramel bullets, dolly pears, bung caraways, ching-changs and ogo pogo eyes. And that was just some.

Having mastered his trade and firmly established his business, there was only one route now for Tom McColl to take – expansion. But that required capital and he was short on that. The banks weren't particularly convinced about the prospects of such expansion, but when he discussed the prospect of brother Bob joining him in the business, there was to be an immediate reaction from the man himself in Newcastle. He had made his mark in football and it was more than obvious that while there might be considerable fame, there was no fortune to be made in the new national sport. He would have to find some alternative form of living when his playing days were eventually over, and playing the way some of these opposing players did with their turbulent tackles and gauche gamesmanship, you just never knew the day when that might be. And all too often it was sooner rather than later.

The prospect of teaming up with his brother in business sounded just the answer to what Bob McColl would do for a life after football. Having the reputation he had at the time, there was an immediate response from Glasgow when he made it known he would like to return to his home city. The club which was to so eagerly sign him was Rangers. And once more Bob McColl was to become a star attraction of yet another side, quickly settling into the Ibrox team, where he was an instant favourite with the crowds. Training commitments at the Govan park in those days were considerably less than in the more highly professional days of later years and Bob McColl was able to devote much of his time with his brother Tom to building up the business they had decided to rename. For very obvious marketing purposes that name was to be the same one which had so often appeared in the press and in top football team line-ups – R.S. McColl.

He had invested £100 in the company they formed, which was enough to fund the beginning of their expansion programme. Two shops had been acquired in that first stage of their development of the chain which was to grow at a pace which was beyond their wildest dreams. Like everything else in life, their forward planning had to be put on hold during the First World War, in which both men volunteered for the services. Because of his poor eyesight, however, Tom had been rejected, but brother Bob was enlisted and served for the duration as a sergeant in the army.

It was straight back to the sweet business at the war's end, the brothers' first move being the reintroduction of their expansion programme. The quality of their product had already become a byword in the city, every new outlet they opened being an instant success, the business prospering so much that the demand for R.S. McColl's sweets was far in excess of what Tom could produce at his Albert Drive shop.

The next stage was a factory with production staff, a small plant going into production in nearby Langside Road. But even that wasn't big enough for the amount of shops they now had and bigger premises had to be established, this time a factory unit in North Woodside Road, not far from the hall where William Smith some decades previously had founded that famous movement which was to spread throughout the world, the Boys' Brigade.

Having established their sizeable factory there was now virtually no limit to the amount of sweets they could manufacture in shapes and sizes as bewildering as their names, any half dozen or so of which most kids could rhyme off in a blink. And Bob and Tom McColl were on their way to being the kings of a wonderful ching-chang, ogo-pogo-eyed world where dolly mixtures, gold mines, liquorice straps, jelly babies, tiger nuts, sojers' buttons, conversation lozenges, bullseyes and yellowmen and other weird titles would be just some of their trading lines.

It was also a world where the recompense for hard work, sacrifice and risking their capital was to bring them deserved rewards. Deserving and considerable rewards. Rewards that in the case of Bob McColl could never have been met as a champion footballer, even by someone that had reached the heights of professional sporting stardom such as he had. For with that name over the shop fronts, combined with the quality of the product his brother had created, they were to expand at a rate no other confectioner had ever achieved before.

It was in the days when time and motion studies and other marketing practices were in their infancy, but the McColls had created their own highly efficient, cost-cutting operation, applying their own methods to all departments. Each shop chargehand, for instance, had to keep a tally of items running low on stock. Vans from the factory toured the shops on a fixed route, the appropriate supplies for each shop being assessed from the chargehands' daily lists, meaning every shop was always fully stocked. The customers' favourite sweets were always available. To speed deliveries, they had custom-built vans to carry layers of specially made sweet trays.

The vans' runs were always on fixed routes, first deliveries loaded last at the factory, last deliveries loaded first to speed delivery time at the shops.

It was competency in confectionery the likes of which hadn't been seen before and it was to be by such efficiency that those two shops Bob's capital had helped secure were quickly to grow to four, then to eight – and ten; then 20, 40, 50, 100; another 100 – and upwards towards yet another 100. With over 1,000 employees, it was to be the greatest empire of its kind ever created. The sweet smell of success was all theirs, making the brothers the sort of fortunes that equalled that of the foremost captains of industry.

In today's terms, of course, they would be termed millionaires or multimillionaires. Their lifestyle perhaps describes their financial achievements better than mere numbers. For Tom and his wife and young son Donald, there was first of all the handsome villa in fashionable Pollokshields, then, as his fortune grew, a move to a mansion near Eastwood Toll. It was in the days before electricity had reached the furthest part of Giffnock, but that was no worry for the McColls, who installed their own electricity generating plant, their house unique in the area with its own inside and outside electric lighting. And when they added on a huge party room at the rear of the house, built on lofty columns, they incorporated an elevator from the kitchens below for the use of staff to bring them whatever was required.

Likewise, R.S. had a property of similar dimensions a mile and a half away in Newlands, complete too with its own staff. It being the late '20s, it was the days when professionally qualified staff, such as chauffeurs, gardeners, cooks, nannies and maids abounded, many of them living in, as they did with the McColls, and even joining them on their annual holidays. Tom and his family had a summerhouse at Seamill and they would hire a yacht, complete with crew, the two families with friends often sharing cruises.

For their vacations, Bob and his wife Helen (but known as Elie) and their two children would usually hire a house, somewhere in Scotland, of similar proportions to their mansion in Newlands, places like Elie in Fife or Pitlochry being favourites. And the staff would load up one of the bigger of the company vans with their trunks and bikes and other paraphernalia for the summer hols.

Making money, such as they had, is one of life's major hurdles. Keeping it can often be a harder one. And for the McColls there was a time when it might all have been lost. The Wall Street crash of 1929 had a profound effect on business people who had invested in the American market. There was to be no leaping out of skyscraper windows for Bob and Tom at the considerable losses they suffered with investments they had in American steel. They had been too prudent with the egg-keeping, but nevertheless their somewhat reduced financial status was to be a grim reminder of just how fickle fortunes can be.

These remarkable two empire builders were also survivors and were able to continue the company's progress, acquiring even more sites in England and Northern Ireland, and to be in a position by 1933 to be given more than covetous glances by the other giants of the confectionery trade. In the case of one, the legendary Cadbury's, the acquisition of a chain like R.S. McColl's with their 250 shops would be a dream deal, giving them in just one clinch the biggest outlet group in the country. So they targeted the Glasgow company and after some considerable negotiations a merger deal was done, Cadbury becoming the controlling partners in the concern, both Bob and Tom being retained as joint managing directors of what was now the R.S. McColl division of the sweet conglomerate.

Their futures secured financially, the brothers got on with their lives. Like so many other footballers, Bob McColl had an equal love for golf and, along with brother Tom, was to be one of the founder members of East Renfrewshire Golf Club. But he was determined to play competitive football as long as possible and was a big favourite with the Ibrox crowd. Because of his continual scoring potential, he was invariably one of the closest marked men on the pitch. So vital was it to keep him constantly monitored, it was the famous Celtic defender, the legendary Dan Boyle – the man they said would create a national calamity if absent from his team – who was to so memorably emphasise just how important this was. Warning one of his team-mates to keep his eye on McColl, he shouted, 'Follow him everywhere he goes. Even if he goes off to the pavilion . . . follow him!'

R.S. was to stay with Rangers from September 1904 to August 1907, playing 55 games in which he scored 37 goals. However, he was not to win any Cup medals during his years at Ibrox. It was one of those times! When Rangers get it good, it appears, Celtic get it bad. And likewise in reverse, as it happened to be during this period when the Parkhead team were on one of the highs which dot the history of both clubs, Celtic on this crest winning six successive league championships and Robert Smyth McColl sadly ending his career with Rangers without a Cup medal to show for it. Injury even cost him a place in the two Glasgow Merchants' Charity Cup finals which Rangers did manage to contest.

When in 1907 at the age of 31 he decided that it was time to end his days in the paid ranks, he was to apply to rejoin Queen's Park, the first professional ever to make such a request with them. They gladly welcomed his return, making him one of the rare players in soccer to resume amateur status after a professional career. His first game with them, incidentally, was to be against Rangers, an Ibrox historian (and obvious fan!) noting that 'many considered he played a finer game on this occasion against the Light Blues than he had ever played for them'. Perhaps the 3–1 score in favour of Queen's Park also influenced his comment.

The sport continued its amazing growth in popularity and the year after McColl's return to his home ground at Hampden it was to establish a new world record attendance of 121,452 to watch a Scotland v England international, the previous crowd record having been 110,802 for the English Cup final at Crystal Palace.

His remaining years in the sport he loved so much were to see him top off a remarkable career. In all he had played some 180 games for Queen's Park, scoring 112 goals for the Mount Florida club. And some of his finest performances were to be in those return years as an amateur, when once more he was to be one of the club's most prolific scorers. If ever any player went out on a high note, it was R.S. In his last three games with the club he was to score nine goals – two in their 2–1 defeat of St Mirren, six in their 6–1 defeat of Port Glasgow Athletic, and one in a 2–2 draw with Aberdeen.

He was still there in the members' stand at Hampden at every home game for years afterwards, and being the great family man he was, he would usually be accompanied by his daughter Agnes and son Robert, both of whom were to serve in the army in the Second World War. A quiet and reserved man, McColl was a professional footballer with the kind of character you would associate with a Lineker or a Bobby Charlton, never the boor, never the boozer, never ever the taint of tabloid tittle-tattle about his personal life. He enjoyed nothing more than his regular reunions with the other players in that fabulous Scottish team of 1900 which had beaten England 4–1 and in which he had scored one of his three international hat-tricks. He enjoyed their company so much he even paid to take all of them with him on visits to see the two home countries' international at Wembley. For soccer historians those ten team-mates of Bob McColl were Harry Rennie (Hearts), Alec Raisbek (Liverpool), Nicol Smith (Rangers), Jacky Robertson (Rangers), John Campbell (Celtic), Alec Smith (Rangers), Robert Walker (Hearts), Neil Gibson (Rangers), John Drummond (Rangers) and Jack Bell (Celtic).

It was shortly after D-day that there came the saddest day in Bob McColl's life. His 21-year-old son Robert, a brilliant scholar and a former dux at prestigious Strathallan School, had foregone going to Cambridge in order to serve in the army. He had been a tank commander and after the invasion in France had gone on to Holland where, while trying to free a small village together with Scots infantry-men from the Black Watch, he was killed in a fierce engagement with German troops. A cairn commemorating his brave action was erected by grateful villagers near his grave at Bergen op Zoom.

The McColl brothers were to continue as executives with the company until their retiral in 1946, Bob McColl being by then 70 years of age. He died 12 years later at the age of 82, brother Tom being

83 when he passed away in 1967. The vast sweet empire the McColl brothers had created out of that little shop in Albert Drive and which had become part of the huge Cadbury corporation had, in more recent times, been on a roller-coaster of financial development. In 1970 the chain was bought by James Goldsmith of Cavenhams then sold on to the Southlands Corporation of Dallas, USA. In 1985 it was to change hands once more, this time being acquired by Guinness who combined it with their Martin Newsagent chain, which made R.S. McColl's part of the biggest confectionery, tobacconist and newsagent group in the UK, known as the Martin Retail Group. It seemed there was no end to the McColl financial big dipper ride, the Martin Retail Group being sold to a consortium of Australian investors who were to form the Panfida Group PLC. In January 1993, ownership of this group was effectively transferred to a syndicate of banks and by the end of 1998 was acquired by the TM Group, owners of the Forbuoys newsagent chain. They in turn formed TM Retail who operated more than 300 branches throughout the UK under the banner of either R.S. McColl's or just McColls.

With that kind of financial history, who knows what will be the next development, who will be the next owner, or who will take over who. But one aspect, it seems, because of its prestige, has been largely retained and will survive whatever. It's the name of Scotland's first ever football star, Bob McColl – the man who gave us R.S. McColl's.

CELTIC'S SADDEST DAY

Today he would have been known as *the* goalie. There was no one around to equal him – he was brilliantly rare. As testimony to that, combined with the everlasting respect there is for him, is the fact that no one since has earned the title by which John Thomson was known – the Prince of Goalkeepers.

The short life and most dramatic death of this outstanding footballer is one of the most legendary of sporting stories in the history of Glasgow. Had it not happened, a scriptwriter might have penned it for, as a work of fiction, it would have had everything. The young lad from the nowhere of a Scottish pit village, hacking it out at the coalface at the tender age of 14. The hero of his locality for his sporting prowess on neighbourhood soccer pitches; the absolute chance discovery by the talent scout from the big city and his subsequent signing by the major football club; the goal guardian who was to become the darling of his club and country, with his remarkable displays of fearless ability and unequalled prowess which were to make him a household name; the courage that was to cost him his life and the sad years to follow for the player who caused his death. The remarkable story of John Thomson has everything. His story is stranger than any fiction.

The Glasgow of the millennium years is a vastly different city to the one of the early '30s to which John Thomson was to come and where he revitalised the top-league soccer scene with his uncanny daring and spectacular saves that were to raise the levels of goalkeeping to new heights. It was a little more than a decade after the Great War which had scarred almost every household in the land. Thankfully he had been too young to be a soldier although, a schoolboy at the time, he remembered the sadness in the homes of friends and family whose menfolk had gone to the trenches where they were to lie forever.

He had come to the city from his home village of Bowhill, Cardenden, in Fife, where he had been a miner since leaving school at the age of 14. Without the facilities or the wherewithal, young men travelled little in such times, the county or nearest big town being about the stretch of their limits, and often their imagination. In John Thomson's case that nearest big centre had been Kirkcaldy, the Lang Toun, as they called it, just a few miles south along the shores of the Forth. The prospect of Glasgow, therefore, was no less than something awesome for him, with its still rising population of a million, a fifth of all who inhabited the entire country, and its status as the second city of the empire. And when you played football like he did, then there was just no place like it, not in Scotland, not in Britain, not even anywhere on the globe, what with match attendances of 80,000 being commonplace in the city that boasted the three biggest football stadiums in the world. What a place to be for a footballer!

It was other days with other ways in that early week of September 1931. While some of the world and local events of the time make it feel so long ago, there were aspects of other happenings which manifestly demonstrate how some things just go on and on. In the wider world, all the talk was about the strange little man who dressed in bedsheets and was called Gandhi and who, in his unique fashion, was illustrating that if you are clever enough, such as he was, changes could be brought about by peaceful means. He was in the news once more and again his novel and unusual ways were dominating conversation. The legendary spiritual leader and social reformer was on his way by ship for talks in London and had been fascinating accompanying passengers and pressmen by refusing to accept the first-class cabin he had been offered for the voyage, opting instead to sleep on a crude wooden bench he had brought along for the purpose, together with ten gallons of specially pasteurised goat's milk as sustenance for the long sea passage.

Another most admirable legend, this time one of our own countrymen, the great Olympic and national champion Eric Liddell, was also in the news. Perhaps, and ironically so, he's better remembered today as the fabled runner featured in the award-winning film *Chariots of Fire* (1981) with its haunting hit theme music by Vangelis. Liddell was returning for a year's study course to a church college after completing six years' missionary work in China and said he intended going back there for more such work after his stay here. A famous sportsman giving up everything to work for the neglected!

In Spain they were doing the kind of thing for which Spain was

better known in those days. They were disposing of striking workers –
by shooting them on sight.

In the Glasgow of 1931 you could buy ten cigarettes for 3p, a lady's
tweed coat for just over £1, a gent's suit for £3.15, a seven-piece
furniture suite for £18.50, go on holiday to Rothesay where full board
was on offer at 38p a day, and see big display advertisements in the
newspapers urging you to head towards 'Milngavie for health', that
being the lure to buy one of builder Gordon's new bungalows in the
semi-countryside. They were going for £625 each, or a down payment
of £25.

There was no Child Support Agency in those days, but they did
have their way of dealing with those who abandoned wives and
children, a city court case being told that week they were looking for
over 1,200 such recalcitrant fathers. Two of them had just been arrested
for such neglect and the court doled out the typical punishment of the
day for what was then a criminal offence – 30 days in jail, with hard
labour.

Other happenings are still the litany of life today. There were
forever problems with the IRA, or Fenians as they were better known
then. The Scottish Nationalists were loudly attacking the former
Labour government for what they said had been 'their failure to tackle
the problems of Scottish industry and welfare'. But it wasn't only the
former government that was copping it from the Nationalists.

The Tory administration of the time was described as being merely
an 'English national government'. And that same government,
incidentally, was about to announce details of the new budget and the
inside word, which everyone knew anyway, was that taxes would be
going up. You would know, of course, on which commodities –
tobacco, beer and tea!

One of our procurators fiscal was loudly criticising the prevalence
of young men going to local dances and taking with them supplies of
whisky. They had never heard of BSE or E-coli, but nevertheless there
was a food poisoning scare in the city, this time in Calton where 17
were rushed to hospital having become ill after eating sandwiches
made from tinned meat. And just as there is today, there was that
presence in our midst of that type of character who, in their pursuit of
the drink, while not meriting any special admiration, do at times lend
that little special flavour, albeit a piratical piquancy, to the overall
character of the city. Although today's breed seems more or less

confined to men in white vans doing breakneck return trips to Calais and Boulogne, yesterday's counterparts had to rely on some rather spectacular tricks for their ill-gotten refreshments. The hilarious efforts of one gang was all the talk that Saturday in early September 1931 as the crowds converged on Ibrox for the big match, and when you say the big match in Glasgow, that means just one thing – Rangers v. Celtic.

The story had gone the rounds, first of all by word of mouth, then it had appeared in the papers. Even without the resulting embellishments that such stories gain, the bare facts were a riot in themselves. Apparently, there had been about half a dozen of them, although the precise number is not known for only one of them remained and was in custody when the incident was discovered. It was around midnight after the last of the staff had left and the premises were, they thought, safely secured when they broke into the Theatre Royal at the top of Hope Street.

Their target – the theatre's bar. Undiscovered and objective achieved, they had then settled themselves in to enjoy the wee small hours with what, to them, had been a form of paradise, albeit a temporary one: free and unlimited booze. Then, one by one, more than lightly refreshed, and no doubt when they could consume no more, they had stealthily sneaked out into the night again, all that is except for one who could obviously last the pace longer than the others, or else had less discretion about his ways. He was to remain on his own, but not just content with the drink and scores of cigars to which the gang had also helped themselves, this last man wasn't for switching off the lights. He had them on, for he wanted to see what he was doing, fulfilling what was probably the ambition of a lifetime. He was still there when the cleaners arrived at seven in the morning, all on his own in the centre of the theatre's stage hilariously performing to the empty theatre an elaborate Indian club act, his clubs being pint-size screwtop beer bottles. His fate at the hands of the authorities was not to be known for some time in the future but the story did lend some considerable cheer to the day.

But to many, especially those on their way to the big football match that windless and mild Saturday afternoon of 5 September 1931, there were much more important things to dwell on than tales of nocturnal purloining revellers, men on the run from wives and children, or of Gandhi and Eric Liddell. He hadn't said it then, but the man they were all to know who was to make the memorable pronouncement that football was more important than life or death might well have said it some decades earlier. For by the early '30s the sport that was to dominate the culture of Glasgow and Scotland, was already a way of life. And John Thomson, the young lad from Fife who had come to Celtic via such rough and tumble soccer training grounds as Bowhill West End, Bowhill Rovers and Wellesley Juniors in Fife, was very much a part of that way of life.

He was just 17 when Steve Callaghan, Celtic's chief talent scout, went to Fife on the tip-off that the young lad in goal for the Denbeath team was one to be watched. It was in the days when the top Scottish clubs went to Motherwell rather than Milan, Bathgate rather than Belgrade, Lanark rather than Lisbon for their players. Callaghan paid close attention to the young player he had come to watch, but was to end up spending more time studying his rival, the other boy defending the goalmouth at the opposite end of the park on behalf of Wellesley Juniors. And particularly so after he saw him save a spectacular penalty. He was often to tell the story.

'We needed a goalkeeper at the time and we had been told about this young lad in Fife. It was a long journey in those days and it had to be a strong recommendation to get me to travel, but the reports on this player were so good that I made the trip. The game started and I had a look at this particular goalkeeper and, just like we had been told, he did look the part. But then I found myself watching the fellow in the other goal and as the game went on I couldn't take my eyes off him. And before the game was over I was obsessed with him and thought that I had to sign him for the club.'

Callaghan said he had rarely seen anyone with such lively and responsive reactions. As he told others later: 'This scrawny fella can spring like a cat.' Callaghan needed no further convincing than that one game in which he studied the junior they called Thomson. John Thomson. And when the game was over he was to spend two hours with him giving him the message, which was no glib spiel, that there was a future for someone with a talent like his. And that future was in Glasgow, at a place they called Parkhead. A team they called Celtic. But the 'scrawny fella' needed some convincing. Surprisingly, there was a rare reluctance from him about making a deal which would see him leaving home and playing for the big club in Glasgow. He was worried about his mother whom he knew would never agree to such a proposition for she had told him about a dream she had experienced about her young son.

That dream had been that he was badly injured while playing in goal and it had been so frightening to her that she had told him about it. The story emerged during their long talk, but Callaghan persuaded even more. Dreams were just dreams, after all, he said. What he was offering was what to countless young Scots lads was the reality of a dream come true.

The fact that Thomson was from a Protestant family who read the Bible every night and were all teetotal members of the Church of Christ, a sect whose services are conducted by lay preachers, was neither noted nor mentioned. But what was discussed was money, although there was little debate about the amount, Thomson agreeing to that and to putting his signature on the contract Callaghan produced and which he signed atop the fuse box of the roadside telegraph pole by which their two hours of discourse and negotiation had taken place. Then Callaghan handed over the fee that was to make Thomson a member of one of the biggest clubs in Scotland. The sum was £10. To put that figure into perspective, players today at the Glasgow club can earn as much as several thousand pounds – per day! Another perspective is that in 1931, Celtic announced what they termed the most 'highly satisfactory' profits for the year and that was a total of £6,000. Yet another perspective was that Jimmy McGrory, one of their greatest stars of that era, was on a wage of £7 a week. And, as a final perspective, and doubtless the one held by the young John Thomson that day in Fife, the signing-on fee represented more money than he had ever held in his life. It was more than he earned in a month in that most grim and arduous of workplaces, the Fife coalfields.

Everything else also being in proportion, there were no Kilmacolm, Bothwell or Newton Mearns mansions for footballers in those days when players were almost entirely known for what they did on the park rather than what they got up to after dark. And so digs were arranged for the young Thomson just along the road from Glasgow Cross, in the Gallowgate.

In order to help with his transition from those lusty junior soccer battle zones in Fife, Celtic had their promising young star put on loan to Ayr United reserves for a part of his first season. But, knowing his potential, they were anxious to utilise his services and, after just three games, and not many days after his eighteenth birthday, he was to make his first appearance for his new club in a league championship game against Dundee.

There was little wonderment that day in Dundee among the hardened and experienced Celtic team – one of the club's all-time great squads with fabled names such as McGrory, Peter Wilson and the McStays – for they had got to know the lad briefly. And they had made their notes about him: that he was raw and country-boy-like, his clothes looking like they were hand-downs from big brother, the big bunnet pulled down over his eyes in a fashion that might have been modish in Methil, but was certainly not gallus in Glasgow. The accent, too, was the full Fife, dotted with 'ye ken' and the like. Like Callaghan had said, he was scrawny, at 5ft 8½ in, weighing in at just 10½ stone. There was none of the bunch-of-five banana hands that were a traditional mark of the good goalie, none of the muscle bulk either. But, goodness, when they saw his movements in that goalmouth, he was something else. This was thoroughbred stuff. This was a class act, an athletic genius who appeared to have the rare ability to actually twist and change his directional thrust in mid-air in what appeared to be some new virile, physical dimension. Forget the dressing-room laddie, on the playing field this young man was about elegance and bravery, with a confidence, courage and co-ordination the like of which few had witnessed before.

Celtic won 2–1 that first day, their new keeper making one clumsy mistake by letting the ball slide past him as the result of a bad fumble. It was a silly and sloppy error, the kind that he never made and of all days when he had to make it by acting so carelessly, it was on this vital first appearance for Celtic.

That one error by those who saw it closest was put down to debut tension and was not to overshadow an otherwise flawless performance, although he was later chided by the formidable club director of the day, Tom Colgan, who told him, 'You did quite well, young fellow . . . but you had better not lose too many goals like that one today.' Which was to bring the earnest response from the young Fifer that it wouldn't happen the following week. The innocent assumption that he would be playing the following week proved justified, manager Maley nominating him once more as the number one keeper.

Celtic were back at Dundee that following week, this time in a Scottish Cup match at Dens Park, and Thomson played the kind of game they were to talk about for years to come, confirming everything that scout Callaghan had predicted of him. The club had a new star and from then on he was to be a permanent part of the club's first eleven, joining with his team-mates for their special pre-Cup training sessions at Seamill Hydro, the hotel which has become almost synonymous with the Parkhead club for their more selective preparations. Such training breaks and the prospect of living in top hotel surroundings were about the sum total of luxury and achievement for young soccer players of the day. Bottle was only about bravery, not Bollinger, and bevvy meant a pint, not a binge.

Seamill Hydro was a long shot away from the seafront at Kirkcaldy and at the Ayrshire resort John Thomson was to take to all the diverse activities on offer, these being a means of inculcating greater team spirit among the players with the theory that just as they relaxed in each other's company as a team, so too would they play like one. Thomson had never before played snooker or badminton, let alone stepped on a golf course, yet he was to astound his colleagues with his instant rapport between cue, bat, club and ball. There was the same uncanny co-ordination and quick response which he demonstrated on the soccer pitch. And on that very first outing with the team, John Thomson within days was to become a better than average badminton player and golfer and his first series of games at billiards was to win him the club tournament.

Thereafter John Thomson and his dramatic displays in goal were to become the stuff of sporting folklore when mates would tell other mates in the most graphic of detail how this man could jump, spring, thrust and stretch, flick, catch and stop a ball better than any man they had ever seen before. Like the time he was confronted by 'Peerie' Cunningham of Kilmarnock, a legendary character himself, given his nickname for the unbelievable way he could pivot and who was reckoned to be one of the most dangerous shots in the country. He had lashed at the Celtic goal and it appeared that the ball was heading for the right-hand post, the keeper diving in that direction only to find that he had misjudged its course and that the ball was going the other way. They said he had virtually twisted in mid-air, turning back in the opposite direction and getting enough of his fingers on the ball to keep it from going in. Those players nearest the goals had stood dumbfounded at what had been the most spectacular save they had ever witnessed.

He did much the same thing when stopping one of Andy Cunningham's cannons in the Glasgow Cup final against Rangers. Then in Birmingham, when he was keeper for a Scottish League team being hammered in both defence and attack by the English, Thomson prevented a humiliation for his team by failing to block the ball on only two occasions. One of his saves was a 20-yard rocket that seemed destined for the netting. Thomson had been on his knees at the time when the ball left the attacker's foot and it was heading for just under the crossbar. The leap he made from his crouch was the kind you only get from Olympic gymnasts, as he reached the heights in time to tip the ball over the bar, earning him the loudest and most sustained applause of the entire game.

Thomson was there, too, in what was probably the most important match of his career, the 1931 Scotland v England game at Hampden Park. If crowd sizes were the hallmark, these were the golden days of football in Scotland, with its unique collection of three giant stadiums in Glasgow and the attendance at this game being some 129,810, a record number to have ever been to a sporting event of any kind, anywhere in the world.

The Scottish team wasn't fancied for the fixture, a new rule decreeing that clubs could not release players for internationals on the day they had a league fixture, except for their own association. This prevented Scotland from choosing their nationals playing in England, the Anglos on whom they had always relied. The result would be a foregone conclusion, at least so everyone was saying, and that was that if the Scots won the kick-off toss then that would be about all they would win. But then when it comes to soccer, Scotland rarely does what is expected and by half-time neither team had scored. Not long after the start of the second half, Scotland took the lead through Stevenson, then Celtic's legendary Jimmy McGrory, who at one time held the record aggregate of league goals in British football, made it two up. That really stirred the English, who stormed revengefully at the Scottish goal, a Liverpool attacker letting loose what was said to be the finest shot of the day and which Thomson moved to catch.

Then, in a blur, the ball was deflected off another player, and Thomson, in mid-air, again with that uncanny flash decision and response of his, made an even further stretch than he had first anticipated. The English team was understandably dejected after witnessing that most astonishing save, wondering if they would ever get a ball past a man in form like this. It certainly didn't look like it. And they didn't. And Scotland had one of its finest victories in the international series that is now just a memory.

Thomson had by then become one of the most talked-about players in Scottish football, his various appearances for club and country being praised to the highest degree. It wasn't just the amazing athleticism of the man, it was his bravery that equally thrilled. 'See John Thomson,' they would say. 'Fire a cannonball at his goal and he'd try to save it.'

Perhaps the hyperbole wasn't all that far from the truth for the man was undaunted in the line of fire.

He was to pay dearly for that courage in a 1930 game when Celtic played Airdrie in a midweek match. He had gone for a ball in circumstances which would have seen most keepers make another move, one which might have had body and soul more in mind. But not John Thomson. It wasn't boots and limbs and torsos coming at him that he saw. His eyes were only for a ball. The consequences that day meant him being stretchered from the field, the injuries including a double fracture of a collarbone, a shattered jaw, the loss of two teeth and a broken rib. And when a member of the family warned him that his boldness would have to be curbed, he answered, 'I know.' And then, as though to justify his daring, he was to add, 'But the only thing I see there is the ball. Nothing else.'

But there were sensations other than physical in the Glasgow soccer scene. The great Protestant–Catholic divide had baffled him, like it does most Scots with a non-Glasgow or West of Scotland background. He had known about it, of course, but had not expected the bizarre bitterness with which each side gives you an instant label as soon as you pull on the opposing side's colours. Perhaps it affected him even more as, despite coming from the kind of working background more associated with the rough rather than the refined, Thomson was both a gentle man and a gentleman. And as a Church of Christ Protestant, he was never really to comprehend the insults he could hear in the chants from other Protestants, the Rangers' fans, when playing against their team. Even worse, there were the religious epithets professional players would often hurl at each other. Why such intolerance? Why such hate? He would often ask that of fellow team-mates. Once, when Jimmy McGrory, the club's great centre-forward, noted Thomson sitting subdued in the dressing-room at half-time, he had asked what was wrong.

'It's their centre,' said Thomson, obviously disturbed by the player in that position in the opposing team. 'He keeps calling me a papish bastard.'

'Come on, John. Don't let that worry you,' said McGrory comfortingly. 'I get called that every week.'

'But it's all right for you,' replied Thomson, perhaps more in innocence than insouciance, 'for you *are* one!'

After several weeks he was fully recovered from his injuries received at the Airdrie game and was back in action again, showing there was no appreciable sign that he was any less a man than before he was injured. The pluck, the verve, the skills were all there, just as before. But he had taken the precaution of finding himself work in one of the city's many gents' outfitters of the day in the realisation that as a professional soccer player, he was in the most ephemeral of occupations. The name of this 1930s game wasn't wealth or riches. And for a star like John Thomson it was just work and wages and you lived in digs up a close in the Gallowgate. Yet, humble though the returns might have been, there were all the other trappings of popularity and stardom, that being brought home to R.E. Kingsley, the legendary sports writer who wrote under the pen-name of Rex. One day, outside the gents' shop, he had met Thomson, whom he always referred to as Johnny, and within minutes there was such a crowd gathered round in the city centre just to gaze at the young footballer who had in such a short time become a household name, he had to cut short his walk with Rex and flee back into the privacy of the shop.

In 1931, Thomson was still headline man in the sports pages. Inevitably, he was to inspire the great debate of the day – who was the best between him and the other legend of goalkeepers, Jerry Dawson, one of the Rangers club's greatest ever stars? R.E. Kingsley said the number of times the question was put to him 'nearly drove me crazy'. But he did answer it, albeit in that undying sports writer's fashion which manages to keep both feet dry: 'Dawson was everything you wanted in a keeper. Lithe as a panther. Brilliant in position. And every bit as daring as Johnny Thomson. He [Dawson] saved Scotland many times and inspired her every time. Yet I believe he would have had few caps had Johnny Thomson been living, because Johnny was the boy in possession. Dawson was the greatest I have seen over a long spell. Consistency in a goalkeeper is a gift from the gods and Johnny Thomson didn't get the chance to prove his.'

In the August of that year, just a couple of weeks before the tragic accident, one of his saves, when his team had been playing Aberdeen, was described as a 'masterpiece'. They were just as lavish with the acclaim a week later when Celtic beat Hamilton Academical 6–1, much of that score due to Thomson's brilliance. By now he had made some 187 appearances as a top-flight goalkeeper, logging a total of 64 shut-outs, which simple arithmetic shows that in one of every three games in which he played, the other side were denied the chance of getting a single shot past him.

On the scene at the time was a young journalist, a tall gangly man of well over six feet who, together with his family, was to become a well-known figure on the Glasgow scene. He was the late Archie McCulloch, a household name in his own right from the '40s right through to the '60s as journalist and entrepreneur. His wife was Kathy Kay, the well-known singer, and one of his sons is Ken, the entrepreneurial hotel owner, founder and chief executive of Malmaison hotels and brasseries. McCulloch senior was just 18 when he was writing a column in which prominent sports stars revealed the secrets of their particular success. It was just a week before John Thomson was to make his 188th and tragic final appearance as a goalkeeper that he had been interviewed by McCulloch.

Thomson was to tell him:

> If you want to be a good goalkeeper you must keep your position, keep your eye on the ball and note when to come out and when to stay in. Never leave your goal if you can avoid it. If you have time to lift the ball, never kick clear, and when you are saving, endeavour to get not only your hands but also your body behind the ball. When taking bye kicks, always try to place the ball to an unmarked man. Always stand in such a manner that you are able to spring in any direction. Don't be glued to one position by standing on your heels. Poise on the balls of your feet and keep your feet a little apart so that you can spring in the event of the ball being deviated. Never stand too near the post next to the person who is shooting. It is easier to spring forward than go backward. Agility is very necessary and you should practise springing in the air and also gripping the ball in a confident manner.

When dealing with crosses from extreme wings, care should be taken to judge the cross and in the event of the winger deciding to shoot, the thoughtful goalkeeper will take up a stand a yard or so out from the goal according to the position of the man in possession. Such a position will render it practically impossible for a goal to be scored. When gripping the ball, care should be taken to pull it in towards the chest. This will prevent the ball from squirming out of the keeper's hands. The great thing in goalkeeping is to keep cool and never lose your head.

Saturday, 5 September 1931, and just under 80,000 crowded into Ibrox stadium and paid their 5p (boys 2½ p) to crush together on the steep terracing, or 20p for a seat in the centre stand, to watch the game which is about a lot more than football. Rangers v Celtic is not the kind of meeting that wins any accolades for being a sporting occasion, being more of a sort of hate-fest where passions are at an abysmal primeval level, and if you try to reason and ask just why, the simple retort is that it's all because one team is about Protestants, the other about Roman Catholics. If you really wanted to comprehend it better than that simplistic analysis, a doctorate in sociology would be useful.

Despite the venom, there are often many exciting meetings between the two clubs, with splendid football fought out at a level and pace to equal the best games in Britain. But this Saturday in September was not to be one of them. In fact, it was so poor that 'Dreadnought', the pseudonym of the *Daily Record*'s man covering the game, was to write about the first half as being 'a deplorable exhibition'.

'The crowd had been looking for thrills and for a battle of craft and cleverness,' he went on. 'But of thrills there were none, of scientific football there was a complete absence and of craft and cleverness not one suggestion.' Players were booting each other as much as the ball and 'not a minute went past without the referee's whistle blowing for some sort of infringement or other. Trainers and assistant trainers were the busy men.'

As well as lacking in thrills, there was a complete absence of goals, and when the game resumed for the second half, both sets of fans were hoping for better things to come, although their teams by now had all the appearance of being much more concerned with not losing rather than with winning.

Into the fifth minute of the ultimate 45 minutes and a counter-attack from the Rangers men looked hopeful. The ball had gone to the young Rangers man nicknamed 'Doc' Marshall, being a medical student, and from him to the big captain, Davie Meiklejohn, and from him to their burly winger Jimmy Fleming, positioned on the touchline a few yards on the Celtic side of the halfway line. Peter McGonagle, the Celtic back, sped across to challenge, but Fleming managed to dodge him, kept the ball low and raced up the park chased by his team-mate Sam English, a recent signing from Ireland who had just passed a fitness test that morning in order to play. The Rangers fans were roaring the loudest they had roared the entire game, for what they were now seeing had all the signs of a goal in the making as English and Fleming raced in full flight towards goal.

Keeper John Thomson, in his distinctive scarlet jersey, had noted everything. 'Never leave your goal if you can avoid it,' he had told McCulloch the week before. But in his view there was no avoiding it on this occasion. English had the ball by now and Thomson went out to meet the speeding challenge. It was just at that moment when English's right leg pulled back for that last thrust that would take it forward for the final kick that Thomson dived.

The maxims by which he played his game were, as always, all in place, all being effected. 'Keep your eye on the ball and note when to come out and when to stay in . . . It is easier to spring forward than go backwards . . . The great thing in goalkeeping is to keep cool . . .'

Football boots in the '30s were designed more for artisans than athletes, their tough pig-leather toecaps covering steel inserts. But that wasn't to deter John Thomson, his eyes as ever on that ball as he dived for it at the same time as English's right leg made its final pendulum for the kick that seemed certain to score the vital goal. The yells of the crowd crescendoed as the pair clashed, English's attack instantly nullified as he crumpled to the turf, Thompson spreadeagled by the collision, his efforts yet again succeeding, the ball being deflected and going wide of the target.

Thomson lay motionless where he had fallen, as sometimes footballers often do for those first seconds or so when injured or badly winded. There were gasps in the main stand, a single piercing scream being heard from a horrified young woman. It was Thomson's lover and fiancée, 'Micky' (Morag) Finlay, watching the game with Jim, one of his brothers. There was another kind of reaction from a section of the Rangers crowd, a gratifying cheer, but then in this kind of game, injury to one is joy to another, and that same response would have come from the rival fans had it been the Rangers man who had been likewise stricken.

Those closest to the prone goalkeeper could immediately determine there was no perverse joy to be had from this fallen opponent, English limping to his feet being perhaps the first to know something serious was wrong, especially when he noted the blood spurting from a small wound to Thomson's left temple. Rangers skipper Meiklejohn, furious at the continued cheers from the terracing, dominated by his own supporters, ran towards them, arms outstretched, with the kind of gesture which had only one translation, and it depends on which reporter's pen is believed as to how quickly his appeal for silence and respect was effective.

Centre-forward Jimmy McGrory and the other Celtic players, including manager Willie Maley and the club doctor, were to rush over to the goalmouth area and surround their fallen colleague. It was the look on their faces that told much of the story. These were men who knew all about injuries on the football field, most of them having had their share, or having seen those who had, in a time when the heaviest of shinguards were necessary, together with cotton-wool and bandages, when shoulder charging was permitted and it was considerably more of a contact sport. They knew all about the bruises and the concussions, the gashes and bashes, the special agony of the fracture and the individual reactions there were to each and every one of them. But the sight they were to see was a very different one from any they had seen before, and their faces were saying just that.

McGrory, one of Celtic's all-time greats as player and manager, remembered seeing the blood spraying from the unconscious goalkeeper's temple. He had looked so still and pale, he said, and the blood kept squirting from the wound, 'like it was a small fountain'. Then he heard one of the Rangers players who had also come over make the comment that there wasn't much wrong with the goalie. McGrory was later to confess that for the first time in his life, 'I wanted to strangle a Rangers player'. But before making the move to do just that, skipper Meiklejohn again intervened, firmly ordering his rash team-mate to make no further loose comments.

A team of six smartly uniformed St Andrew's ambulancemen then rushed to the spot and, under the supervision of Dr William Kivlichan, administered temporary first aid, carefully bandaging the head wound then stretchering him to the dressing-room. Kivlichan was one of the most experienced of soccer team doctors, having been a player himself and who, uniquely for the time, had played for both Rangers and Celtic and even scored winning goals for each side.

With Thomson now off the pitch and being as there's no business like this football business, they went on with the show, the referee calling for play to continue, with substitute Charlie Geatons taking over as the Celtic goalkeeper. The following 40 minutes were to be the longest period in a football match any Celtic team had ever known, each and every one of them more than anxious for it to be over and learn how their injured team-mate was faring. Little wonder the soccer writer who wrote under the pseudonym 'Dreadnought' was to say, 'None of them played as we know they have the ability to play,' although he went on, with little thought of what had happened that day, to make the comment on all the players that, 'They can all be lumped together, packed up in the same parcel and labelled "poor stuff".' It may have been kinder to note that the 0–0 final score was perhaps some form of testimony to a day which wasn't one for winners.

Having been taken to the dressing-room, John Thomson was given a closer examination by Dr William Kivlichan who was to diagnose a compressed fracture of the skull. Without regaining consciousness, Thomson was then rushed by ambulance to the Victoria Infirmary.

By early evening, Thomson's parents, John and Jean, and his two brothers, Bill and Jim, surrounded his bedside in Ward 5 together with medical staff. It was in the days when there were no life-support machines, no monitors, no mechanical life aids, no high-tech equipment, and no miracle drugs to sustain existence through a crisis like this, just patient, doctors and nurses hoping there may be some form of recovery, whereafter what vital skills they had at the time could be applied. But there wasn't even to be the slightest flicker of response from the comatosed young footballer. And just six hours later, at 9.25 that night, the thousands who had congregated outside the Glasgow Southside infirmary were told that without regaining consciousness John Thomson had died. He was 22 years of age.

The Celtic players had waited too, tensely anticipating any news of their mate, all of them hoping that somehow he would pull through. McGrory was to describe his death as the greatest on-the-field tragedy in the history of the Scottish game. It still has no on-field parallel. It had such an effect on McGrory at the time that he was to consider quitting the sport. He said the players would have liked nothing better than to have followed John Thomson's stretcher off the field and had never been so thankful when eventually the game did come to an end.

Writing later about it, McGrory was to say that when at the end of the game they were told how badly Thomson was injured, they never thought the worst. 'Despite the gloom, I never thought in a hundred years that he would die,' said McGrory. But then, when he heard the news, he was so shocked he was to say, 'That was the only night in my entire career that I wanted to quit football. I was sickened. I was never afraid of physical contact or taking a knock, but to experience a team-mate dying playing a game of football was just too much.'

John Thomson's death was to mark an extraordinary chapter of mourning, the extent of which no other Scots athlete has ever received. They stopped work in the pits and works in Fife and villages emptied as mourners converged on the little graveyard at Bowhill, Cardenden, to be there for his funeral, where the service was held at Thomson's Church of Christ, conducted as always by a lay preacher, perhaps appropriately for the occasion, a miner. Six Celtic players (McGrory, Thomson, Wilson, McStay, Cook and Napier) carried John Thomson's coffin, adorned with his international caps and a wreath in the shape of goal posts, the half mile from the home of his parents to the graveside. They were witnessed by the biggest crowd ever seen at the one time, the one place in Fife, estimates putting it at between 30,000 and 40,000. There were 20,000 alone at Queen Street station in Glasgow just to watch the mourners leave for the funeral.

They came too from other further coalfields to be there for the farewell to one of their sons. Special trains had been commissioned to bring thousands who wanted to pay their last tribute. And they trekked from Edinburgh and from Glasgow, hundreds of them walking all the way, sleeping out overnight in fields. Well, that was the way of it in those early '30s when you were unemployed and the 20p return on the train was virtually enough to keep you for the week.

The great outpouring of feeling was as much, perhaps even more, for the man rather than the goalkeeper. Of course, there were plenty of rough diamonds on the fields of soccer glory, but fortunately there was no shortage either of the kind of men who rode their own chariots of fire. John Thomson was most certainly one of them. The

Rangers Bridgeton Supporters' Club wrote to newspapers apologising with the understandable explanation for their cheering and jeering: 'We just didn't know.'

At the first of two packed and remarkable memorial services conducted in Glasgow, David Meiklejohn, the man who had rushed towards those Rangers fans that day, read the lesson. And the conducting minister, Revd H.S. McLelland of Trinity Church, was to say: 'The simple truth had been for tens of thousands of Glasgow citizens and hundreds of thousands of Scotsmen, that John Thomson had been the *beau idéal* of Scottish sportsmanship.'

They're old men now, those few who remember the life and times back in the early '30s and that most sad day in Fife, with all its accompanying spectacle, the day they buried John Thomson. Tom Kirk, a retired joiner, was just a schoolboy at the time and was 77 years of age when I spoke to him about his memories of the occasion. Such was the impact that day made on all those in the local community, it lives on with him like it just happened yesterday. Tom had been friendly with the Thomson boys, the one he knew best being John's older brother Jim, the brother who had been at the match together with John's girlfriend Micky on the day he was killed.

Although he was just nine years of age at the time of the accident, Tom Kirk's memories of John Thomson are as someone who had lost a member of his extended family, which was the way with these mining communities in the villages of Fife, rather than memories of a man who had become a sporting hero. Just simple memories of working men going about their daily lives doing the very ordinary and routine things that were part of life then, in and around the place they called the ABCD village because it was made up of Auchterderran, Bowhill, Cardenden, Denend and Dundonald, the five sections of the Auchterderran parish. He vividly recalls those Sunday mornings so long ago when most people would be going to their respective churches, John Thomson, like the rest of his family, an enthusiastic Baptist and dressed in his best suit with plus-four trousers. They would point him out, of course, him being the personality he was.

'Mind you,' says Tom, 'there was five of them from in and around here who were all good enough to sign for Celtic: John Thomson, of course, then there was John McFarlane, who also played for Scotland, Willie Fagan, Paddy Rodger and John Conway. I played in a game against Conway myself, by the way. It was at the Central Park in Cowdenbeath.'

Memories too of his old pal Alex Reekie who, during the 1926 strike, would regularly meet John Thomson at the Jamphlars Pond coup. Alex was an apprentice joiner at the time and he would be at the coup to burn sawdust and shavings from the workshop where he was employed and John Thomson would be there spreading the ashes from the ash carts, earning a few coppers at that to make up for the wages he would not be getting due to the strike. And those regular chit-chats between the pair at the coup were all remembered, then passed on and woven into the local folklore of the man from among them who had become the sporting legend.

Tom speaks too about Arthur Burt, another pal, who for years had treasured the horseshoe given to him by John Thomson, it being the custom then for supporters to present their goalie with a good-luck horseshoe before cup final matches.

And Tom had shared those same experiences John Thomson would have had in their little home of Bowhill. Saturday was their best day, for you got the half day off work and there was Sunday to look forward to with no need to be up before dawn and down to the colliery. Saturday was the busiest day of the week in Bowhill, the main street packed with housewives doing their food shopping, or getting their messages as they would say, many coming in from Dundonald, Woodend, Jamphlars and further away from Brighills and Kinglassie to shop at the 'store', the name everyone in Scotland gave then to their most popular grocer, the Co-operative.

Just like John Thomson, Tom as a youngster would have been given his Saturday penny for the matinée film show in the Goth picture house in the morning and when they were older and working it would be either the cinema at night or the Masonic Hall or the Bowhill Institute for the dancing, then heading for the busiest venues of all on a Saturday night, Davie's, Curatti's or Adamson's, the local fish and chip shops.

Then there's Tom's very own recollection of that beautiful early autumn Wednesday in September of 1931, the day the world, it seemed, had come to their village. His thoughts of it are seared into his memory, for there had never been a day like it in the village, nothing like it in all of Fife for that matter. It was the biggest crowd they had ever known. There were convoys of buses, trainloads including two 'specials', and long lines of men who had walked all the way from Glasgow, and that was more than 50 miles away, all wanting to be there when they buried John Thomson. And every shop closed up and all the houses had their blinds down or curtains drawn out of respect.

'You know, the crowd was such that many of those living near to the little cemetery at Bowhill had to clamber up on the roofs of their houses in order to see the funeral pass by. Hundreds of boys who had come up from Glasgow, most of whom had walked all the way, slept the night up at the Crags (that's a well-known plantation nearby) and others bedded down by the pit bings. And, do you know, at the actual graveside you could look up and see the bedroom of John Thomson's house up at 27 Balgreggie Park.'

As he speaks, each little memory recalls another. 'Our bands were all there, the Bowhill Pipe Band and the Bowhill Silver Band. And I'll always remember the special wreath with the hearse. It was this big piece of trimmed turf, like a miniature football pitch, with goal posts etched on it in small white flowers. And then, just at that moment, an aeroplane landed in the Daisy Park.' And that really was something to remember in the Fife of 1931. The plane, apparently, was on a special mission from the national newspapers, ready to rush the pictures back to eager printing presses.

Jim Ferguson, a retired architect, was an old schoolboy pal of John Thomson's and probably the only personal friend of the legendary goalkeeper still living. He was 90 years of age when we met and he recalled his own fond memories of those days in another age in and around these little Fife villages. John is from one of the best-known families in the community, his father having been the long-serving – 42½ years, no less – manager of the No. 1 Goth in Bowhill. Goths are not something that impact on the lives of many Scots outside of Fife and the Lothians, but people from these parts know all about them. The Goths were the very hub of their communities, being the local public houses, but public houses with a very big difference. They had their origins in the novel and commendable way of running such drinking establishments in similar working communities in Sweden, hence the name Goth, that being a shortened version of the name of Sweden's largest port, Gothenburg. Being local ventures, all their profits were ploughed back into the welfare and other good causes of the community.

'I had known Johnny since our schooldays. He was at Auchterderran school and I was at Denend and we played against each other in our school teams. And, do you know, I had the honour of scoring a goal past him. My memory of him as a young lad was that he was football daft and always near a ball of some kind, and in those days the ball was more often an old tin can or a pile of old newspapers tied with string. Like John, we were all football mad, I suppose you could say. And we were good at it as well. You know, at one time the young men from this locality who had been signed and were playing for the big teams could, on their own, have formed a full first division side – plus reserves. How many other places in Scotland – or anywhere – do you know could do something like that? And on top of that there were those five lads who played for Celtic.

'And after we left school we went about our various ways in life, Johnny going to the pits, the Bowhill Colliery, where his dad worked, and myself starting my long training to be an architect. But we still kept in touch and when Johnny became good enough to be signed by Celtic we would still see each other. I remember the time when he was badly injured in a match while playing for Celtic [the game against Airdrie in 1930 when he fractured his jaw, ribs and collarbone]. We had met up after the game and spoke together about it. I remember it so well for he was to tell me that, as a goalkeeper, it was the ball that you always kept your eyes on, not the player's feet.

'Then we touched on the subject of a really serious accident happening on the field and he turned to me and said: "Well, if I ever get a serious kick then I hope that's it." And by that he meant he didn't want to be crippled – he would rather die.'

Jim, with John Thomson and his girlfriend Micky Finlay and John's brothers Bill and Jim and sister Ella and other friends, spent many happy times together following the pursuits of typical young people of their age and in those times in Fife. There would be local dances. 'Oh, aye, there was plenty of them. And hikes in the countryside. 'We would walk for miles and miles.' And other simple pursuits of a more uncomplicated age, all of them happy and dear memories of huckleberry friends looking for the same rainbow's end.

Jim Ferguson's whole family were deeply affected by John Thomson's tragic death. And that day of the funeral, too, lives on like it was yesterday with Jim Ferguson.

'You know, the place looked as though Glasgow had emptied itself of people and they were all here. There had never been such a crowd in Fife, nor has there been since. The first we had got to know about the accident had been early on the Saturday evening. I was at the local cinema with some friends, including Hugh McFarlane, who played for Celtic, and they put a flash up on the screen about the accident. And that was the end of the show, for everyone was so shocked at the news they just got up and walked out.'

The day of the funeral had been little Bowhill's saddest day, but such were the lives and times of these little hard-working mining communities in Fife it was soon to be eclipsed by an even sadder day for them. On Wednesday, 4 November, exactly eight weeks after they had laid John Thomson to rest in Bowhill cemetery, the crowds were back again, but this time they were without the world as witness. The previous Saturday, 31 October, a scenario had been played out in Bowhill that has been replicated in so many books and films. The pit horns had blown without stop and houses and shops emptied as knowing relatives, the screeching horns still ominously blaring, rushed to the pit head where the first of the rescue teams were readying for the hazardous task of heading below. There had been an explosion hundreds of feet down in the bowels of the earth and it had been so devastating the rumblings from it were heard around the village.

It had been caused by the dreaded firedamp and the ten men who had been working that morning on repair and maintenance duties were all instantly killed. Some of them were men who John Thomson had laboured beside as a lad when he had been a miner at the pit, and others were nearby neighbours like Jim Anderson who had lived just across the road in Balgreggie Park. And in the pouring rain and biting wind of the almightiest of storms that early November day, their bodies were laid to rest nearby that of the man of whom they had all been so proud and whose funeral they themselves had attended those few weeks previously.

An analysis of the accident that had killed John Thomson was to show that Sam English had been absolutely blameless for Thomson's death, and that was not just the general feeling but the verdict of an ensuing fatal accident inquiry. It was revealed that it had not been the toe of his boot which had connected with Thomson's head. Instead, it was his left knee which had crunched into the Celtic goalkeeper as he came out, those eyes of his, as he so often said, fixed on that ball he was determined to save.

The tragic death of Thomson was to haunt the Rangers man Sam English, despite his complete innocence, for the rest of his life. Capped twice for his native Ireland, English was a player of some considerable merit, establishing an all-time record for the period by scoring 53 goals in the 1931–32 season, a record that was to remain unbeaten in the Ibrox club for more than 30 years. However, following the Thomson tragedy, he was only to play for a further two years with Rangers before going south to join Liverpool, moving on again this time to Queen of the South followed by Hartlepool United. He gave up his professional playing career just six years after the accident which killed Thomson. They had not been the happiest of years for him, the abuse from the terracings, the taunts from rivals on the field continuing. Little was heard of him after his retiral from Hartlepool, although that was the way of it with most players of that era. When the football was over, it was back to the trade they had left in order to play full time with a club, if they were lucky enough to have a trade, that is. English had been a sheet-metal worker and settled with his family in Dalmuir, keeping in touch with the sport as a trainer with Duntocher Hibs.

In 1965 English was in the news for the first time in years when at the age of 57 it was mistakenly reported that he had passed away. The assumption had been made after he had been off work for some time, but English laughingly dismissed the story as something of a joke. Two years later, however, on 12 April 1967, after a long illness, Sam English died. He had described himself in one newspaper interview as 'the second unluckiest footballer in the world'. A small assembly of just 100 attended the funeral at Cardross Crematorium, Dunbartonshire.

THE PETERHEAD PAPILLON

He has been in prison for maist o' his days,
An' 'I must have ma freedom' is a' that he says,
There are nae horizons in a twenty-foot cell,
And bitter the music of a hard prison bell.
– from *The Ballad of Johnny Ramensky*, by Hamish Imlach

Not many Glasgow criminals have won the respect or the admiration of their fellow citizens, their fellow *honest* citizens, that is. Nary a Robin Hood among them, but plenty of robbing hoods, to use an expression. But one alone stands apart from his fellow felons. He never drank; okay, he had the occasional stout. He never smoked. He had a detestation of drugs and the drug trade. He never used violence. But the man who called himself John Ramsay, but was known better as Johnny Ramensky, did steal, usually from places where no one else could steal; or from locked boxes, strongrooms and safes which no one would ever consider could be broken open or into. For John Ramsay was a serial safe-blower. The most famed safe-blower of his time. More likely the most famed of his like in Scotland in all time.

Stealing was John Ramsay's profession. And he did it in what he considered a professional manner. He would think nothing of shinning up the most vertiginous of buildings. He would clamber along the most precarious of roofs and ledges to get at his haul. He was an expert with oxyacetylene equipment, with gelignite, fuse wire, tamping sticks, detonators and all the stock-in-trade equipment of the men they used to call cracksmen – the safe-blowers. Ramsay's targets, whether houses, shops or business premises, were chosen only from the most wealthy, or else those whom he considered could afford whatever haul he might get away with. Had he carried business cards, they might have read: anywhere, anytime . . . distance no object. For while Glasgow was his adopted city, Johnny Ramsay worked at his trade all over the country . . . a bakery safe in Aberdeen, a bank in North Yorkshire, one in Oban, another in Rutherglen, a Woolworth's store in Paisley, another store in Ayr, the factor's office in Stirling. And that was just a few.

When compared to others in his trade, John Ramsay was star material. And if you were to believe much of what was written about him, the man was pure Hollywood. Big star Hollywood. But in between the fact and the considerable fiction about the man who was probably the most colourful Glasgow criminal of this century, the true story of the man who was to spend most of his life behind prison bars and the sensational escapes which he performed from various penitentiaries is still the kind of stuff the scriptwriters of American dream factories go weak at the knees about.

John Ramsay, the name he legally adopted and used, was much better known in his day as Johnny Ramensky, the name alone having all the ring of the lead character in a movie, as did his nickname 'Gentle Johnny', first coined for him by the police for the self-imposed standard he had set by never offering any form of violence. What few years he did enjoy of liberty were spent in the East End, but mainly the Gorbals area of Glasgow.

As his name indicates, Johnny's forebears were from other parts. He was born Jonas Ramanauckus on 6 April 1905, at 11 Ashbank, Glenboig. His parents had come from the little town of Marijona Grigosaityte in Lithuania, where they had married. Like their fellow countrymen who came here, they had been subjected to the brutality of living in a Russian-dominated state where if you didn't serve in the tsar's army you either starved or were shot. For the Lithuania of 1899, just think of the Kosovo of 1999. It was as horrible as that.

The Ramanauckuses were to be among the lucky ones able to flee, doing so by the usual route which was by trekking all the way to one of the Baltic ports where for a few shillings, usually about £1 per adult, they could get a passage to Leith. There was work, they were told, in the place they called Scotland. That it was the harsh rigours of the coalfields or the steel mills were of little concern: it would give them enough to eat. More importantly, it would give them that precious commodity of which they had known so little in their lives – freedom.

Like many of their compatriot nationals who established themselves in and around the coalmining towns of Lanarkshire, the Ramanauckuses were to settle in what was then the little village of Glenboig, where their young son John was born in the first years of the new century.

As did most of their countrymen, the Ramanauckuses changed their knotty Baltic name to something more compatible with Scottish tongues, their family name going through several forms before settling on Ramensky. Despite changing his own name to Ramsay, their son was never able to shake off the name by which he had first come to the attention of the press and public and he was to be forever known as Johnny Ramensky.

He was just seven years old when his father Vincas died. Vincas had never fully recovered from the horrors of life as a fugitive refugee combined with the rigours and primitive working conditions of a miner's life in turn-of-the-century Scottish coal pits. Mrs Ramanauckus, crippled through the loss of an arm in an accident, was left to rear their three young children, Johnny and his two younger sisters.

They moved to Glasgow just after the First World War and it was the old and predictable story for the young John Ramensky after that, the fatherless young boy growing up in some of the toughest parts of Glasgow. Trouble began early. He was just 11, in fact, when his name first appeared on offenders lists. Again it was the predictable: petty crime at first, thieving whatever he could, housebreaking and shoplifting – the underworld undergraduate.

But even early on along the road his life seemed destined to take, he was to set himself different standards than the others on the same route. Standards that were to make that Lithuanian family title of his a household name; a name that meant daring and bravado; that meant courage of the highest order; that meant audaciousness of the rarest kind. His exploits as a prisoner and as a patriot were to comprise one of the most remarkable of true-life stories.

Such was the legend that was to grow around the man that on one occasion when being sentenced in the High Court, the judge, Lord Russell, was to tell him that he had listened with the utmost attention 'and with a certain amount of respect' to the story that had been outlined by the defence counsel. Even the very policemen who on so many occasions had to arrest and detain Johnny Ramensky couldn't help but like the man, hence the title 'Gentle Johnny' they bestowed upon him.

It was about six years before the outbreak of the Second World War when Johnny Ramensky first came to the attention of the general public, as well as the authorities, as being a prison inmate of considerably different dimensions than the normal prisoner. He was in Barlinnie prison at the time, having been convicted once again for his particular speciality, that of a cat-burglar. The old cat-burglars were a daring breed, breaking into locked premises of various sorts – large houses, offices and the like – which invariably involved considerable risk as well as an element of patience and precision and no small degree of pluck. It's another profession that has gone downmarket, as it were, the latter-day burglar opting for the much easier life of simple housebreaking, there being no shortage in today's homes of the kind of easily lifted and disposed of items they are after. But Johnny Ramensky had all of the qualities required by the professional cat-burglar – in abundance. But what caused him to hit the headlines on that first occasion back on a warm summer Sunday in July 1931 was his flair in demonstrating to the authorities that he was a man to be noted, a man they would have the greatest difficulty restraining.

He had been in 'E' hall at Barlinnie prison, Glasgow, when he dashed from under the very noses of the warders guarding him, out into the yard, and although his chasers were just inches from his heels he was to reach a ronepipe and shoot 70 feet up it to the roof of the building in a fashion that left his pursuers gasping in awe. They had never seen a man climb like that before, and in his stocking soles at that, Ramensky, just prior to bolting, having untied his laces in order to throw off his boots as he ran.

Having reached the roof of the building, Johnny let loose a barrage of slates on the warders below as a warning to keep clear. Some tried to come through one of the hatches on the roof and they too came under a hail of slates and quickly backed off. Then they sent for the fire hoses which would be sure to do the trick, only to find to their dismay that the pressure wasn't sufficient to get the water that high.

By the time the newspaper reporters arrived, crowds had flocked up from Carntyne and there were more than 4,000 standing along Lethamhill Road and neighbouring fields being entertained by one of the best Sunday events they had seen in years. Having spotted them, Johnny was to give the crowd one of the best displays of gymnastics they had seen. Being the keep-fit man he was, he knew all the routines, even simulating dumbbell exercises and standing precariously on the edge of the high building – on one foot.

Hearing the bawls from the crowd, Johnny was to shout down to them: 'Can you send me up some boiled eggs?' They laughed at his simple request like it was Tommy Morgan at the Pavilion. 'Well, if you cannae send me up some eggs, how about getting me some fresh air?' They laughed at his continued cheek even more, doubtless the inspiration for the *Scotsman* newspaper headline for their story the next day. It read 'Amusing Incident'.

Having entertained the crowd below enough, Ramensky was then to strip off his shirt and lie down and relax in the warm sunshine for the rest of the day. It wasn't until dusk when the governor approached as near as he could and made a plea to Johnny to end his stand, whatever it might be for, that he quietly surrendered and clambered down.

When the governor made his own inquiries into the background of the incident, he was to be told by one less-than-discreet inmate, or a 'grass' as his mates would have said, that the reason for Ramensky's display was only to demonstrate to the other prisoners that he was 'a big man', someone for whom they should have respect.

Ramensky strongly denied that when it was put to him by the governor, maintaining that he had done it as a protest for being refused work outside the prison in the quarry, this stemming from a fight he had had there with another prisoner, a rare episode for Ramensky who was never to be known for any form of violence. And while such work might seem the most dubious of privileges, the fit prisoners, such as they were, appreciated that it did at least break the monotony of the long hours they spent incarcerated in their cells.

As punishment for his rooftop performance, it was decreed he should be detained elsewhere and Johnny was dispatched to Peterhead prison to serve the remainder of the five-year sentence he had been given, safe-blowing being included in the burglary charges he had faced. Peterhead! The very name had all the resonance and meaning of the most feared and famous of penal institutions, places like Dartmoor or Alcatraz. At other prisons in Scotland you were there to be locked up and kept away from society. You were there for that too in Peterhead, but also to be more securely locked up, its very design and structure combined with the bleak surrounding countryside making it virtually escape-proof. And you were also there for the punishment they called hard labour, which meant working all day long in all sorts of weather, breaking stone in the quarries.

Peterhead was opened as a result of a committee set up to consider 'the employment of convicts'. Their report in 1881 was to recommend that the 'most likely prospect for benefiting the shipping and fishery interests of the country at large and at the same time profitably employing convicts, is the construction of a harbour of refuge at Peterhead in Aberdeenshire'.

Five years later they began building the prison there so that its labour could be used to build that harbour. Just as they had been since the day the prison opened in 1888, prisoners, including the new boy Ramensky, were taken to and from the quarries by train. And the very dress of the warders made it demonstrably clear that this was not the kind of place from which you should even think about escaping. Every guard inside the prison wore a cutlass and scabbard and it was the strictest of rules that no prisoner should stand closer then five feet from any prison guard, otherwise the cutlass would be drawn. And the guards on duty with work parties at the quarries or elsewhere outside the prison walls were under orders to use their rifles should anyone be foolish enough to try and make an escape.

None of which was to daunt the irrepressible spirit of Ramensky, who was to find himself back in Peterhead in 1934 not all that long after having completed his first sentence there. He had been arrested in the March of that year together with his brother-in-law Marco Demarco. Police had detained them after what was described as 'a thrilling chase'. It was in the days when it was not all that uncommon for fleeing criminals to make their getaway by public transport, in this case . . . by train. The police had been looking for the two men after a safe in the premises in Mount Street, Aberdeen, was blown open with explosives and more than £200 stolen. The two men had raided the premises over a weekend, but as soon as the police made their examination of the robbery when it was discovered on the Monday morning, they were to note what, even by now, were the well-known hallmarks of Ramensky. Other forces throughout Scotland were notified of the raid and Ramensky and Demarco were spotted on the train at Perth, heading for Glasgow. Police moved in quickly and arrested the men, but Johnny shortly afterwards escaped from their custody by jumping from the train, whereafter that 'thrilling chase' took place. Surprisingly, it was the same railway staff, obviously some very fit railway staff, who succeeded in running him down and detaining him until police arrived once more.

At the High Court in Edinburgh two months later he was sentenced to five years' penal servitude, in other words, hard labour, his brother-in-law getting 18 months. And that hard labour to which Ramensky was sentenced meant Peterhead. The prospect of serving the next five years in that grimmest of prisons was to be too much for Johnny, and as soon as he was incarcerated there, his first notions were to formulate a plan of escape.

It was there he was to demonstrate that his skills at hauling himself up ronepipes with all the agility of some long-armed primate could be put to much better use than merely entertaining audiences below. Cutlasses and loaded rifles and the surrounding wilds of Buchan appeared to instil no fear whatever in Ramensky who, in the next few years while incarcerated in Peterhead, was to make a series of sensational escapes, all of which ended in his eventual recapture and further punishment. But it was in that first escape in November of 1934, just six months after being sent there, that he was to defy all the odds, not only in his method of escape, but also in the way he was to elude the dragnet searching for him.

The authorities were to confess that in his escape he performed two feats which they had considered absolutely impossible, the first being how someone was able to get over the prison wall; the second, how he was able to evade his pursuers.

Prisoners had escaped from Peterhead before, the last one being in 1932. But this prisoner had made his flight from a work party at the quarries and was shot dead by armed warders in the process. No prisoner, however, had ever got out over the enormous granite wall surrounding the main prison blocks. It was so obviously daunting, none had even tried a bid for freedom by that route. Oblivious to the freezing cold and the flurries of snow on a bitter Sunday in November, Johnny Ramensky, with two pairs of socks covering his feet, but with no shoes or boots, somehow – no one knows how – in the darkness of early evening climbed up that vast wall and leapt over 20 feet from its summit to his freedom on the other side.

It was around 6.30 p.m. when they first noticed he was missing and immediately a cordon of police surrounded the prison to prevent him getting away from the immediate vicinity, while inside the buildings they were conducting one of the most intensive of searches, still unconvinced that anyone could successfully have scaled that formidable wall.

That night a lorry driver was to tell newspaper reporters that he had never known such 'excitement', as he called it, in the fishing town of Peterhead. He went on to tell them about the warders, civilians and police who were searching everywhere. 'They were searching the outskirts, particularly among the rocks (by the sea). If ever there was a night for an escape. It was inky black and a drizzling rain was falling. We were stopped and interrogated by a uniformed policeman and a plain-clothes officer at the Bridge of Don,' he said.

A day and a half later, they finally caught up with Ramensky on the main Aberdeen–Peterhead road about eight miles north of Aberdeen, and 20 miles south of the prison. He was still without footwear and had survived a night of the most bitter north-east weather, including several snowstorms. Apparently he had got as far south as Ellon by the early hours of the following morning, breaking into the loft of a garage on the outskirts of the town, where he had slept and stayed until the following day. As darkness fell he had got on the move again. His obvious way south would have been to cross the River Ythan, on the south side of Ellon, and the police had put a heavy guard on both the old and new bridges there. The river at this point, as it heads towards its estuary, is broad and treacherously deep. It was also in spate at the time and the waiting police considered there was not the slightest chance of him crossing it and thought that he would fall into their trap.

They never knew how he crossed the river, although it's said he did it right under their noses by swinging his way across under one of the bridges. Whatever, he was next spotted south of the river by a police inspector and sergeant who gave chase in a car. But Johnny took to the fields and they lost him again. About five miles further on, he was seen again, this time on a bicycle which he had acquired, and so a police motorcyclist gave chase, whereupon Johnny tossed the bike away and took to the fields once more. He was to get about another five miles further before being spotted again, this time at Balmedie, on what is now the main A92, where three officers were to capture him as he walked along the side of the road.

There were more escapes, each as spectacular as the others, giving Ramensky, the great fugitive, something of a wonderman reputation. He was anything but a wonderman, however, to the more than somewhat embarrassed prison staff and authorities who were to decree that with the facilities they had at their disposal at the time, more severe methods should be utilised in detaining him, in a fashion which would make escape impossible. Solitary confinement was one. Leg shackles were another. And Ramensky was given both.

Word of the barbaric way in which he was being held at Peterhead was to reach the press, who spoke to the veteran Glasgow East End MP James McGovern. He tabled a question in the House of Commons asking the Secretary of State for Scotland if the reports were true, particularly the use of primitive leg irons. A reply via the Prisons Department in Edinburgh was to confirm that, in fact, they were, but that 'they are used for the purpose of preventing escape from these [solitary] cells and are only considered necessary in exceptional cases as that of John Ramensky who is a man of singular athletic capability and considered daring'.

Nevertheless, the leakage of the conditions in which the now well-known and somewhat celebrated prisoner Ramensky was being held was to cause no little embarrassment to both the Secretary of State and the Government, and in December 1934 the Scottish Secretary was to announce that the leg irons were to be removed from Ramensky and that this form of restraining prisoners in Scottish prisons was never to be used again. But it was not to be the last the Secretary of State was to hear about prisoner Ramensky.

The removal of the leg irons had been mainly due to Ramensky's own actions by petitioning the governor and others. It was to be one of the most significant lessons he was to learn as a prisoner: as there was little likelihood of beating the regimen of prison life, you therefore played along with the procedures, you ran with the rules, you digested all the decrees and you played them to your advantage, just like he had done with those leg irons.

Prison life was all about routine and system. You washed, ate, worked, relaxed, slept and behaved according to the system. And you made sure too that that same system played the rules by you. If you had a complaint, you therefore did that by the system too, by petitioning the governor. Which he did, regularly. By the mid-'30s he was as much part of the prison system as anyone, having spent much of the previous 15 years in and out of a variety of jails. And he was to demonstrate that this Gentle Johnny was never to be a Reticent Ramensky, becoming as much a thorn in the side of authority for his petitioning as he was for his escaping. He petitioned them in Peterhead to be given leave to attend his wife Daisy's funeral in 1937. This was refused on the grounds that 'he was more risk than the normal prisoner and an unusually unruly character'. That particular refusal had understandably upset him, Daisy having been his childhood sweetheart and having died suddenly from a heart attack. He had been so depressed at not getting to her funeral, he was admitted to the prison hospital – then promptly escaped.

The petitions continued: for being allocated a mere three pints of water for washing when full washing facilities were available; for being vocally abused when taking brief respites between swings of the 16-pound hammer while smashing stone in the quarries; for being refused the *Noon Record* (a horse-racing newspaper); for not being allowed to write his memoirs; for being turned down for a trusty's job; and for a transfer from an English prison, while serving a long sentence there, to one in Scotland. The list went on so long that questions were asked of the Secretary of State for Scotland about them. And when he made inquiries a governor in his official reply was to state: 'This convict writes petitions on subjects of which he has no personal knowledge. He shows a total disregard for truth and common decency in his petitions.'

Ramensky was to finish his latest sentence at Peterhead without any further escapes, but he wasn't to have his freedom for long. By the outbreak of war, he was once again serving one of the eight sentences he was to receive for the way of life he could not resist. Burglary and safe-blowing were an irresistible form of gambling to him. As one prison official was to say of him: 'Johnny Ramensky is no shilling each-way gambler. He goes for the big one every time.' Which he did . . . and would invariably end up in jail for it once again.

Johnny was in his late thirties and the Second World War was into its third year before he was to get his latest release from Peterhead. He had been desperately anxious for this release, much more so than usual, as he wanted to demonstrate that whatever they might think about Johnny Ramensky the convict, one aspect of his life could never be questioned: his love for and loyalty to his country. There was little point, he considered, in merely volunteering to be an ordinary soldier in an ordinary regiment in the army and although he enlisted as an infantryman in the Royal Fusiliers, he immediately searched for a unit which could use his specialist services. After his initial training was complete, he was to volunteer for the Commandos, the élite corps composed of the fittest and toughest men in the army at that time.

Johnny Ramensky couldn't have found himself in a more compatible form of soldiering. Here he was in a unit that was teaching them how to use explosives! How to break into premises! How to climb up various structures! How to get into strongrooms! How to jemmy open lockfast cabinets and safes! How to blow them apart if necessary, without destroying what they contained! How to operate without being seen or heard, and without being detected! To most of the volunteers this was the brave new world. For Johnny Ramensky it was more like nursery school. And because it was, and because, it is said, senior officers, including Brigadier-General Laycock, C.-in-C. of combined operations, were made aware of the new man on the staff, Ramensky was earmarked for special assignments.

Soon it was Johnny who was doing the teaching, and in and around the old hospital grounds at Noranside, near Forfar – ironically now the site of a new prison – Johnny Ramensky was teaching his Commando comrades the finer arts of explosives, the small details at first, like how many ounces were required for a particular job and of the use of a specific type if you wanted to blow something upwards, another if you wanted it blown downwards, and yet another if you wanted it blown inwards. And if you made mistakes at this game, you were the one that got blown – in any one, maybe even all, of these directions.

Soon, too, there was to be more hands-on work with his Commando unit, hands on the enemy, that is. With some others he was sent on a specialist parachute training course, then posted to North Africa for work behind enemy lines. They dropped him to link up with Italian partisans fighting in the mountains. They were to help get him to various German command quarters where Ramensky was to break open a variety of safes and strongrooms holding vital war plans. Once in Rome he blew open four strongrooms and ten German safes within a few hours. What a life! Blowing safes and not getting jailed for it. It seemed like he was on one long busman's holiday, and absolutely enjoying every minute of it.

His work as one of the army's most proficient safe-blowers and became so famous, it's said the Americans were to request his secondment to their special unit doing the same work. The story goes that their men had been baffled by the workings of safes in one of the Japanese consulates in Italy and needed someone with that extra touch. Johnny Ramensky had it and was to gain entry to the strong boxes that had defied all others.

Discharged from the army with certificates of merit and gratitude, his army paybook – the military's equivalent of a passport – marked 'exemplary military conduct', Johnny Ramensky settled back into civilian life once more in Glasgow. He had planned to go into business as a bookmaker, but it was not to work. It just wasn't his trade. Safe-blowing was, however, and the next one he was to tackle wasn't to be of German or Japanese design. This safe was to be much simpler than any of those foreign consulate ones.

It was also one without the prospect of being shot on the spot should he be caught in the act. Nevertheless, it wasn't without its problems, for the safe Johnny was to blow in Cardonald Post Office, Glasgow, was done with all the hallmarks of his profession. Too many hallmarks, that is. And that was Johnny Ramensky's big problem in his career as burglar and safe-blower, for he was never able to overcome the fact that only one man tackled and blew safes the way he did. Every job he did was like leaving his signature behind. And when the detectives inspected what was left of the door of the Cardonald safe, they just shook their heads and wryly smiled at their conclusion. Johnny was back in town. They might even have joked that perhaps he had been in the Cardonald PO's safe looking for his post-war credits.

There was to be little post-war sympathy, however, for the man who was totally addicted to this way of life and, sadly, that was Ramensky back in prison once more; which had been, and was to continue to be, the pattern of this unusual man's life. Another location; another safe; another robbery. And because he was such a one-off, the trademark would be there again and he would be back in custody once more.

The litany of his life had become a monotony. Another High Court appearance, another sentence, another jailbreak, another recapture, another addition to his sentence. As the late criminal counsel Nicholas Fairbairn was to so aptly put it, Ramensky had this compulsion to break into whatever he was outside, and out of whatever he was inside.

Outside and inside, his colourful but largely wasted life was to bring him into contact with an immense variety of other equally compelling characters. On one of my visits to Barlinnie Prison – as a writer, that is – I met one of its most distinguished governors, the late Duncan Mackenzie. A former merchant seaman who had risen through the ranks from prison officer to Governor of Peterhead and then Barlinnie,

Duncan Mackenzie was the son of a crofter. He was an enormous alp of a man, his stature alone being in the form that must have been more than useful at various times in his career for winning instant respect, although it was those soft speech tones of his which were more indicative of the benevolent person he really was, being the gentlest of men and full of compassion for the wayward charges put in his care. He knew Johnny Ramensky better than any other prison official, rating him as one of the most remarkable criminal characters he had ever known.

Duncan Mackenzie was in charge at Peterhead for many of the years Johnny Ramensky served sentences there. In one of these periods Johnny had escaped from his tough and isolated jail three times in the one year, bringing him one of the harshest of sentences, that of ten years' preventive detention. It was a sentence passed in order to prevent him from committing more crimes and carried no automatic reduction of sentence for good behaviour while in prison.

He hated that sentence more than any other, angrily telling Governor Mackenzie that he felt he was being punished twice. Mackenzie understood his fury, although, being a civil servant engaged in the administration of the law and its penalties, he could do little more than express his sympathy for Ramensky's feelings.

'If I don't get justice, then I'll take it,' warned Ramensky angrily, changing to an almost apologetic tone in an expression of the respect he held for Mr Mackenzie. 'I wouldn't like to harm you in any way, or hurt your career as governor. But I'll escape whenever I want to.'

The words were more of the brave than the bravado and Mackenzie knew it, knowing him as he did as one of the fittest prisoners he had ever come across in his long career in the custodial service. He knew that getting out of prison when he felt like it was as much an art form of Johnny Ramensky's as blowing safes. And not many weeks after that threat he had given the governor about being off again, he was. In fact, in one year alone during Mackenzie's reign at Peterhead, the governor was to suffer the embarrassment of having his star inmate flee from his confines on three occasions. It was the third of these escapes which Mackenzie himself in an interview was to describe as the most sensational escape he had ever known from a Scottish prison. It was to rank, he said, with some of the most dramatic of wartime escapes from German prisons, and every festive and bank holiday TV viewer knows how incredibly sensational they can be. And this particular escape of Johnny's was most certainly one of these.

The governor had often watched Ramensky, as keen a footballer as he was a gymnast and keep-fit enthusiast, taking part in matches in the prison exercise yard. Always, when the ball ended up on the prison roof, there was only one man the other prisoners would look to in order to retrieve it. And once again he would be watching Ramensky flashing up a ronepipe like he was on home territory. Little wonder, he thought, that soon he might be off once more.

That thought, however, had been the furthest from his mind one bitterly cold winter's day when he had watched Ramensky exercising in the yard, thinking that this would certainly be no weather to be contemplating another jailbreak. But Johnny Ramensky had other thoughts. He had been busy planning what was to be his Oscar performance as an escapee. Despite regular searches and being watched more vigilantly than the others, he had somehow managed to become equipped with a chisel and a screwdriver. And, incredibly, he had found the appropriate cloth in order to measure, cut out and sew together a smart suit while working in the prison's tailor shop.

Because of a fault in his cell-door spy-hole – and who might have created that? – the flap over the small aperture didn't close properly, enabling Ramensky to peer through the tiny hole on the lookout for patrolling warders. Despite the brutal weather outside, Ramensky had gone to work with his chisel and screwdriver on his cell door after being locked in for the night. He had managed to chip and scrape his way through the wood all right but to his dismay was then to discover it was merely a covering over an impenetrable steel plate. His night's work had been in vain, leaving him faced with the problem of somehow covering up the mess and the considerable damage he had done to the interior of his cell door. But when it came to enterprise and resourcefulness, this man was as much Houdini as he was Ramensky, his amazingly agile escapee mentality quickly opting for a solution to this new problem. The answer was to be a mixture of chewed bread and compressed porridge, which made an instant DIY filler after which he rubbed it down then smeared it over with boot polish. No one was to ever suspect that door had been hacked through to its metal core.

The door escape plan having failed, he was to tackle an even more blatant form of escape. One morning later that week, when the doors were opened with the customary brusqueness, Ramensky was to leave his cell as usual at 6.15 a.m. for the routine of slopping out. He was looking somewhat bulkier than usual, having donned his new tailor-made suit, which he had somehow secreted in his cell, on top of which he had on his normal prison garb.

In the mêlée of prisoners rushing around the gallery landings to the lavatories, it wasn't noticed that Ramensky was in his stocking soles, his shoes tied round his neck. The prisoners usually moved briskly at that time of day, many of them often running as the quicker they performed their ablutions and cleansing-out ritual, the quicker they got to the dining hall and the pick of whatever there was for breakfast. Like the others he, too, was moving swiftly, but with a vastly different intent.

With all the surrounding hustle and bustle, it had been easy to dash unnoticed as he had done towards the end of the gallery, where he was to suddenly make a spectacular leap into the air. A prisoner who was there on that memorable occasion in Peterhead told me it was the most amazing sight he had ever seen inside: 'It was as though you were watching a man that had turned into a cat.'

There had been a gas pipe running up the wall, the old two-inch iron variety, and although it was nearly flush with the plaster surface, it was to provide sufficient grip for Ramensky to scale right up it. The pipe led him up to a window ledge which he used as another spring-off point, leaping this time several feet upwards in order to grab a roof beam with one hand. From one beam he swung to others leading to a skylight window where, hanging once more by just one hand, he used the other to smash the window with a shoe, then clamber through it onto the roof.

Peterhead was like a second home to Ramensky. He knew every inch of every roof, of every yard, of every wall. Going down was easier than going up. It was also faster and it took just seconds to slide down the slates of the sloping roof to a rone he knew was positioned at that point, and then an even more speedier and vertical descent, this time about 60 feet down to a quiet courtyard which bordered on the main outside prison wall.

There was a workmen's hut there; he knew all about that too, and about the vital piece of equipment it held at that moment – a ladder. There were also two dustbins there and with one on top of the other and the ladder on top of them, there was now in position a visual form of escape by reaching the summit of the main wall. A ladder atop two hastily positioned dustbins! In appearance, any chance of a man reaching the top of that precarious ascent seemed more theoretical than practical. It was the kind of thing that only a madman would attempt. Or someone like Johnny Ramensky.

The first sign that there had been an attempted escape was when nightshift staff going off duty in the morning heard the sound of breaking glass – the noise he had made when smashing open the skylight window. Despite his frontal flight from that busy gallery, he had, remarkably, still not been observed and this had been the first intimation that someone was doing something they shouldn't. Within minutes of hearing the glass breaking, the nightshift men promptly returned to the guards' offices and the alarm was raised. But it was too late. Johnny Ramensky was out and free once more.

Any time Ramensky had absconded in the past, subsequent inquiries had delved into not only the method of his breakout, his planning, his route, but also the precise timing of his escape. These had been timed to the very split second in the hope that the knowledge gained would prevent future flights. Once again they were to put the stopwatch on this, the most daring and spectacular of the Peterhead Papillon's getaways. The results of their timing inquiries were to be as remarkable as the physical feat he had performed in getting out of the prison. From the moment they had opened his cell door that morning till he was free and on the public highway it had taken him less than four minutes. And he had done it all without one prison officer having sighted him at any point along his entire escape route. Like they said, Johnny was Hollywood and this was an Oscar performance.

Once again Johnny Ramensky was headline news throughout the country, the manner and audacity of his escape capturing no little admiration from a public who had for years become fascinated by the man who had become not only a legend in his own lifetime but something of a hero as well. Despite a police dragnet for miles around Peterhead, roadblocks and guards on every bridge crossing in the surrounding area, they weren't to catch Ramensky for a week, during which he had survived one of the worst spells of weather that winter, days of incessant rain, sleet, snow and the most bitter of easterly winds. It had been so bad, in fact, that Governor Mackenzie was convinced that the next they would hear about Johnny Ramensky would be the finding of a frozen body somewhere. But the toughest man in his charge was alive and well when they captured him near Aberdeen that week and Duncan Mackenzie was so relieved to hear the news he went to the city's police station to collect him personally. And when he got there he had to struggle his way through a huge crowd of admirers who had gathered outside and were chanting 'Good old Johnny'.

The utter futility of Ramensky's escapes, of course, was the fact that that face of his, those distinctively high and prominent cheekbones of the Balt, the fair hair, the hollow cheeks, made him one of the best-known profiles in the country. Okay, with those Mayfair contacts, Lord Lucan might have made it to South Africa or South America, but Johnny Ramensky couldn't have made it further than the Southside – the Southside of Glasgow, that is. His pals were not of the order that could fund him a trip to the veldt, the pampas or the prairies and he would be forever condemned to be the recaptured man, as he was yet again on this occasion.

He refused to tell Duncan Mackenzie where he had hidden or how he had eluded the police forces of the nation for a week, only smiling to say that he was keeping it for the memoirs on which he had been working in various prisons for years.

Within days of his return to Peterhead, Governor Mackenzie was summoned to the Scottish Office at St Andrew's House in Edinburgh for important talks about the man who was making a laughing stock of the country's prison service. Mackenzie was issued with the clear-cut directive that Ramensky must never escape again. Which was easy in a way, really. All they would have to do to ensure that would be to put him under visual watch 24 hours a day! And that's precisely what they had to do in order to be secure in the knowledge that he could never escape again. Six prison officers were personally selected by Governor Mackenzie to supervise Ramensky for 24 hours a day, 365 days a year, to which Johnny was to react with his customary defiance, warning them that he would still have a go at getting away. But when he realised just how effective his constant guard was to be, even he knew that was now out of the question and he made no further escape attempts.

After a year and a half of the perma-vigil and concerned for the mental and physical welfare of the special prisoner he considered he knew and understood better than anyone, Governor Mackenzie wrote to the prison authorities with the plea that Ramensky be transferred to an open prison. The application was met with incredulity and Mackenzie was asked if his decision-making processes were in order.

He maintained they were and that as they had obviously got the better of the man, there was little point in persisting with the treatment to which Ramensky was being subjected. Given the chance in an open prison Mackenzie was confident Ramensky would not try to escape again. Governor Mackenzie's insistence with the authorities was to pay off and the request was granted. Ramensky responded by being the model prisoner and enthusiastically joining a Training for Freedom course in preparation for the day when he would eventually be released.

If Duncan Mackenzie was the man who knew Johnny Ramensky on the legitimate side of the fence, as it were, better than anyone, one of the men who was to know and understand him equally well was on the other side of that fence. Johnny Ramensky was already something of a star criminal when Sonny Leitch first got to know him.

Sonny's real name is William, but it was a popular name among relatives in his big and widely respected family in Craigneuk, Lanarkshire, so they called him Sonny as a boy and it stuck. There were other names, of course, one of them being 'Danger Man', which in a way summarises a fairly extensive, but past, way of life in which he got up to a wide variety of nefarious tricks, some being of a similar genre to those of Johnny Ramensky, like safe-blowing and jailbreaking.

Sonny was just a young lad when he made his very first contact with the man he was to meet in later life in such selective places as Barlinnie, Saughton, Craiginches and Peterhead. It happened when Ramensky was visiting friends in his home town. While there, he had performed a little 'homer', as it were, breaking into the surface works of the local Shields coalmine from where he stole a battery unit, the type miners carried with them at the time to power the lamps of their helmets. Johnny's underground plans, of course, had a whole different conception to those of the men who worked at the coalface, the battery unit he had taken being the ideal equipment to work in conjunction with the new electric detonators then being introduced in the various industries which relied on explosives. And in Ramensky's case, that included his own private industry as a safe-blower.

When the break-in had been discovered, National Coal Board officials carried out a quick investigation into the missing battery, tracing it to having been one assigned to the care of Sonny Leitch's miner father, William. He, of course, had been totally innocent of any implication in the stolen piece of equipment, but nevertheless he was called to appear as a witness in a subsequent trial against Ramensky at Hamilton Sheriff Court following his arrest for the theft.

'We were in awe – at least I was – of this man at the time for he was already a legend where I lived for his various exploits.' It was to be many years later before Sonny Leitch and Johnny Ramensky came into contact again.

This time it was in Glasgow. Barlinnie Prison in Glasgow. The war had come and gone, 'Gentle Johnny' now having the enhanced reputation of courageous Commando added to that of colourful convict and Leitch, too, having notched up some status marks in the demi-monde side of his life, having not only served with the Royal Navy in Korea but also having experienced what are termed in the forces as military corrective establishments. Which is forces-speak for jail. One of the sentences he was to serve was at what is probably the most infamous of these establishments, the Shepton Mallet Royal Military Prison, in Somerset. He was there with two other men, old pals of his from Scotland. And these same two, as it happened, were in his company once more when Leitch and Ramensky met again.

Leitch and his mates, together with Ramensky and a group of others, were, it certainly can be said, 'a most rarefied collection'. If you were an officer in the CID or someone who belonged to the underworld, then you might view this collection as something of an all-star cast of Scottish criminality. For many others, however, there would be a completely different view of them, maybe something along the lines of them being players with the principal roles in your worst-ever nightmare.

The conversation between them had been the usual this and that of small-talk about prison life; what they had been up to, who they knew, whom they had met, where they had been, where they were going and that sort of thing. The three who had come up from the military prison mentioned an exploit which had occurred there and which, in the way of things, was good chat.

Sonny tells the story about the episode. 'We had been ordered to clear up this hall at Shepton Mallet which was adjacent to the shed where men sentenced to death were hanged. And, by the way, do you know they did it the Australian fashion down there? That is, instead of being dropped, they had this device which shot the men up the way where they dangled to death. Anyway, while we were clearing up this hall, we came across all these big eight by four feet boards, at least that's what they appeared to be, each one carefully wrapped up. Being the inquisitive bunch we were, we started tearing off the paper from them to discover they were paintings – paintings of all the German leaders. The first one had been Eva Braun, then there was Goering, and Hess and Himmler and Hitler as well. Now, when he heard the story, Johnny, to our surprise, conducted what was almost like a court hearing on each one of us individually, questioning us all about what we had seen and getting each one to describe it. Not knowing us, he wanted to get at the truth of this story which is why he asked us separately. Later on, we found out why. It turned out, you see, that Johnny had seen that very same collection of paintings but not at Shepton Mallet. He had seen them all while he had been on one of his raids in Germany during the war. He had been ordered to break into some big house and it had been one which Eva Braun had stayed in. And all these very same paintings were hung on the walls there. Then, when our troops eventually invaded Germany, the paintings must have been collected by our people, then brought back and there we had been in that store hall of the military prison ripping the paper off them and not being all that gentle with them either. Anyway, Johnny was convinced we had been telling the truth and from that time on we became firm friends.'

Johnny Ramensky and Sonny Leitch were to come across each other many times after that in, as it were, all the old familiar places . . . with the familiar names we all know as our foremost penal institutions. In fact, it had been while they were together at Craiginches, which is at Aberdeen, that Johnny was to perfect yet another escape plan, only on this occasion he was not the one to perform it. It was for Sonny Leitch. It was during the time of the postal strike in the early '70s and Sonny had been anxious about news of his father, an ex-miner who was seriously ill at the time. He had requested permission to make a phone call which had been refused and warned the prison authorities that if he couldn't hear from his family, he would escape.

'They just laughed back at me for Craiginches wasn't the easiest of places to get out of,' says Sonny. 'So I told Johnny what I planned and because I had already escaped from prisons he joked, "What, are you out to beat my record?" When I told him why I had to get out, he immediately recognised my need and sat down with me to draw a plan. The main wall there, you see, is about 40 feet on the outside, and because of a banking, about 28 feet on the inside. The plan he came up with was to make a sort of springboard out of two planks of wood. He reckoned that if they were positioned at the proper angle up against the inside wall and if I could run up the first part then jump in the middle, the planks would flip me up towards the top of the wall. Do you know what – it worked like a dream and I was away for six weeks and was able to see my dad, all thanks to the man who had become my close friend, Johnny Ramensky.'

Obviously tired of Ramensky's total disregard for the law, questions were raised in 1959 by the Scottish Secretary about his war record, it being regularly trotted out as a plea of leniency every time he appeared for sentence. Files on the subject were classified as secret and not to be released for 40 years. They are stored in Register House, Edinburgh, and after their release I examined them. They were to reveal that as a result of the Scottish Secretary's questions, a Scottish Office report was to deny one aspect of the claims that had been made more than once in court about Ramensky having been specifically released from prison in order to serve in the army. And it somewhat sniffily added that they were 'sceptical about the press reports of his exploits'.

Details, too, had been revealed in the *Daily Express* of his army discharge papers which made little mention of his behind-the-lines exploits. In fact, they had simply stated that his military conduct had been 'exemplary', then, going on in more detail to record: 'An honest and reliable man who has been employed as an officers' batman [that is an officer's personal servant]. He carried out these duties well and showed that he possessed initiative and has a sense of responsibility. A cheerful and likeable character.'

Various interpretations could be made of the wording of that kind of discharge reference. A civil servant with a non-military background could easily read them to mean that Ramensky had merely worked as some officer's servant and therefore hadn't seen the action claimed for him, particularly as there had been no mention of his bravery and daring, so often mentioned by defence lawyers on his behalf. This would undoubtedly have been the basis for the Scottish Office's scepticism.

So just why, then, was there no mention of the widely reported raids he had been on or of gallantry medals he may have been awarded? One book which contained a version of his life story was to detail the fact that he had been awarded the Military Medal, an award given to other ranks and non-commissioned officers. The medal is normally awarded for an outstanding act of bravery.

At my request, the Ministry of Defence searched their files for any record of this award to Ramensky, but none is listed. However, with the slightest knowledge of military workings, a much different interpretation could be placed on the comments in his discharge papers. Ramensky was not demobilised from the Commandos until more than a year after the war ended, therefore the discharge comments in these papers would more than likely have been about the work he had been doing in the period immediately prior to his discharge. Only the best and most trustworthy of soldiers were given jobs as batmen, it usually being a perk for being a soldier of merit and for previous good service. And when the officer they serve goes into action, the batman is right there beside him, aiding and protecting him in gaining the objective of the mission.

Ramensky had been detached from his parent regiment, the Royal Fusiliers, to join a unit of the Commandos. Each and every member of such units did the most intensive of training and they experienced the heaviest of casualties on their many raids behind the lines. The fact that Ramensky wasn't awarded the MM merely puts him in line with the vast majority of all the comrades who wore the green beret.

My research through former secret papers on Ramensky was to confirm the views I have just listed on his career with the Commandos. I was to discover from these papers that because of the tone of the Scottish Office's comments to the Scottish Secretary in the '50s, the War Department had been asked for their observations on the doubts raised about Ramensky's war record. Their views were to be contained in a letter from the then Secretary of State for War, signed by R.M. Hastie-Smith. The reply was brief and to the point. It read: '6482307 Fusilier John Ramsay served in the army from January 1943 to September 1946. He was enlisted in the Royal Fusiliers and was employed with the Commandos on special duties including parachutist duties until July 1945. I am afraid I can't give you any details about his career in the Commandos but clearly there is a considerable element of truth in the story of his military career.' The question of his army record was never raised again, nor was there to be any further comment from the St Andrew's House scoffers.

Following Governor Mackenzie's request to the authorities that

Ramensky be given a fresh start in life, he had been sent to Penninghame Open Prison, near Newton Stewart, on Mackenzie's recommendation and was also to be the first prisoner enlisted for the new Training for Freedom scheme. He served under this scheme at Saughton, getting day release and sometimes weekend release, as well as being helped with coping with the many aspects of ordinary life which can be a major problem to the institutionalised, the effect of that being no little handicap to the long-term prisoner. Johnny had vowed to try his best and was to write to Mackenzie in appreciation of all his help, a letter which was to reveal much of the basic honesty and integrity of the man.

> I realise better than anyone the impossible task you have. It must be most disheartening when your efforts are rewarded with ingratitude and deceit. I know what you would like me to promise, but I don't think prison is the place to make a solemn vow. The real test is on the outside where temptation and opportunity abound. It would be easy to deceive you and myself with a glib promise but it wouldn't be fair to you. You have been let down so often by ungrateful prisoners that I wouldn't like to be just another name added to the list.

He obviously wanted to be the straight man and be finished with the life which till now knew little about freedom. But the real test, as he said, was on the outside. That outside where temptation and opportunity abounded, and by opportunity Johnny Ramensky wasn't referring to that word in its basic and innocent sense. It was, as he said, temptation and opportunity – like they were in the one. And, alas, it was not to be long after he had completed his training for freedom and had qualified once more for a life beyond bars that both temptation and opportunity were to cross his path once more. His life recital, that litany of crime, capture, conviction, was to continue its predictable ways.

There had never been anyone with a record to match his awesome list. There were convictions that dated back as far as 1916, when he was a young lad of just 11 years of age. He had served sentences in the '20s, '30s, '40s, '50s, '60s and it was now approaching the '70s and still it went on. He had been in borstal and in prisons in England and all over

Scotland. He had served time in solitary; he had been incarcerated back in the days when men like him wore leg irons and were guarded by warders armed inside the buildings with cutlasses and outside with loaded rifles; he had received four sentences of five years, one of ten years. In a period of 56 years he had received sentences totalling 56 years, spending something like 42 of them locked away from society. And still! When temptation and opportunity abounded!

* In March 1967, by now 62 years of age, it was four years for breaking into a bank and blowing a safe. A further charge of police assault was found not proven, his title 'Gentle Johnny' remaining intact, but the judge, Lord Thomson, did comment on his 'extraordinary record of criminal activities'.

* In March 1970 police found him semi-conscious and seriously injured in the Bank of Scotland's car park in King Street, Stirling, having been called out when the manager of the nearby Crown Inn reported noises in the early hours of the morning. Johnny, who was living in Queen Elizabeth Square, Gorbals, at the time, was detained in Stirling Royal Infirmary with a fractured skull, thigh and wrist, police saying 'charges would be preferred at a later date'.

* Three months later he was wheeled in an invalid chair into a specially convened court on four housebreaking and explosives charges. A month later, still in a wheelchair, he was jailed for two years. He pleaded guilty to breaking into an office and a pub. He had fled empty-handed from both raids, and in escaping from the pub had fallen 50 feet from an icy roof.

* In December 1971, free once more, he was back in the dock yet again, this time at Edinburgh Sheriff Court. The charge – illegally possessing explosives and 'other tools of his trade'. And everyone knew what that trade was!

He was by now 66 years of age, white-haired and arthritic, with failing eyesight due to cataracts, and separated from his second wife. It was a rather sad image of the younger and fitter man so many remembered, the one with the gaunt face of the marathon runner, the barrel chest of a weightlifter, the shoulders and arms of the gymnast and whom Governor Mackenzie said had been the fittest prisoner he had ever known. The sheriff on this occasion was to tell him he had looked not only at his 'considerable record', but at his medical report, and that, 'It is deplorable that a man of your age should run the risk of returning to prison.' Then, with some considerable compassion, he allowed him to go free on a deferred sentence for six months to prove that he was willing to give up crime.

In May 1972, just five months later and into his sixty-seventh year, he was in court once more, this time in Ayr where he was to admit a charge under the Prevention of Crimes Act. The court was told that Ramensky had been found hiding on a roof in the town by two policemen. It was also mentioned that he was on deferred sentence from Edinburgh Sheriff Court.

As he had invariably done in the past, Ramensky pleaded guilty to this latest charge, his ethics being that if you had committed an offence and were caught, then you pleaded guilty to it and didn't conjure up any spurious defence pleas. Joe Beltrami, the prominent Glasgow lawyer of that period, was once again called on by Ramensky in an effort to persuade the judge to exercise some form of leniency. Having appeared for him so many times in the past, it was by now difficult to come up with anything new in the Ramensky saga which could be put forward by way of mitigation, apart from the fact of his advancing years, stressing, in view of his obvious medical condition, that should he be given the maximum sentence there was every probability that he might not leave prison alive.

Beltrami decided to flavour his plea with a little piece of humour, hoping it might mellow the proceedings in some way. He mentioned to the sheriff that his client had been on more roofs than the now famous Fiddler. It might have brought some smiles in the courtroom, but there were no noticeable ones from the direction of the bench. He was jailed for a year, a deferred six-months sentence being added at Edinburgh Sheriff Court two months later.

This was to see Johnny meeting up once more with Sonny Leitch, doing one of his longer stretches at the time – 12 years for armed robbery! Their sentences were to be served at Perth prison, the oldest general prison in Scotland, building work on it having started back in 1840. 'He was really getting on in years now,' recalls Sonny, 'but was still as fit as ever, doing the keep-fit routines he had been doing for years and always taking advantage of periods in the exercise yard to keep walking. He always liked to keep on the move. Yet, there were still aspects of his character which had never changed. Do you know, he was the kind of man who would take no favours from anyone. He had been speaking about his need for a new pair of trainers and I knew if I got him a pair he wouldn't take them, that would have been considered by him as some kind of favour. So I said to him that I had a new pair which needed breaking in and on that condition he wore them – for me, as it were.'

So once more it was back to the old routine for Johnny Ramensky, doing time for his 32nd conviction. It had been many years earlier, while in Peterhead, that Johnny Ramensky had, in his own eloquent way, revealed just how enmeshed he was in the unchanging pattern of his peculiar and extraordinary life. This was in a somewhat poignant letter addressed to Lily, the woman who was to become his second wife, living at the time in Eglinton Street, Gorbals. It was his first letter after his recapture following yet another escape from that prison. The punishment for that would mean more time added to his sentence and he felt he had to explain just why this latest episode had befallen him.

It had all started, he wrote, after a row in prison with a guard he described as a 'cantankerous old copper'. The warder had complained of being assaulted and the thought of Johnny, as a result, losing his job at the time as a 'trusty' had genuinely upset him. Matters such as getting a good job while in prison can be paramount to an inmate's spiritual welfare, affording him some variation in that curse of prison life – routine.

His letter went on:

> Instead of 'keeping the heid', I broke out without any plan or idea of what I wanted, except the urge to run away from it all. But it's not easy to run away from trouble as I should have known. Only more trouble follows up and that is how it is now. I will be punished in a few days' time and maybe I will be unable to write to you for some time. Don't worry about me for whatever punishment comes my way I will be able to take it. After all, they must feed me something! And regarding other matters, I will manage along. I am sorry, love. I am such a source of worry to you but honestly dear, I can't help it. The

impulse was too strong to resist so I fell for it. Don't worry, love.

That letter says a lot about the life of Johnny Ramensky, the incredible survivor who could take whatever punishment they gave him, with impulses that were too strong to resist. This time in Perth there were no trusty jobs, just the grinding old routine. It was a Friday in early November 1972, five months into his sentence, and Johnny was sitting with Sonny Leitch and some other prisoners enduring some of that routine, working on mailbags. They were the old-style bags made of hessian and the job was to fix metal tabs round the bag opening to allow them to be hung on the pegs of the stands used by the Post Office sorters. Friday was perhaps one of their better days. It was the day before the weekend, and therefore a day when they had something to look forward to. For weekends were special. Other than the normal work routine, there were other things to do, and while they may just have been very ordinary things, like seeing a film, watching a football match, even going to a church service, they were the most precious of moments for the prisoners – a break in the agonising monotony of weekday life; a break in the tortuous routine that seemed to go on and on, so that you became a part of it. So much a part of it that it took away your ability to think, for you didn't have to think; the routine did that for you. You didn't have to contemplate or speculate on what you might do next, for the routine did all that for you. The morning slop-out. The head count. The shuffle to the dining hall. The same breakfast. The same workshop. The same mailbags. The same tabs. The same everything at the same time every day. Except at weekends.

As well as working on the mailbags, the group with Johnny and Sonny that Friday in November had been playing the game known as Scrabble on the outside, but called 'Wordy' by those inside. Ramensky had been complaining of very bad headaches and kept rubbing his forehead just over one of his eyes. Sonny tells the story: 'He said they had started after being hit by a baton when getting arrested one time. Anyway, the last I saw him there was this big red patch moving across the side of his face he kept rubbing. On the Saturday evening before we were locked up for the night, Johnny had left his cell wearing the new trainers I had given him – but absolutely nothing else. Now, that was not Johnny Ramensky's style. No way. The warders saw him and asked what was wrong and he told them he wanted outside to go to the pictures. They knew right away something was drastically wrong with him and after being taken to the sick bay from there they took him to hospital.'

When the prisoners at Perth got the shock news that Sunday morning of Johnny Ramensky's death in Perth Royal Infirmary the night before, Sonny Leitch fondly retrieved a piece of paper from his meagre cell possessions and once again read the words written on it. They were some lines written by Ramensky which he had given him some time before. They read:

> Way up in Scotland's north-east coast,
> Just outside Peterhead,
> There stands a grey prison
> That holds the living dead.
> Bereft of all humanity,
> Devoid of all but pain,
> I hope I never see its inside
> At any time again.

And there the story of Johnny Ramensky might suitably end, but for a curious observation, together with the revelation of the last puzzling item in the life of this most unusual man. I referred to Ramensky as the Papillon of Peterhead. It is no mere flippancy to use the comparison. For, indeed, there were some parallels in the lives of Johnny Ramensky and the man from the Ardèche in the south of France called Henri Charrière, whose sensational escape from Ile du Diable (Devil's Island), the dreaded French penal colony off the coast of French Guiana in South America, was to become the subject of the outstanding best-selling book and hit movie with the title that was his nickname – *Papillon*.

Ramensky and Papillon were born within months of each other in the first years of the twentieth century. They both were to die some 67 years later, again within months of each other. Each made the same number of escape attempts from prison. Each wrote jotters full of notes on their harsh and deprived lives while in prison. Their stories part at that point, Papillon eventually escaping to freedom and seeing the success of the book about his amazing life. For much of his time in prison, Ramensky was not to enjoy the freedom Papillon was given to record his story.

When he first sought permission to record the details of his life, the Scottish prison authorities even refused him the writing materials he required. In rejecting his request for pencil and paper, officials cited the regulation that 'books or paper may only be issued to prisoners to take full advantage of approved courses of study'. Recording the details of his various escapades was most certainly not in that category.

The first recorded refusal to keep notes was in 1939, around the same time that Papillon was planning the last of his escapes. Ramensky persisted with his requests and had to wait for 12 years before one prison governor relented and said he could keep notes. Three years later, however, when word of this reached a Sunday newspaper, the authorities clamped down once more, declaring that the particular governor had acted without proper approval and that 'it would not be in the public interest' to have Ramensky's life story made known. Despite that, however, some of his wartime army exploits were published in a Sunday newspaper. He was later permitted to make more notes, but on condition they should not be removed from prison. The prison authorities noted at one time he had filled as many as 32 jotters with notes. So what happened to these memoirs which may have become Scotland's very own *Papillon* book? Sonny Leitch is the only person who knows the full details about that.

'He spoke about them, his notes that is, quite a lot. He would say things like, "I wonder if I can publish this or that." He was fearful that some of the true details could have got people put in jail and he was very apprehensive about that as well as telling some of the secrets he knew. It probably would have been all right, of course, but it worried him. He was a man of ethics, you know. He didn't want to be accused of betraying anyone. He wanted everything to be right. So he decided to get rid of them all. And we did this together by making a lamp base in our handicraft workshop. It was a thick wooden base, but what no one knew was that we had the core of it hollowed out. And when I left prison I was allowed to take my piece of handicraft with me, stuffed with all Johnny's notes. And at his specific request I had them all destroyed.'

Which is why the full story of the Scottish Papillon, in his own words, never was, and never will be, told.

GUYS AND DOLLS AND SAMMY DOCHERTY

So we switched to the Jeffords' entry and got differed out
of over half a unit, or $550, when Pot o' Luck won. Good
Time Charley sat as if stunned for a while and then
delivered himself of a truism that I must pass on to
posterity. 'I have often wondered why people go broke at
the race track,' Charley said. 'Now I know. It is because
they are always trying to pick something to beat the best
horses.'

> – from *Where to Find the Common
> Man*, by Damon Runyon

Perhaps the fact that some of this particular Great Glasgow Story
was written while staying in New York has more than a little to
do with these introductory lines by the legendary observer of
that city's scene and lore. But then they may have appeared here
anyway, being, as they are, an appropriate way of looking at an aspect
of a way of life that has disappeared from our very own Glasgow
scenario. A way of life from which was to emerge one of the greatest,
one of the most amusing, most captivating, and certainly most talked-
about stories of the day. A story that is best appreciated by first recalling
the way of life and the times and events of the early '60s.

The Swinging Sixties they called them, the reason for that mainly
being that a slick sub-editor on an American news magazine labelled
them as such. And the label stuck. Sure enough, a lot was swinging in
those days of the '60s. A lot wasn't. The Second World War had been
over for nearly 20 years, but there were still post-war doldrums, hang-
ups and hangovers, like shortages of various kinds. It seemed that, apart
from foodstuffs, with almost anything else you wanted to buy, the
answer from shop or store would be, 'It'll take six weeks. Ye see, it's to
come from England.'

The '60s may seem like yesterday to many, yet in so many ways they are an age away. An age when television was a much smaller box in a much smaller room, where the black and white picture on the two available channels (BBC and STV) invariably came via set-top aerials made of strangely shaped pieces of anodised wire, the telescopic one called 'rabbit ears' being the most popular. And if you moved around the room at certain angles to the box, the picture fuzzed. But then it often did that without anyone moving, which meant more fiddling with those rabbit ears.

It was an age when women wore hats and professional men bowlers and you went to the football in collars and ties and cloth caps, the only casual clothes being flannels, blazer and open-neck shirt collar primly folded over the jacket collar, and you wouldn't dare go to the game dressed like that! Churchill was still alive, Greece had a king, dictator Franco's cops strutted the streets in Fascist Spain, there were 240 pennies in the pound, there were no calculators or computers, no curries, no pizzas, no karaoke and no McDonald's; you said 'hello' never 'hi', you said 'fellow' never 'guy', and you said 'queer' never 'gay'. And that word 'gay' was used only for its original meaning – happy and carefree.

It was an age, too, when a variety of restrictive laws curbed lives and lifestyles. If you wanted a drink, you had to think about doing so in the early part of the evening for the last drinks in pubs were at ten o'clock. You couldn't go out and have a pleasant glass of wine with the family because young people weren't permitted in places selling alcohol, except in hotel dining-rooms. And on Sundays you just forgot about having a drink at all, the pubs, like the kids' swingparks, and anything that resembled fun or amusement, being all closed. And if you were an ordinary working man, you were virtually barred from putting a bet on the dogs or horses, unless you committed an illegal act by giving your wager to an illicit bookmaker. And if your street didn't have one, the next street to yours certainly would have.

In the major industries and big factories, management and unions played silly games and because they couldn't, or wouldn't, get their act together, others reaped the benefits, which meant that motorbikes and cameras came from places like Yokohama and Yokosuka instead of the Midlands and mid-Lanarkshire, and factories and yards in and around the Ruhr, the Rhine and the Rhône turned out the ships and cars we used to make better and more of than anyone.

In May of 1963 there was momentary cheer locally when beaming bosses announced they had £30,000,000 worth of orders on the books as the first production model of their attractive new car rolled off the assembly line in the spanking new factory over the Paisley boundary at Linwood. They called it the Imp. Then 20 days later it was 'all out, boys'. The workers had gone on unofficial strike for more money. The bosses offered them 1½ p an hour, which wasn't exactly the kind of ball game the men had been thinking about. They wanted a rise of £1.25 an hour, a figure that was way beyond the norm of the day, considering that the average wage was still under £20 a week. 'This is a tragedy for Scotland,' said Scottish Trade Union boss James Jack, adding, 'It's not helping the country in its present plight.' And that same spring week, one of the famous Glasgow shipyards, Connells of Scotstoun, announced they had just lost a huge order to Japan, boss Sir Charles Connell announcing he was 'completely mystified' at the shock news.

Package holidays to exotic places hadn't happened, the bustling skyscraper holiday towns of Spain and the Balearics being just remote and primitive fishing villages. So, instead, holidaymakers enjoyed themselves in Blackpool where a week with full board in a good hotel was £1.50 a day, and boarding-house tariffs started at 95p a day; and there were full cruises on the *Maid of the Loch* around Loch Lomond, train fare from Glasgow Central included, for 70p. Many didn't go on holiday at all, principally because they couldn't afford it, and instead enjoyed what there was to do in the city, the uptown theatres still being a big draw. Anyway, between Max Bygraves supported by Bob Monkhouse, Yana and David Hughes at the Alhambra, Lex McLean at the Pavilion, Jimmy Logan in *Rob Roy* at the King's and a down-the-bill single act called Frank Carson at the Metropole, with the demolishers not yet having seriously decimated the city's 130 cinemas, there was more entertainment available in Glasgow than most seaside resorts.

Those pleasant evening diversions, it seemed, were so often dispersed with the contents of the following morning's papers, invariably displaying yet another batch of grim industrial and financial figures coupled with forecasts and outlooks which made daily newspaper editors crave for the story that would cheer their readers. They would grasp at anything which would take minds away from politicians and their preachings, trade unionists and their predictions, one lot on about the gathering gloom, the other lot about days of doom. Little wonder those editors were on the lookout more than ever for more uplifting news.

It was in November 1962 that the media were to get the first word of what promised to be one of the best of such stories to take everyone's mind away from those downcast days. News had come from the Outer House of the Court of Sessions in Edinburgh that the judge, Lord Cameron, was about to give judgment on a case before him which had everyone in Glasgow talking. And that judgment would be whether or not a man called Sammy Docherty, one of the best-known Glasgow bookmakers of the day, could proceed with a case against the Royal Bank of Scotland which, if he won, would mean him collecting a small fortune. Not that the money would be a new-found fortune for the bookie, his claim being that it represented the actual sum he had lodged with the bank. The bank, in turn, however, were claiming otherwise and that the sum was only a fortune because one of their tellers had mistakenly and unfortunately, for them that is, inserted another '0' in the sum which had been handed over.

It was the kind of situation which fantasies are about. Well, imagine it! You give the bank £10 and they mark your credit slip with it having been £100. Perhaps, even, it was £100 you gave them and the receipt they give you is for £1,000. Or, in the case Lord Cameron had before him, the bank said the bookmaker had lodged £9,995 but the receipt they had given him was for £90,995 – at least that was their story. The bookmaker had a different tale. He claimed he really had handed over the £90,995 and as he had a counterfoil showing that was the amount, he was claiming the bank for it. And in today's terms that £90,995 is the equivalent of over half a million pounds – £636,965 to be precise. Little wonder newspaper editors wanted to tell their readers every detail they could about the story that had all the city talking, and soon the entire country.

Because of the nature of their profession, albeit being an illegal activity, few people were better known than the street bookmakers of the city. They were an essential part of the fabric of Glasgow life at the time, coming somewhere in importance between doctor and undertaker, and to many even more essential than the former, certainly much more welcome than the latter. But every bit as vital.

The city's bookmakers and all the surrounding individuals involved with them were Glasgow's very own Guys and Dolls, with characters who matched, and sometimes outmatched, the likes of Harry the Horse, Charlie the Bug, Dapper Dan, One-eyed Solly, Gloomy Gus, aye, and the Lemon Drop Kid too. Everyone knew the name of their street bookie. Perhaps they, the bookies, more than advertised the fact that the game in which they participated was, as so many said, a mug's game, and by the standard of their dress and lifestyle, it wasn't they who were the mugs. But that was accepted, and overlooked, for they represented a chance that the next time you handed one of their runners that scribble which indicated a horse, a time and a race, in return you would collect the pile you always dreamed about. They were in the days before 'It Could Be You' and where millionaires, it seemed, happened only in the movies, and while the winnings you might collect from them wouldn't require the assistance of a financial adviser to help you cope, they still answered a lot of prayers.

Being an illegal institution, everything about the street bookmaker was done on the side, as it were. A wink here, a nod there, a little sweetener to the man in uniform to mind his own business, a gentle reminder to anyone encroaching on their territory that they had helpers who didn't appreciate moves like that, helpers with the kind of faces that immediately made you think of words like 'sorry', 'please' and 'thank you'.

The street bookmakers existed because of the grossly unfair laws on betting at the time. It was perfectly legal to place a bet, of course, but only providing you were a person of sufficient means in order for a legitimate bookie, more prudishly known as turf accountants, to accept your custom. You would first of all have to establish your worth to them, it being much more difficult then than it is today to get a loan from the bank, and once having assured them of that worth, they would then put you on their books as an account holder. Thereafter, and in absolute respectability and conformity with the laws of the land, you cold bet your heart out.

On the other hand, if you were the average working man, one of the real punters, who lived up a close and who measured collateral in what next week's wage packet might contain, then you were deprived of a legal bet. Few laws were more obviously divisive between rich and poor than the archaic early '60s betting laws.

Having no official legislation to govern their operations, the illegal street bookmakers operated within their own code and in conjunction and by 'arrangement' with local police. Having carved up their own territory on the simple basis of this street and that street is mine, intruders beware, they would then establish their 'offices', invariably the open window of a ground-floor tenement house by one of the closes in the street. The tenant would receive an arranged 'bung' for the use of their open window through which they would collect 'lines', or bets, which, in turn, would be collected by one of the bookie's runners. The operation would be guarded by lookouts, the operation being immediately suspended with their call 'edge up', meaning simply that patrolling beat policemen had been sighted. And if it looked like the cops were on one of their raids, the 'edge up' call would be shouted in a tone that meant runners, watchers and householders should get rid of every scrap of evidence which might indicate there was an illegal betting operation in progress.

Evidence included items such as betting slips, the blackboard which had all the details of races, runners and results, chalk, notepads, pencils, even copies of the *Sporting Life* and *Noon Record*, the punters' newspapers, all of which, rather than be destroyed, would be quickly farmed around other friendly houses always willing to do the bookie a good turn.

Of course, being the kind of game it was, there were times when not everything would go to plan, the friendly houses on occasion taking panic measures in their efforts to hide the betting material with which they were suddenly landed, efforts somewhat reminiscent of secreting away the spirits in *Whisky Galore*. On one occasion during a raid in Florence Street in the Gorbals, all the vital betting slips handed into one housewife were thrust by her into a large handkerchief and when the police looked like bursting into her house, the hankie and its contents ended up in the copper boiler together with the rest of that day's laundry. Another wife, who hadn't even the time to get to the back-court wash-house, mixed the slips she had been given together with a plate of veg then bundled the lot into the day's pot of soup. And each passing week, somewhere around the city there would be yet another 'Bets Galore' scenario.

The police, of course, were as much a part of the betting burlesque as the watchers, the runners, the tenants of the houses with the open windows or the other friendly houses, being regularly paid to avoid over-harassment. What? Bent coppers? Call them what you like, tut in disapproval or raise a sceptical eyebrow, but they were all part of this eventful game of the streets, a two-way deal with an unwritten code in which the bookie played his part, the police theirs. It was also a part of the charade that, in order to demonstrate they were actively engaged in curbing the illegal trade, the police would perform regular raids on an 'it's your turn' basis, the bookie being forewarned so that it was always one of his runners, never him, who would be arrested and charged.

They all knew the routine at the various police courts in the city where they would appear. As a young court reporter I witnessed hundreds of cases in the old police courts dotted around the city: the Marine in Partick, the Northern in Cowcaddens, the Southern in Craigie Street, Crosshill, the Eastern in Tobago Street, Bridgeton, one at Maryhill just past the old barracks, and the busiest, the Central, in Turnbull Street just off Glasgow Cross. When each fresh case appeared, the police fiscals would wearily read out the charges against the accused in that routine fashion of theirs, holding the charge sheet before them but rarely looking at the words, knowing them as they did by heart: 'You are charged under the Street Betting Act of 1906, in that any person frequenting or loitering in streets or public places on behalf thereof himself or any other person for the purpose of bookmaking or betting or wagering or agreeing to bet or wager or receive or settle bets shall for a first offence be liable to a fine not exceeding £10 and for a second offence be liable to a fine not exceeding £20 and for a third and subsequent offence, and were it proved that there was a betting transaction with someone under 16 years of age, be liable to a fine not exceeding £50 or to prison with or without hard labour for a term not exceeding six months . . . how do you plead?'

The answer from the accused was invariably the same – 'Guilty' – as was the sentence, which would normally be the prescribed minimum fine. It was all part of the big charade of the police and the courts demonstrating that they were enforcing an unworkable, unjust and unwanted law.

In turn, the bookie would play his part in the farce by ensuring there would be no unruly behaviour near his pitch, and that when there was a raid there would be no obstruction of the police, those caught would go quietly and plead guilty, and on the evening of the raid the bookie would be back at his pitch in order to make his payments. All by, as it were, the 'arrangement'.

Senior officers, of course, were aware of such arrangements, most having come through the ranks and undoubtedly having taken part in the widespread gambling gambol. From time to time they would upset the system by sending in men to make raids from different areas of the city, men who had no allegiance to local bookies' deals, although more than likely they did have on their own regular beats. These raids met with varying success, the bookies' own bush telegraph often getting the appropriate tip-off prior to the police incomers making their swoop.

Some bookies, being the kind of entrepreneurs they were and in an effort to avoid the regular, disruptive and costly police raids, devised more unconventional methods of collecting bets other than by the obvious street corner or the kitchen window of the house nearest the close. One of the most enterprising of these was to use a mobile method of collecting bets. It was in the pre-war days when cars were more of a novelty than a necessity and one particular bookie, who operated in the St George's Road and Possil areas, used his car to lift betting lines from runners and other bookies at specified street corners. Like the others, however, he too was eventually to be caught when the full story of his unusual collection methods was revealed in the Northern police court.

The court was told that it was the first-ever occasion on which such gathering procedures had been noted in the city. A police inspector in evidence said they had received information about a car frequenting numerous streets in the vicinity of St George's Road and Possil Road and plain-clothes officers, as well as a police observation car, were detailed to make a surveillance of the operation.

Police witnesses then went on to tell the court that it was their impression the car was collecting packets containing bets from various stances run by bookmakers. They said that they saw the car stopping at a street corner near St George's Road. A man walked up to the car and handed the driver a packet or envelope. The man jumped on the running board of the car and the car moved off. After the car had proceeded some distance, this man jumped off and ran into a close, returning with an envelope which he threw into an open window of the car. The car continued and at various points this man plus another from the car repeated the operation. At certain locations the car slowed down to about five miles per hour but never stopped. It was seen to do this on several occasions.

The police continued to follow its operation as it went northward from St George's Road to various street corners where more envelopes were thrown in. Eventually the police stopped the car in Possil Road and three men were taken into custody. When searched at the police station, 12 envelopes containing 52 betting slips were recovered.

The driver of the car admitted it was their job to collect lines thrown into the car as they drove slowly past. The prosecution then asked what happened if the men collecting the envelopes missed the open window when tossing them into the car. He replied: 'They never miss.'

He was then asked if he stopped the car, would the envelopes still be thrown, to which he answered: 'Most certainly not. The car never stops on any account. That is part of our instructions.'

The driver was fined £2, his assistants, who had pleaded not guilty, were found to be 'not proven'. The fine was of little concern to the bookie who paid up on behalf of the driver, the worst aspect of their being caught was that his novel bets collection scheme had been discovered and they would be on the watch for him and his mobile runners' car in future.

Such illegal gambling, of course, was a gnawing concern to many in the country, mostly, it seemed, to those who lived in the pleasant suburbs or in county towns and who never gambled, or if they did, could do so discreetly with a phone call to whichever commission agent held their account. There were regular pleas from them that something must be done to stamp out the activities of the street bookie and illegal gambling, usually saying things like it was a scourge on society, overlooking the point that it was the law which was the scourge, not the poor punter.

A conference on the very subject had been held at the Berkeley Hall, near Charing Cross, attended by a wide representation of churches, teachers of voluntary organisations, various dignitaries, such as the Duchess of Atholl, Lord Polwarth, the Chief Constable, a clutch of colonels and a retinue of reverends. Everyone, it would appear, except the bookies and the punters. A House of Commons Select Committee had been looking into the question of gambling and was considering a tax on all betting, which at least was something constructive on the part of the Government as another means of revenue. The Select Committee had put forward a figure of some 30,000 illegal bookmakers operating in the country, one Glasgow witness telling them that he took £5,000 a day in bets in the city. And at the Glasgow conference, delegates were enthusiastically applauded and supported when they warned of the 'terrible vice of gambling' . . . that 'in betting there was the main root of crime' . . . that 'it exercised a poisonous influence on sport' . . . 'an incalculable handicap on industry' . . . 'a pernicious effect on home life' . . . and was the 'source of individual degeneracy'.

A teacher from a school in Woodside was to shock delegates by informing them that the amount of betting going on in schools would surprise them. He personally had a list of 38 pupils in one department of a city school who ran to the bookies for their parents. There was loud applause when he asked that bookies should refuse to take betting lines from children under 16 years of age and there was unanimous support from the hall when the Revd John White moved that betting should be curbed because of the 'grave concern it was causing in the country'.

All of which were the furthest thoughts of the man in the expensive Crombie coat or the runners and the watchers and the ones who shouted 'edge up', or those who collected the benefits from that morning's tanner each-way bet. The law had ostracised them from society and to compensate for that they had created their own rules.

By the '50s and early '60s the betting laws had fallen into such disrepute that most of the street bookies had progressed from their corner pitches to setting up their own betting offices in vacant small shops, former dairies, newsagents and the like, usually in a street just off the main thoroughfare, with neither signboard nor name over the door indicating what might be taking place inside, although everyone, including the police, knew. As for planning permission or city council rules, a combination of *laissez-faire* and blind eye seemed to be the rule. Furnishing in the offices was non-existent, the only facility being a gent's urinal (women punters were a rarity), the walls' sole decoration the pages of the racing papers, and the focal point the loudspeaker announcing the course and race details from the Exchange Telegraph racing service. The usual staff would be two or three collecting the bets, known as 'takers-in', a couple of clerks, the men who made up the betting lines and figured out the winnings, a boardman who marked the blackboard with the races and prices, and a manager, invariably the bookie himself.

The police would raid them in the same routine fashion they had operated with the street bookies, who would smartly absent themselves but pay the involved punters' fines, usually £2, and usually give them £1 for their 'inconvenience'.

The £1 inconvenience money often created its own scene, however, the most streetwise of the punters rushing to the bookie's shop the moment they got word of an impending raid in order to qualify for their quid. Daffy Jack and Ears Acosta would have been proud of that lot for that would be their kind of enterprise. Daffy and Ears would have been proud, too, to have been there the night in Glasgow when the bookies assembled for one of their Protection Association meetings and the controversial subject under discussion was the new and increased levies the dog tracks wanted to impose on their betting shops.

The betting shops had become so popular with the punters, the dog track owners were claiming it was taking business away from them, the tracks until then being where the majority of punters went and where they could legally bet. Because of the success of the shops, the track owners wanted to charge them a new levy on a per-bet basis. The norm until then had been for each bookie to pay the tracks a flat rate of £33 for which, in return, they would be given a relayed results service. Now the owners – the principal Glasgow ones being White City, Carntyne, Albion and Shawfield – wanted a levy of £2 for every bet placed. The bookies were furious and it was to be the stormiest of meetings with loud and vociferous calls from various parts of the hall instructing the committee and chairman as to what they should tell the track owners. And the measures they were advocating were in no uncertain terms. The 'f' word, in the most emphatic of forms, was coming from all parts of the gathering, suggesting all sorts of dire warnings and remedies for the track owners. But there was no mistaking the consensus call, which was in the simplest of terms: 'Tell them to fuck off!'

The office-bearers and committee heard them out and when they calmed the meeting somewhat, the chairman said they would do things in the regulated and proper way by taking the most appropriate action against the owners. That would be by forming a deputation which would go and meet them.

'And what will you be telling them?' came a shout from the meeting. The reply was that when the deputation met the owners, they would convey the feelings of the meeting to them and that would be, he said, by telling them 'to fuck off'.

And wouldn't Daffy and Ears and all the Guys and Dolls gang have just loved hearing that!

Many of the respected and legitimate turf accountants and commission agents who could advertise their services from their commodius city offices had more than a passing knowledge of the street bookies. Many operated in conjunction with them, illegal street bookies acting as their agents and being paid on a commission basis for the bets and business which they brought them, the bookies running a two-way service between street and uptown office, taking care to operate along what they considered safe routes as cars were included with all other betting apparatus and liable for confiscation if caught by the police. Some ran a two-way operation, one part of it uptown cosy and legal, the other part downtown dreary and illegal.

Many, perhaps most, of the uptown betting agents had come up through the ranks of the street corner or illegal shop owner. They were men of the street and as streetwise as they come, Sammy Docherty being one of them. He had all the appurtenances of the big-time operator: the expensive clothing, the handsome house, the car with the private registration plate – in a day when they were the rarest of commodities, his being SD 147, that number not only representing snooker's maximum break but the number of his office address in Renfield Street. As well as being head of that flourishing and prosperous business, he was also a boxing promoter, rivalling some of the biggest sporting entrepreneurs in the country, people of the calibre of the larger-than-life Jack Solomons, hardly a big fight taking place in the country without his name being mentioned in some connection. Mainly for his boxing activities, Sammy was regularly featured in newspaper articles, being associated with some of the major fight nights which were a regular part of the Glasgow scene at the time.

The story about his rare conflict with the bank had first broken in November of 1962, when the judgment was made in the Outer House of the Court of Session in Edinburgh as to whether or not there was a case to be answered in what was simply referred to in court terms as *Docherty* v *Royal Bank of Scotland*. Docherty was suing his bank for £81,000. Docherty was so insistent that the bank was wrong that he raised this action against them. Before it could proceed to proof, the word used in civil cases for trial, a decision had to be made as to whether or not there was evidence for that. Hence the hearing in the Outer House of the Court of Session.

The first legal hurdle to be debated at length by the judge, Lord Cameron, was which party should be given the chance to lead evidence first. This is an important legal point, as the side which leads with their evidence can be said to be at a disadvantage in that while being first to reveal their case, it forewarns the other side of just what testimony they have and what proof they possess, at the same time alerting them of the points they require to counteract the claims. The normal rule is that the counsel for the pursuer, in this case Docherty, should lead his case first and the judge acknowledged that point. But he was to indicate, however, that if this was to be the procedure in this case, he would have to anticipate the various explanations of what went on inside the bank and this could prejudice the presentation of his [Docherty's] case. He said he had given considerable consideration to this submission and that as it appeared there would be no such obvious prejudice suffered by the bank if they were to lead first, he ordered that this should be the case.

That legal preamble having been settled, it was to be another six months before the court was to get down to the real serious question: did dapper 42-year-old Samuel Docherty, well-known Glasgow character, bookmaker and boxing promoter, lodge £90,995 with the Royal Bank of Scotland, as his counterfoil showed, or was it a mere £9,995? Forget the strikers at the Imp factory, the big ship order at Connells going to Japan, the promises, preaching and posturing of politicians and union bosses, and the rest of the doom and gloom of the day. There was only one story that mattered on Glasgow street corners, in pubs, in workplaces or wherever people met – was the bank doing one of Glasgow's well-known sons out of a fortune? Or, was Sam at the scam? It was the very story daily newspaper editors had been craving for ages, particularly when they looked at their news schedules for that week, stories including the news that while the Imp employees had gone back in, the BMC truck men had come out. They were on another unofficial strike, the claim this time being that a foreman had sworn at one of their men.

The bookie versus the bank action was to be heard again before Lord Cameron, one of the most distinguished figures of the Scottish bench, having been a sheriff, a Dean of the Faculty of Advocates and a decorated war hero with the Royal Navy.

The case opened on a cold spring day in March 1963, in the Court of Session, Edinburgh, the highest civil court in the land. The opposing parties were represented by two of the most able and respected Queen's Counsel of the day, Mr G. Gordon Stott QC for Docherty, and Mr Manuel Kissen QC for the bank, both in time to become Law Lords. And it was to be a week of non-stop page-one headlines for the most sensational civil case of the era.

The bank gave their version of the affair first, their principal witness the bank teller who had given Docherty's messenger the counterfoil for £90,995, that fact in itself being one which was not in dispute. He was a 29-year-old, slim, boyish-looking man named Prentice and he was to tell the court of the day – virtually to the day a year previously – that he made a mistake, an £81,000 mistake, and although not putting it precisely in such terms, it had been the biggest mistake of his banking career.

Prentice, who had worked for the bank for 12 years, was to frankly admit that his error had been 'a stupid mistake' in arithmetic. 'I thought ten times £100 came to £10,000,' he was to confess. He went on to describe how Docherty's messenger, John McSweeney, had come to the bank with the money in a zipped bag. The messenger had told him he didn't know how much money was in the bag, but he did say that 'Mr Docherty knew'.

Prentice said that on the morning of that day, Docherty's messenger had been in the bank to collect a packet for which he had a receipt. The packet, Prentice said, had been small enough to carry away in his one hand. McSweeney had then returned in the afternoon carrying the zipped bag containing money. The money in the bag was in ten bundles and each bundle had ten folds, or notes, held together by elastic bands. They was no pay-in slip and when he asked him how much money there was in the bag, he said he didn't know but that Docherty, his boss, knew.

'McSweeney appeared to be unaccustomed to bank procedures and I made out a pay-in slip for him. There were ten large bundles – some were £20 notes, others £5 notes – and ten smaller bundles in each of the large bundles. I formed the impression there was £10,000 in each bundle. One of the bundles I found to be £5 short and I made the total to be £90,995, which was the sum entered in the pay-in slip.'

The money had been the biggest sum he had ever had to handle in the bank and when shortly afterwards an employee had come to collect some documents from him, he had excitedly commented to her, 'How's that for a day's business – £100,000!'

It was then that he had second thoughts on the actual sum, it dawning on him that he had made an error and that, in fact, the sum deposited by the messenger only totalled £9,995. In fact, he had made two mistakes with the counting of the sum brought in by McSweeney. The first had been when he thought ten times £100 made up £10,000 instead of £1,000. And mistake number two had been that £100,000 less £5 was £90,995, the amount he had marked on the counterfoil, his reckoning again being out as obviously it should have been £99,995. By the time he had spotted his mistakes, messenger McSweeney had left the bank. However, the moment he had realised the error he had mentioned it to a machinist working beside him, saying there had been a mix-up with the cash and she returned the pay-in slip to him. He had also immediately informed the manager about what had occurred and was told to telephone Docherty about it.

'I told him [Docherty] I had taken the lodgement to be £100,000 instead of £10,000. When I said it was £5 short he explained that he had expected that.'

The teller had then asked Docherty to return to the bank the counterfoil with the £90,995 marked on it and Docherty had told him, albeit in a jocular fashion, 'You are in trouble now.' At that point he didn't realise for one second that Docherty's comment was to be no mere joke.

In reply to a question from the bank's counsel, Mr Kissen, the teller said that when he had spoken to Docherty he had held him to be an honourable man. And, as such, he had thought that he would return the mistaken counterfoil. Instead, the next he heard of the matter was when a lawyer's letter arrived. Mr Kissen was then to put his next question to the teller, doing so most delicately: 'I am sorry to put this to you, but there may be a suggestion that you took this money away.'

Kissen had cleverly predicted the line Gordon Stott, Docherty's counsel, would take in his cross-examination. Among the points Stott was to suggest was that there were £100 notes among the bundles handed over by the messenger, that the teller was in financial difficulties at the time, and going on to inquire whether or not he had a key to the bank or if a friend of his had arrived after the messenger had left. All very suggestive inferences, and all of which the teller strongly denied. And when they were called as witnesses, the machinist confirmed the teller's phone call to Docherty and the bank manager said he couldn't see how the teller could have taken such a sum out of the bank.

When he was called on the second day of the hearing to give his side of the story, bookmaker Docherty was to prove, as everyone had anticipated he might, that he was the star turn in the case which not only was the talk of the city but of the whole country. There wasn't a street corner gossip group or bar-room debate that went without the words Sammy . . . the bank . . . ninety thousand . . . the cheek . . . what a character! And more. Forget the fact that we couldn't make cars or trucks for strikes and the strikers. Forget even more gloomy news on the jobs front and that we couldn't match Germany, Norway or Japan at making ships and another Clyde shipyard was laying off men. There was just one story, one subject that everyone was talking about that week in 1963 – Sammy Docherty and his claim for a lost fortune. Or was it one he wanted to gain? But that, of course, was the big question. The £81,000 question.

Docherty's first day in the witness stand was to be a day of sensations, the like of which seldom accompany the customary more placid, more pedantic, often quite boring nature of civil cases. And perhaps one of the first surprises of the day was to come with a preceding witness and the reading of an exceptional testimonial relating to the character and financial standing of bookmaker Docherty. This glowing commendation was to describe Docherty, among other things, as being a 'highly respectable man of comfortable means' and that his financial position was such that he would have no difficulty in meeting his financial commitments while abroad. But the surprising element of the enthusiastic reference for the man at the centre of the case was the fact that it came from none other than Mr William Elder, the manager of the branch of the bank which Docherty was suing. The reference, it was said, had been supplied by the manager when Docherty had requested some form of character and financial status endorsement in order to get a visa for a trip he had made to Brazil.

Questioning him about the reference, QC Stott was to make the comment to the bank manager: 'You wrote that his financial position was such that he would have no difficulty in meeting his financial commitments while abroad?' to which Elder replied that he had believed that at that particular time.

The bank manager, in cross-examination, was asked if there had been 'other serious mistakes in the branch', replying there had been merely trifling ones, involving shillings, maybe perhaps as much as £1.

But when it was put to him that there had been 'quite serious difficulties' in the bank's balance, he was to turn to the judge to inquire, 'Do I have to answer that?'

When told that he did, he said there had been 'a thing concerning another customer, but a much smaller amount than this'. It had arisen, he said, because of the unusual way the money had been paid in.

The bank manager's evidence concluded, the court sat up smartly for the appearance of what had been anticipated as the star act, bookmaker Sammy Docherty.

Dressed impeccably, as always, Mr Docherty was to answer questions put to him by the bank's learned counsel in a fashion which was as much eyebrow-raising as it was eye-opening. He began by recalling the day in question the previous March when the money had been deposited with the bank. There had been a phone call from them early in the day to say that he did not have enough in his account to pay a cheque for £10,000 which had been presented to them. He assured them there would be no problem in meeting the cheque and that he had lodged with them in one of their safe-boxes what he described as 'a parcel' containing about £15,000. He had added about £12,000 to this sum. His messenger had then collected this 'parcel' and at his office he had put the money together with another sum he had brought from the house that morning. That sum had been for around £50,000, which brought the first wave of astonished looks and exclamations from those in the court. To put that in perspective in the values of the millennium age, the sum Docherty had so casually brought from his house would now amount to almost £400,000!

There was plenty more breathtaking stuff to come as Docherty went further into his story. Having got all the money together in his Renfield Street premises, 'I started counting out the money in the office and comments about how much was there were passed by others in the room. I began to realise that too many people were seeing what was going on so I put it all in a bag and told McSweeney to take it to the bank. He was driven there and came back later with the slip for £90,995.'

At that point, Mr Kissen considered appropriate some cross-examination, asking if it were not the case that Docherty was paying up instalments on a car, a Bentley, at which point he flavoured the question with a smiling remark about the prestigious car being the one 'that is taking up half of Parliament Square at the moment!'

(Parliament Square being the locus immediately outside the Court of Session building).

But there was a more salient and less jocular point to be made about the Bentley – just how was it being paid for? Docherty was to agree to Mr Kissen's surprising question that he was buying the car on hire purchase, paying it off at £295 a month.

Intrigued at that, and obviously having himself noticed the sumptuous car in question, Lord Cameron was to lean over the bench to inquire: 'Is that the Bentley standing outside?'

Smiling, Docherty replied, 'No, your honour. That's a new one, this year's model,' the reply being met with a loud burst of laughter.

From one merely making observations, Kissen switched his approach to a more stringent line by suggesting that perhaps the reason he kept money in a parcel, as he did, had been to avoid paying tax.

That brought another comment from Lord Cameron, this time a word of advice for the man giving evidence, that advice being that there was no need to answer any question which might involve him in criminal proceedings. The advice was quickly taken, Docherty promptly replying, 'I don't wish to answer that.'

The QC adopted another line, perhaps not expecting the surprise answer he was to get. 'Do you usually go about with thousands of pounds in your pockets?' he asked Docherty.

The superb cut of the suit virtually subdued the imperceptible shrug of the shoulders which accompanied the bookie's reply with a slight nod of the head: 'More or less.'

Kissen wanted him to be more precise and asked how much he had on him at the moment. The reply was that he had between £3,000 and £5,000 in his pockets, but couldn't be more precise than that. Kissen, probably as surprised as anyone in court, commented that he personally hadn't seen a £100 note for some time. Which was as good an invite as any for the counsel to be given a demonstration of one, Docherty thrusting his hands deep into his trouser pocket and pulling out a bulky wad of money which would have brought louder gasps from the varied assembly had it been in a theatre not a courtroom. As it was, what was happening before them was pure theatre, the pile of notes Docherty had pulled out being so enormous he couldn't hold them all in one hand, many of them fluttering to the floor of the witness box. The learned bewigged were so amused that Lord Cameron strained further forward in his chair to view proceedings as the surprised and smiling counsel strode over to Docherty in order to retrieve some of the spilled notes before turning to the judge and saying, 'Yes, they are £100 notes.'

Kissen then decided it was appropriate to introduce another unexpected note into the proceedings, asking Docherty if he considered his messenger McSweeney to be an honest man, to which he answered simply, 'Yes.'

'Has he been in trouble?' Kissen went on.

'Yes. I know he's been in jail, but I don't know what for.'

'Does it worry you that he has been in jail for something involving dishonesty?'

'No. He's been working for me since he got out of prison.'

Counsel persisted, switching this time to the amount of money lodged with the bank. 'You didn't know to within £10,000 how much money was lodged in the bank?'

'That's what I'm telling you.'

Lord Cameron again thought it time for a question of his own, this time one which was not to induce any smiles or laughter: 'Are you asking this court to believe that you lodged a sum amounting to £80,000 or £90,000 in the bank, sent by a man you knew had been in jail, and you didn't bother to ascertain how much money you were lodging?'

Docherty's reply came in one word: 'Exactly.'

He was to add to that in reply to counsel that his trusting of the £90,000 in an unlocked bag with the ex-prisoner was exactly what had happened and that money meant nothing to him. 'I've been put here to tell the truth and that's what I'm doing,' he said convincingly.

It was that same day another bank manager was called to give the court lessons on the counting of money. Earlier it had been stated by the bank teller Prentice that it had taken him 20 to 30 minutes to count the money lodged on behalf of Docherty on the day in question. But William Swan, who had been the accountant at Jamaica Street and was now manager of another branch, said he had carried out some experiments in counting notes.

'We took 1,000 notes and they took two minutes five seconds to count. Those notes would be double-checked and I would assume it would take roughly four minutes to do that. For a lodgement of £90,000, according to my figures, it would work out at about four hours.'

Resuming his evidence the following day, Docherty was to introduce something of an international element into the proceedings when he brought up an incident involving the famous Harlem Globetrotters basketball team. It had occurred about a month after he had lodged the disputed sum with the bank. Three of the Globetrotters had come to his office in town and wanted to place a bet on the last horse-race of the day. The bet was for £790 on a 6–1 chance in the race. One of the Americans had waited in the office to hear the outcome of the race and, in order to cover the bet, Docherty said he had sent a clerk to the bank in order to cash a cheque for £2,000. He would have needed around £5,000 to cover the bet, which was why he required the £2,000, the rest of the money either being in the office or on his person. However, the cheque bounced, the bank saying there was insufficient funds to cover it and claiming his account was overdrawn because the bank disputed the amount paid by him on a previous date, that being the specific sum at the centre of the court case.

As Docherty continued his evidence, Lord Cameron said, 'You did not tell us what happened in the last race.'

'The horse lost, sir.'

'That solved the problem, then,' said the judge, smiling, at which the court erupted in laughter once more.

But there were to be no smiles later on when a much more sombre note was introduced into the proceedings, this time by yet another international witness. For nearly an hour the threat of being sent to prison hung over this key witness who had been called from the Republic of Ireland to give evidence. He was publicly warned in court that he would end the day behind bars if he continued to refuse to supply the answer to a specific question being put to him by the counsel for the defenders.

The witness was a Dublin architect named Vincent MacEoin who was to tell the story of a friend of his in Belfast, an accountant called Burke, who had been in touch with him two years previously with the word that Sammy Docherty had required the loan of a large sum of money. He had been told that he needed the money for a year and there would be interest of 15 per cent paid on the sum. Apparently some two months later a group of people in Dublin showed some interest in the deal and in February 1962 – about a month prior to the sum involved in the court dispute being lodged by Docherty in the

Royal Bank – MacEoin had gone to Belfast with the money in his luggage. The accountant Burke counted the money and thereafter wrapped it together in one bundle. MacEoin and Burke together with the parcelled money had then gone to a hotel in Belfast to meet Docherty. And there in his bedroom they handed over the parcelled cash, requesting Docherty count it.

Docherty had then asked if Burke had already counted the money and when he was told he had, he had said he needn't bother rechecking. Docherty had then given MacEoin a receipt for the money, a sum of £50,000.

It was at that point the difficulty arose over the answering of a question. QC Kissen had wanted to know from whom MacEoin had got such a large sum of money. Without any hesitation, the Irishman was to reply, 'I am not prepared to answer that.'

Which was the cue for some guidelines to be shown the witness about the powers of the court, Lord Cameron addressing MacEoin directly with a reminder about what happened to people in his court who didn't answer questions. 'If I give you an order you obey it – or else you go to prison,' he said in a manner that left no doubts about his intentions.

But the threat made little impression on the Irishman who quickly countered, 'I can only deal with my own affairs. I cannot involve any other people.'

The judge responded, 'You have not been asked to involve anyone. It is a competent question and one you are bound to answer. If you don't wish the name to be disclosed in open court, write it down.'

MacEoin was still unbending, telling Lord Cameron, 'I am afraid I must refuse.'

'In that case you will stand down and remain in custody of the court.'

Whereupon MacEoin was led from the witness box to an anteroom and placed under police guard.

Some time later, however, QC Stott obviously considered it was time the legal men got together in private to discuss this somewhat unexpected development in the case and was to intimate to the bench that he was 'concerned' about the witness MacEoin and requested that they, himself and Mr Kissen, have an adjournment to discuss the matter with Lord Cameron in his chambers.

The judge agreed and the three left for their private discussion.

Whatever went on in their meeting obviously resolved the matter and when the court resumed MacEoin returned to the witness box to write down the name of the person who had given him the money for Docherty.

In his evidence, Mr Burke, the Belfast accountant, said he had known Docherty for ten years, their connection being through the many boxing promotions which the bookmaker made both in Glasgow and in Belfast. He confirmed the story about the money which had come from Ireland, the first intimation of it being in a phone call from Docherty who had told him he was having a dispute with his bank and that he was very angry about it. He had gone on to give him some details of the dispute, going over the story of giving a messenger from his office money in a bag to take to the bank and, although he didn't know how much precisely had been in the bag, he estimated it to be considerably more than the bank's claim of it being only £9,995. By his estimate he had considered the sum to be about £81,000.

One of the final witnesses was the messenger himself, John McSweeney, who was to admit under questioning that he had a number of convictions for dishonesty. All very embarrassing for the pursuer. But he did testify that when he had taken the zippered bag containing the money to the bank he had stood at the counter while the teller had counted out the contents three times before handing him the counterfoil.

The hearing concluded after four days of evidence with a sombre declaration by Judge Lord Cameron that in deciding whether or not it had been £9,995 or £90,995 he would have to take one very important point into consideration. And that was that one of the two main characters in this bookie versus the bank case was a criminal, the use of that word setting the tone of his approach, and they would be hearing no more humorous asides or laughter in court. Whittling aside the main bulk of the evidence, Lord Cameron, in an initial summary, was to home in on the central pillar of the case in that way the sharpest of legal brains so splendidly do. During the final speech by Docherty's counsel Gordon Stott, he was to say, 'When one comes to the ultimate issue, either £81,000 was stolen by Prentice − or your client has committed perjury and fraud. That is the clear issue and, that being so, one does not need to mince one's words about rascality.

'Either one or other of the principal witnesses is a criminal − and there is no possible room for reconciliation. One or the other must be lying and for a very good reason – £81,000.'

Counsel Stott said he had to agree with that, but on that being so, their character would hang on the result.

To that Lord Cameron added the foreboding prediction, 'And possibly more than their character.'

QC Kissen, for the bank, was the most scathing of the three in his final speech, saying that while the bank had been taunted about making a mistake, at least it had been a mistake, 'not a piece of gross dishonesty'. As a result of being given a counterfoil for the wrong sum, he said, Docherty had used it in an attempt to extort from the bank the sum of £81,000.

'When one comes to the evidence, one thing is crystal clear and that is that the pursuer has perjured himself and has led perjured evidence.' As for the story about money coming from Ireland, Kissen said this had been 'reeking with suspicion' and had the 'taint of illegality'.

The evidence concluded, the final speeches made, everyone was dying to hear the verdict which, in a criminal case, would have been more or less immediately forthcoming. But civil cases don't work in that fashion and, as is their way, it was intimated that Lord Cameron would be 'reserving his judgement'. In other words, he was going off to think about it. And after what he had heard, there was no doubt a lot to think about. There had never been another case quite like it before, at least not that anyone could remember and it was most certainly not a matter for a snap judgement. The judge had already indicated that in the case of the principal witnesses there was possibly 'more than their character' at stake, while there were those stinging words from the bank's counsel about 'perjury', 'gross dishonesty' and 'reeking with suspicion'. They don't usually trade phrases like that in the civil courts.

Some two months later and having shaken off the worst vestiges of a miserable winter, there was the news that the judgment was imminent, reviving new interest in the case which had continued to be the talk of the steamie, that expression being very much in vogue by virtue of those great centres of all things gossip, the steamie wash-houses themselves, being still very much alive and working in many parts of the city. There were, of course, many other events of the day on the tongues of those who exchanged current happenings, events that in so many ways either demonstrate just how much things have changed – or how some things just go on and on. Schoolgirl mothers, often considered to be the scandalous new problem of the millennium years, were very much in the news that week Lord Cameron's judgment was due. New figures had shown a frightening rise in their numbers, over 3,200 babies having been born that year to girls between the ages of 13 and 18, illegitimacy too being also on the rise. And, as always, football was news, a major topic being the problems at Celtic FC, an urgent probe having been ordered by manager McGrory over their 3–0 humbling by Rangers in the Cup final a few days previously, Celtic having fielded for the game their 40th forward line permutation that season. The post-match scenes had been predictable with a spate of inter-fan skirmishes in Shawlands, Gorbals and Bridgeton with more than 70 arrests.

It had been intimated that Lord Cameron would give his judgment on the morning of Friday, 17 May, from the bench of the Court of Session. And once again the case was to be the stuff of sensational headlines, this time much of the sensation focusing on the bookie and the comments to be made about him and the case by the judge. That prediction of his, all those weeks ago, that the verdict would have a bearing on 'possibly more than their character' was to prove so stingingly accurate. For, in the early part of his judgment, Lord Cameron was to express the view that Docherty's action had either been a gamble . . . or a deliberate fraud.

In his conclusion he was to accuse the bookie of 'concocting' his story about the bank owing him £81,000 and so serious a view did he take of this, he was to issue an order that all the evidence in the case should be sent to the Crown Office 'for such further inquiry and action as they deem proper'.

But the bank, too, were not to escape criticism in his lengthy judgment, which was to take more than an hour to deliver. While he did not doubt the honesty of its employees, he considered they had perpetrated an 'extraordinary blunder' and had done remarkably little to rectify it.

His observation of the witness John McSweeney, Docherty's messenger with the bag of money, and the only one of the witnesses to be actually present in court for the delivery of the judgment, was to be on a somewhat softer, even kinder tone, saying that while he was 'a man with an unfortunate record' he had considered that he had tried to give a truthful and accurate account of what he remembered of that day he had delivered the zippered bag with the disputed sum of money to the bank.

Lord Cameron was to begin his judgment in a routine fashion by making reference to previous cases where there had been a resemblance to this one, although without having a precise parallel. Demonstrating just how much homework had gone into his research on such cases, he was to quote from a variety of those, including one in 1941 and others going back to the previous century, one as long ago as 1860. He said he had to acknowledge the fact that it would be unfortunate if banks could be in a position to repudiate their own authenticated receipts of money from their customers by mere denial of their accuracy. This would put customers holding such receipts in the position of having to prove their accuracy in any case of dispute. If that were the law, the receipt would then be a valueless piece of paper because it would only become important if any disagreement arose between customer and bank.

In this case, however, after listening to the evidence he had considered it to come down to who should be believed. The evidence given by the bank teller Prentice had been consistent and coherent and did not creak or crumble under close and careful cross-examination. While he had made an extraordinary blunder he did not attempt to explain it away and 'he gave me the impression of complete honesty'.

The bank's own negligence, however, which appeared to be something between nonchalance and indifference, was not to be missed in his observations. When the mistake had first been noticed and Docherty had been asked by the teller to return the counterfoil with the wrong sum on it, he had not done so. Because they hadn't checked, the bank was not to know whether or not he had returned the vital counterfoil. And because he had heard nothing further from his staff, the manager had considered that all-important slip had been returned for correction in accordance with his instructions. This assumption was to be described by Lord Cameron as 'unfortunate', as neither the manager nor any of his responsible subordinates appeared to have made any inquiry as to why Docherty did not – if he had been asked to do so – send back the counterfoil.

'As days passed and nothing happened, I find it hard to understand why no action was taken. I think the most charitable explanation lay in the manager's reliance on the integrity of his teller and the honesty of his customer. In neither case did he have any reason to have doubts so far as his previous experience went. Indeed, he had himself given for purpose of a passport visa a soberly worded testimonial of the character and financial standing of Docherty within the year. The personal history and character of Prentice was known to him also. These circumstances go far to explain the omission to take any action until the matter reached the hands of Docherty's solicitor.'

The question which was to be perhaps the most central to the hearing was just why Docherty had made his claim for the £81,000. Said Lord Cameron: 'It may well have been in the hope that the bank rather than disclose the circumstances of so extraordinary an error, would be prepared to compromise. But whatever the hope or the motive, I have not the slightest doubt that Docherty all along knew it was false.'

Pinpointing the evidence he considered to be wrong, Lord Cameron said it had been claimed there had been 270 notes each of £100 denomination in the sum lodged that day but there was no doubt that no such number of £100 notes had been remitted to the chief office of the Royal Bank in Glasgow, as they should have been according to the regulations had that kind of sum, in fact, been lodged. 'I find it difficult beyond belief to accept not only that Prentice would steal £81,000 on the spur of momentary temptation, but that as a bank employee and knowing the comparative rarity of £100 notes he would have been guilty of such folly as to steal 270 notes of that denomination.'

Nor did the judge believe the story of the £50,000 it had been claimed that Docherty had received as a loan from a man in Ireland. He didn't doubt that a man such as Docherty whose profession included, as well as bookmaking, the promotion of professional boxing matches, did from time to time require large sums of ready cash at his immediate disposal. And he observed too that sometimes the sources of such sums might not be always easy to trace, or even convenient to disclose, which raised the question of the bookmaker's relations with the Inland Revenue of which, he considered, Docherty had been 'at least less than frank'.

As his judgment went on, Lord Cameron was to be even more critical of Docherty, making it abundantly clear before reaching the conclusion of his verdict just which way it would go. Among his observations of Docherty and his case were that he had not been impressed favourably by him in the witness box, that he had been inconsistent in his recollection of the receipt of the bank's quarterly statement, and that he disbelieved his denial of having received a phone call from the bank regarding the alleged error in the pay-in counterfoil, a point, he said, which was critical on credibility, 'and here I believe Prentice and disbelieve Docherty'.

His Lordship was also to comment that he also disbelieved Docherty's explanations of why he was lodging £50,000 in the bank on current account on that day, his explanation being 'singularly unconvincing'.

While appreciating that the bank officials, including the manager, had found it difficult to understand how the teller had made such a mistake, he said he had even greater difficulty in understanding how Docherty could not know within a margin of £8,000 or £9,000 how much money he was sending to the bank. It would have been the biggest sum in cash that the bookmaker had ever lodged with the bank and there had been evidence to show that in the past he had been careful to count the money.

Apart from the central issue, about who was telling the truth, and who was not, Lord Cameron was to conclude his 15,000-word judgment with his verdict. He said he was of the opinion that whether the onus of proof rested on the bank to overcome the evidence of the counterfoil or on Docherty to establish positively the lodgement of the sum claimed, the bank had succeeded . . . and Docherty had failed. And it was because of his views on this and on the principal witness himself, Docherty, that he said he intended to pass all of the papers in the case to the Crown Office 'for such further inquiry they may deem proper'.

To the lay person not fully conversant with the inner workings of the law, the judge's comments and declaration about this not being the end of the matter all sounded very ominous; that the next time you hear about Docherty would be him being arrested and charged with some serious criminal offence. Docherty's counsel and lawyers, however, seemed less concerned. Judges do, from time to time, huff and puff a bit much and the bookie's legal team was fully aware of the fact that in this case his Lordship was a thoroughly establishment-minded person. Well, he was, after all, a Knight of the Realm.

However, just as Sammy's legal team considered would be the case, no criminal proceedings were to be instituted against him by the Crown Office. And that was the end of the matter, except, of course, the hefty bill of many thousands he would have to pay to his rather expensive legal team for preparing and raising the action. But then Sammy, like all bookies, was a gambler and he no doubt had deliberated what odds to give a case like this, his verdict obviously being that they were good enough for him to have a flutter. That is, of course, going on the assumption that he had taken the action he had on the chance of winning himself some £81,000. Then again, maybe his appeal to the Court of Session was founded on what he believed to be the truth.

The colourful days of characters like the late Sammy Docherty and of the illegal street bookie and the nondescript betting shops they were later to run, have long since vanished from the Glasgow scene. New laws introduced in 1962 under the Betting and Gaming Act provided for the establishment of legalised betting premises, offering at last the ordinary punter the chance of which he had been deprived for so many years. But, as is the way of things, the new order was to bring about unforeseen changes in the bookmaking industry, sanitising it, as it were, out of all recognition from its Runyonesque days.

Before the sweeping changes were introduced in 1962, there had been around 600 bookies' betting shops throughout Scotland. Now there are less than 300, only a handful being listed in the Glasgow *Yellow Pages*. More than half of the 8,000 to 9,000 betting shops in the UK are now run by major conglomerates. Ladbrokes, who proudly boast of being Britain's biggest bookmakers, have around 1,900 of them, William Hill not far behind, Corals just below 1,000 and Stanley Racing about 600. In Glasgow the William King chain is the biggest.

Like so many other businesses that have taken on all the challenges of the modern market place, it's the accountants, marketing executives and public affairs specialists who make the rules and call the shots in today's betting industry. The Lemon Drop Kid and One-eyed Solly don't have a say any more. And as a result, the small man has been squeezed out by the prohibitive costs of running an up-to-date business complete with all its modern requirements. No longer is it the leaky, chipped and yellowed gent's urinal, bare floorboards, a scratchy loudspeaker and enough passive cigarette smoke to make a ten-minute visit feel like you've just inhaled a pack of 20 in crowded premises designed by a pickpocket which Jimmy from up the close fitted out for a bottle of whisky.

Nowadays the shops, like all main-street premises used by the public, come under the supervision of local Environment Department regulations and are regularly inspected to ensure they comply with sanitary, fire, building and any other rules such places require, all of which add heavily to the on-costs. These new shops are bright and welcoming, freshly painted, with carpets, calculators, computers and pretty girls in smart suits taking the bets, with their share of female managers competing with their male counterparts in the *Racing Post's* Betting Shop Manager of the Year contest.

Then there's all the new high-tech communications without which today's bookie can't survive. The days of the old-fashioned board markers and the 'blower', as they called the speaker suspended on a wall relaying betting and race news from the Exchange Telegraph company, have disappeared. Perhaps someone has saved them for a bookmakers' heritage museum. Instead, the new shops come equipped with SIS (Satellite Information Services) with a bank of screens where punters can watch everything from the racecourses on an up-to-the-second basis in the comfort of their bright new betting salon together with a fizzy drink (but no alcohol), a cup of coffee and a packet of crisps. Where once the old 'blower' service cost them only hundreds a year, the latest systems cost thousands, starting from £2,000 per shop and rising by many thousands for the full top-line, on-line package.

By having their own service from the courses, the big firms can do this cheaper, putting yet another burden on the small operator trying to compete. About the only thing that hasn't changed is the fact that the nag you back invariably comes home somewhere behind the winner, today's punters, like those of old, still trying to pick something to beat the best horses!

Many other factors have affected the humbler of the bookies. Betting patterns have changed, the punters now concentrating on races they can actually see, which means there's considerably more single betting, which is less profitable to the bookie than the old doubles and trebles. The Lottery, too, has meant another dip in business, there being only a certain pool of money available for gambling, a cut of that now going in the direction of the big Wednesday and Saturday event which can make you a million or lose you a quid. Some bookmakers did counter with their own numbers system betting, but it entails big liabilities which the small man can't meet. And if the small man dares to open up too near one of the big chain shops, he's liable to be faced with an opposition that lays on all sorts of gimmicks to pull the customers away from his shop.

Fresh paint, carpets, computers, satellite information, those nice girls in the smart suits, Cola, crisps, environmental regulations, manager of the year contests! Little wonder you don't see the likes of Harry the Horse, Good Time Charley, the Lemon Drop Kid and all their mates around any more.

Nor guys who can pull fistfuls of £100 notes from their pocket and take on the Royal Bank.

AXED FOR THE POPE

The greatest and most significant news stories of the day so often affect people in different ways. There is no better example of this than the reaction to what was to be the great Glasgow story of 1982, in fact one of the greatest and most significant stories of that decade. It is the story of an event which would evoke all forms of reaction, raging from sheer delight bordering on dimensions of delirium, to one of utter indifference. To some it was to induce a state of anguish approaching near apoplexy, and perhaps in a few cases the response would be the full-blown apoplectic condition itself. The Pope can have that effect on people. And that effect was to be put to the full spectrum of reactions right from the very first announcement in the first few weeks of that year, confirming that, in fact, there was to be a papal visit to Britain and it was to include Scotland.

Being destined for a city where the most common graffiti refers to either UDA or IRA, 1690 or FTP, none of which means 'welcome, brother' let alone 'have a nice day', it was obvious from the first breaking of the news that this would be no ordinary visit; a visit which might be faced with all possibilities, particularly if one were to listen to some of the things overheard at certain soccer games where nothing seems to irritate referees and agitate fans more than the sign of the cross. And here was the very man whose right hand appears to be in perpetual motion with that sign coming to bless his faithful and, being the good Christian he is, to offer his blessings to the unfaithful.

It didn't take long for the fury to erupt from all the predictable quarters when the possibility of such a visit was first aired early in the previous year, 1981. The Orange Order let it be known they were firmly opposed to any such plans and argued that the very prospect of the man from Rome coming here was – 'unconstitutional'. At one of the major Orange walks in the July marching season of 1981, David Bryce, the Grand Secretary of the Scottish Orange Order, referred to the recent attempt on the Pope's life (he was wounded by a gunman in Rome) and coupled it to the trouble liable to be caused in Scotland. 'If he cannot be protected within the walls of the Vatican, the most Roman Catholic place in the world, then there is no chance of adequate protection being provided in Scotland, which is overwhelmingly Protestant and where a large section of the population is hostile to the visit.'

Ulsterman David Cassells, an Evangelical church leader and friend of super-Protestant Ian Paisley, said he planned meetings with the Chief Constable of Strathclyde in order to discuss marches and plans for demonstrations. He confidently predicted that in Glasgow alone 65,000 Protestants would converge on George Square for a protest meeting on the eve of the Pope's visit to the city. His friend and fellow-Ulsterman Ian Paisley predictably welcomed the protest plans, his feelings about whoever was Pope being well remembered when, on the death of a papal predecessor, and condolences sent to Rome by Belfast City Council, he had declared to the 'hallelujahs' and 'amens' of his supporters at a protest meeting that, 'the Romish man of sin is now in hell'.

Another super-Protestant, Pastor Jack Glass, leader of his own Zion Sovereign Grace Evangelical Baptist Church, a man with some considerable fire and zeal in his true-blue beliefs and, if you want, a sort of Glasgow version of the Revd Ian Paisley, without the stentorian voice that is, would obviously have agreed with such sentiments judging by his reactions. Among them was the issuing of a document titled 'Eighteen Reasons Against the Papal Visit'. In it he was to declare that the Pope, being a controversial figure, was therefore 'a troublemaker'.

'We ban other troublemakers from this country, then why not the Pope?' he was to ask, going on to give the stern predication that, 'The riots of Toxteth could be like a picnic compared to the resentment and riots the papal visit could cause. If this self-styled champion of peace has any concern for the tranquillity of Britain, he will stay at home, but perhaps he wants to cause trouble in this Protestant country . . . The polarising Pope should stay away.'

All totally predictable stuff from Pastor Jack who, over the years, has become established as one of that wide and varied spectrum of human beings who are part of the colourful kaleidoscope of the Glasgow scene. In other words, one of our very own 'characters'. Pastor Glass is a born-again, again and again Christian from the East End of the city who, he has confessed, was totally converted to Christ at the age of 11 in a Salvation Army hall. The effect that conversion had on him, he was to tell a journalist colleague of mine, was that 'immediately my heart was strangely warmed'.

As a protester, few have protested more. Pastor Jack has voiced his objections against pornography, against abortion, the Archbishop of Canterbury, the Moonies, the Catholic Church and against the IRA, among others. And in his protesting peregrinations he's been there to shout and denounce in such places as Dublin, Geneva, Rome and, of course, Glasgow. Apart from labelling the Pope as a 'troublemaker', the Pastor has called him many other things. When he stood as a candidate for the House of Commons in the Glasgow Hillhead by-election, just four months before the Pope was due in the city, he even managed to include the head of the Church in Rome in his election address, saying: 'The Pope parades as a figure of fun, a sort of Buck Rogers sporting a tea cosy ... a Santa Clausian figure embracing little children for the sake of the media.' Which, of course, immediately wiped out the possibility of any remaining Catholic vote from those few who, for some strange reason, had never heard of him before.

So there he was, months before he was even due here, being labelled as 'polarising Pope ... Romish man of sin ... troublemaker'. There was certainly no pretence of humbug about this collection of gut reaction.

But then, that was their way; lots of wind, lots of huff and puff, and at the appropriate time the venting of their feelings by some form of visual demonstration. All in the spirit of what a good democratic society should be. But it was the ones who weren't saying, who weren't sermonising, and who would not be shouting on the days before and during the visit who were to be of more concern to the police and others committed not only to the safety of this holiest of visitors, but for all those connected and taking part in the visit. And it was to them that Special Branch officers were to pay the kind of attention reserved for such groupings. Meanwhile, the plans for the visit of the *capo di tutti capi* of the Roman Catholic Church, their official godfather, as it were, went ahead.

Whatever feelings one might have for such a leader, Pope John Paul II, Karol Wojtyla from Poland, is an impressive man in many ways. He was a humble factory worker nicknamed Lolek – Polish for Chuck or Charlie – before turning to the priesthood, which perhaps more than anything accounts for the down-to-earth pragmatism he has never lost, with a lifestyle which sees him when off duty in the evening unfastening his clerical collar and relaxing in informal clothes like any other working man, and enjoying a personal chat with friends or guests for dinner. The first Polish Pope and the first non-Italian in nearly half a millennium, he is now one of the longest-serving of the 263 Popes in history, and certainly the most travelled, having clocked up something like 700,000 miles, which the zestful will tell you is 2.8 times the distance between the earth and moon. The sardonic will observe that in the process he must have collected quite a pile of AirMiles. His theological teachings are impressive, the bound volumes of them covering ten feet of shelf space, and they include 13 encyclicals, 45 apostolic letters and constitutions, 14 official epistles, nine exhortations and more than 600 addresses or speeches on formal occasions, all of which makes some ask how he gets the time for all those trips abroad.

The amazing statistics surrounding him are of dimensions that would almost constitute a one-man *Guinness Book of Records*. No man in history has spoken personally to such multitudes, to which he has delivered more than 3,000 homilies, his 877 general audiences in Rome having been attended by nearly 14,000,000 people, his group and private audiences averaging five per working day. He has canonised 280 new saints and beatified 798 brave, pious and holy men and women as candidates for future sainthood, has held 12 synods, created 159 new cardinals and consecrated 2,650 bishops.

The invitation to visit the UK from the bishops of England and Wales, as well as Scotland, had been extended just over a year before his arrival and as soon as it was confirmed he would be coming to Scotland, the Catholic Church set about the first moves in the organisation of a papal visit. Such events don't come simple, they certainly don't come cheap. His visit to Australia, for instance, was to cost around £1,000,000 . . . a day. Part of that was paid by the Australian Government, the rest funded by the Church. In Scotland it would be entirely funded by the Church and whilst not in the financial dimensions of the Australian tour – longer distances to travel while down under and the journey there and back bumping up their costs – it would still be in the region of £1,000,000 for his proposed three-day presence in Scotland.

The invite established, a Scottish bishops' conference confirmed that

Bishop Thomson, the Bishop of Motherwell and in charge of fiscal affairs, was given the responsibility of setting up a working committee whose remit would be to assume the full responsibility for the organisation of a proposed three-day visit by the Pope to Scotland. Father Dan Hart – later to become a Monsignor – who had been the deputy director of post-graduate courses at Notre Dame, the Catholic college at Bearsden, was appointed by Bishop Thomson to take charge of what was to be the biggest project of his ecclesiastical life. He left his post in the April of that year and set about his first duties in preparation for the visit scheduled to take place in just over a year's time.

Planning headquarters were set up in offices at the Presbytery of St Joseph's in North Woodside Road – the site of Scotland's first Jesuit church – and a full-time secretary was appointed. Merely as an aside, it should be pointed out that by a remarkable coincidence this same small stretch of road in the West End of the city figures prominently elsewhere in this book: a mission hall there saw the beginning of the world's first ever youth movement, the Boys' Brigade, and also nearby was the first factory of confectionery manufacturers R.S. McColl, founded by brothers Tom and Bob McColl.

When the newly appointed secretary turned up on a Monday morning the following month to start work on her new post on the project, the first question she was to ask was, 'Do I have a job?' Not an unreasonable query to make as that weekend there had been the sensational news of the assassination attempt on the Pope by a crazed Turk who had shot and wounded him amidst the thousands of pilgrims attending mass in St Peter's Square. With his condition uncertain for a few days, it did, in fact, seem that the visit could either be postponed or cancelled. But the secretary did get an immediate answer to her question. Yes, there was a job. And yes, they will begin and continue to prepare for May 1982 – the proposed date of the visit.

The spirit and the will were there and the great day would eventuate and, in fact, virtually within days it was revealed that the Pope would make a complete recovery and that the visit would go on. Overjoyed, Father Hart hung out a papal flag in celebration of the news from their North Woodside Road office HQ. It was stolen that very night!

Papal visit committees were formed, whose varied responsibilities would be to cater for every exigency of the visit. There was one to cater for youth participation; another for the handicapped. One for health, to ensure that water, toilet and other facilities would be catered for at the main sites. Another for inter-church participation. One to arrange the selection and appearance of the choirs. Name a situation and they had a committee which would have that function as their remit, whether that be to create or cater, organise or originate, facilitate or formulate – all on the simple basis of . . . just do it. But being as neither he nor any of the others had ever done anything like it before, Father Hart was to initially seek out some of those who had.

Some years previously, the Pope had visited Ireland so his first call was to Dublin where he met the team who had organised the visit there and they passed on their experiences. That was a great start for him, bearing in mind that the Pope's Irish visit had been to a country where there was universal empathy for the occasion, which did help. Thereafter he headed to Rome where he was to be given more guidance, this time by one of the Pope's principal background advisers at the time, the American Archbishop Paul Marcinkus.

'The advice in Ireland helped me cut lots of corners,' recalls Monsignor Hart. 'They advised me not to attend all the meetings of committees we had set up as I would get too involved and they would be waiting and relying on me to make decisions for them. So I just let them get on with it . . . and that's precisely what they did.'

The American prelate Marcinkus, in a series of meetings in Rome and on visits to Scotland, was to help with some down-to-earth guidance on just what kind of reception a man such as Pope John Paul II would appreciate. 'Concentrate on the ordinary people,' he was to say, 'and don't put any emphasis on who should get preference to meet him, whether it be the head of this or the head of that.'

'He was to apply that philosophy to everything we discussed about the visit,' said Hart. 'Like the choice of pipe band. There were suggestions that the world champions be invited to play or one of the other more famous bands we have, but Archbishop Marcinkus simply asked who we normally had playing for visitors and I told him it was the St Francis Pipe Band from the Gorbals. "Good," he said. "Get them." And that's just what we did.'

A draft programme was then drawn up for the three days the Pontiff was to spend in Scotland, the main guidelines of it being that he should visit both the west and east of the country, and that somewhere a site would have to be chosen where he would celebrate a huge outdoor mass. It would have to be a site capable of coping with something in excess of a quarter of a million people, which would be one of the biggest crowds ever to be assembled in Scotland at one time. A site which would have easy road access, where services such as water and power would be easily available and would not interrupt in any way the flow of normal life in any of the major cities. That latter point was considered to be an essential one by the executive committee, it being made a point that the papal visit was in no way to be an imposition on the non-Catholic part of the population.

Because of that anticipated huge crowd for the special mass, the main event of the visit, it ruled out any of the major soccer grounds, none of them being big enough for the numbers – one of them obviously being ruled out for reasons other than the numbers! Ingliston Showground was considered and would have been suitable but as a majority of the Roman Catholic population lived in the West of Scotland, a site there was preferred. Strathclyde Park came into contention, but the police weren't keen, the easy getaway access to the motorway and other factors giving their security specialists some concern. There were no problems in that direction when Bellahouston Park was suggested and the district council was to give it their immediate and unquestioning approval, no one even hinting that might have something to do with the fact the Lord Provost was one Michael Kelly, a leading light in Celtic Football Club and one of the city's high-profile Roman Catholics.

Then, with just over a month to go prior to the visit, there was the most unexpected of news – news that to describe as being of bombshell proportions was to be more literal than metaphorical. For, to the surprise, shock and dismay of the entire country, the UK found itself in the rarest of confrontations with another nation. Britain's furthest-flung colony, a group of godforsaken islands in the Southern Atlantic had been invaded by Argentina. We called them the Falklands, they called them the Malvinas. We called them British and said they were ours, they called them Argentinian and claimed they were theirs, and to make that latter point in the boldest fashion they could, they had taken them over, capturing in the process the colony's entire population, not all that much of a feat considering you could fit every one of the islanders at the one time into any decent-sized Glasgow cinema.

So, Britain was at war. And at war with a Catholic country –

virtually on the eve of the arrival for a tour by that Church's supreme leader, the Pope. The dubiety of his visit was immediate as the conflict took more sinister turns, a huge armada of our ships, planes, weapons and men known as the Task Force being readied and then setting sail for the other side of the world to do battle for the recovery of the islands and the restoration of Britain's dented pride. Whatever, it was no time for papal visits, the Vatican being fully aware of that, the Pope declaring that his proposed tour could only take place in an atmosphere of peace. But the closer the Task Force approached those distant islands, there was less sign of that. The Exocet missiles were by now on the loose; both sides' jet warplanes were hunting each other down; and there was the sinking of the Argentine's prize battle-cruiser, the *Belgrano*, with considerable loss of life, followed by that of the Royal Navy's HMS *Sheffield*. Nothing seemed more distant than that atmosphere of peace.

Britain's two most senior Catholic churchmen of the day agreed they should hurry to Rome in order to persuade His Holiness that, despite the war, he should continue with his tour. They were Cardinal Basil Hume, whom the BBC usually – and wrongly – described as Britain's number one Catholic, whereas in fact he was simply the head of the English and Welsh hierarchy, and Cardinal Gordon Gray, whose diocese was St Andrews and Edinburgh, the leader of the Scottish hierarchy and the world's youngest archbishop when appointed in 1951 at the age of 40. They were to spend four hours with the Pope on the evening they arrived, pleading for the continuance of the visit. Alas, on their return to London, they were to make the official announcement that the trip would not now be going ahead. It was now May, just 17 days prior to his scheduled arrival in England.

No insurance had been taken out on a cancellation, but that had all been carefully calculated by the tour organisers who had anticipated everything being paid up front. Therefore, with no loss situation likely, insurance wasn't necessary. At the point when word was received that the visit was off, some £600,000 had already been spent in the organisation of the Scottish end of the visit. But it had all been matched by money coming in. And in the hope that it might still eventuate, collections continued, to ensure the avoidance of any extra burden on central Church funds. One Glasgow parish had already paid £4,000-plus of its £6,000. The only nervous ones were those businesses who had made big orders for the hoard of souvenirs, bricà-brac and other gewgaws such as engraved pens, busts, plates, plaques, paperweights, silver spoons and the like. One Glasgow shopkeeper bemoaned the fact he had ordered more than £1,000 worth of such souvenirs. At least he had the consolation of being surrounded by mementoes of the big occasion that might have been.

But to the vast majority it was the loss of the presence of their Pope that was of much more importance than any loss of revenue. There was, naturally, some quite profound disappointment at the news, it being a sharp reminder to all denominations of the nation of just how seriously this war so many considered needless was being taken. Even two senior men in the Church of Scotland – one being the Moderator-elect, Professor John McIntyre, the man due to meet the Pope on behalf of the Kirk – were to publicly express their disappointment at the cancellation news.

And yet, despite the gravity of the situation, so many other events in life were going on as though there were no such things as the *Belgrano*, HMS *Sheffield* and the Task Force, or that the most important man in the Catholic Church would now, it seemed, not be coming to Britain. That very week the Pope had made his announcement, there was the news that irrespective of what might be happening in those southern oceans, we would still be going to soccer's World Cup. Well, as everyone agreed and the maxim said, things like that were more important than life or death. As always, there was plenty of other soccer news to take one's mind off more serious events. John Greig, the Rangers manager, had stated that any talk of a Sunderland player joining his team was 'totally unfounded'. The player had already been given two chances to sign for the Glasgow club and, as Greig said, 'That is more than most people get . . . and perhaps one more than he should have got.' The player's name, incidentally, was Ally McCoist.

Celtic under Billy McNeill won the Premier title for the fourth time in six years, and Aberdeen, bossed by Alex Ferguson and with just one defeat in 24 matches, were to beat Rangers 4–1 (after extra time) to win the Scottish Cup. And for those who either appreciate or else just wish to be reminded of such details, the Aberdeen scorers were McLeish, McGhee, Strachan and Cooper, McDonald putting his name to the Rangers goal.

A few days after the return of Cardinals Gray and Hume, bearing the disappointing news, two more senior churchmen, the then Archbishops Derek Worlock from Liverpool and Thomas Winning from Glasgow, headed for Rome to make one final plea for the visit to go ahead. It wasn't merely because they were available at the time that these two names were chosen. As one Monsignor put it: 'The cardinals were very nice men, but perhaps a bit too polite. On the other hand, the Archbishops Worlock and Winning were very different people . . . a couple of warriors and they would really lay it on the line.'

Winning was also an old Rome hand, having spent almost 12 years there as a brilliant student studying for a degree in canon (church) law and going on to be made a Doctor and Advocate of the Sacred Roman Rota, that latter achievement having given him a valuable insight into the workings of the Vatican. In other words, he knew the right doors to knock, the ones not to knock, such politics in the Vatican being every bit as essential as those necessary to gain access to the real corridors of power in any of the world's major multinational companies. What's more, both he and Worlock had been personal friends of the Pope since before his elevation to being, as it were, the chairman of the board.

The departure of the two archbishops boosted the enthusiasm of the organisers in Scotland, and all those who continued with the last-minute preparations for a likely visit. Among those were the printing of some 200,000 souvenir booklets of the visit (selling price £2) and finalising the arrangements at Bellahouston Park and Murrayfield, the two major visit centres.

Whatever way they put it, the line Winning and Worlock gave the Pope seemed to be showing some results, according to the latest word from them in Rome. The first reaction from the man in the Vatican was to order the Church leaders from both Argentina and Britain to meet him urgently in Rome and by 20 May the word was that the visit was now 'teetering on the brink'. Which at least was one stage better than the previous word, that it had been washed right over the brink.

There was now just over a week to go before the original scheduled date of his arrival in the UK and while the visit prospects were still see-sawing, there was to be no teetering about the prospect of a major conflict in the South Atlantic, for this was now a reality, it having escalated into full-scale war. The Royal Marines had gone ashore on the Falklands and the rest of the armada was readying to land. At the same time five more Royal Navy ships were damaged in action and 17 Argentinian fighter jets destroyed.

Nevertheless, the two archbishops who had gone to Rome persisted with their pleas and eventually, on Sunday, 23 May – just four days before the Pope was due to arrive in London for the start of his British tour – the Catholic Church's press officer in Scotland, Father (later to be Monsignor) Tom Connelly, was to reveal that it was almost certain he would be coming. He had heard from the two archbishops that no further meeting of the bishops was planned in Rome, that fact being a virtual confirmation the visit would be going ahead. Their assumption had been no mere speculation, the Vatican confirming two days later that the visit would be going ahead according to the last plan drafted for the tour.

The plans had already undergone more changes than a Hollywood script. In fact, they were now working on the 42nd drafted schedule of the itinerary, but this was make-your-mind-up time as eager security officials studied the latest plan and made the necessary alterations for the extensive precautions they had already made to ensure the Pope's safety while he was in Britain.

The fact that he really was coming was to create something of a panic at Father Connelly's press office in Glasgow. It was a new role for the man whose work with the Church had been mainly that of a parish priest, although he had assisted in the preparation of religious programmes for radio and TV. In the army, when asked who can play a musical instrument the first two recruits to answer get the job of hauling a piano up two flights of stairs. The parallel wasn't exactly the same with Father Connelly, but the job he had just been landed with was like manhandling that piano up those stairs – on his own. It was the kind of assignment that would have daunted even the most seasoned of pressmen. To help him cope, however, they enlisted on detachment from the Sunday newspaper on which he worked Hugh Farmer, one of Scotland's best-known and most experienced tabloid journalists, celebrated over and above his impressive list of Sunday scoops, that is, for being the newspaperman who made the news on his own accord by being on the receiving end of that much publicised whack when trying to interview comedian Billy Connolly. But that's another story.

There were to be no such dangers in Farmer's temporary role at the papal visit press office, only frustration and the panic that had set in. This had come about when it was discovered that with the Pope really coming and his arrival in the UK virtually just hours away, not one press accreditation pass had been issued in Scotland. Without these passes no newspaper, radio or TV people would get anywhere near the papal party. The problem had arisen through the insistence of the Metropolitan Police in London that they should be the ones to handle their distribution. This was not only an affront to the Glasgow end of the organisation, but also not the best of security arrangements. It meant that the men at the Met, through lack of familiarity, wouldn't have known one Scottish journalist from another and without recognising the Macs from the hacks, anyone could slip through the security net. Something had to be done, and quickly.

Farmer, together with a senior police officer from Glasgow, headed south on the first available flight to Scotland Yard to collect the passes. At the Met HQ, however, they were astonished to learn that the vital passes weren't there: they had gone to the papal office in London.

'And there I got the shock of my life,' says Farmer, 'to discover all the passes lying in a shoebox in one of the offices. So, as I was the one responsible for distributing them, I just lifted the lot. And to this day that office doesn't know how those passes found their way to Scotland.'

The good news that they could now collect their passes then went out from The Chapel to many of the Glasgow media. The Chapel! A whole range of people, from nuns to clerics to news bosses, were told during these hectic days that that's where Farmer and Connelly would be to meet press contacts, and thought little more about it. The Chapel, in fact, was the ad hoc codename given to the nearest pub in Queen Street from the Catholic press office and where the pair were to regularly conduct their press briefings. 'Well, we thought the name of our established meeting place with the journalists should be given a bit more dignity,' explains Farmer on his innovative and effective variation of journalistic licence.

Police chiefs were more than aware that the man they would be protecting was, apart from the President of the United States, the most high-profile target in the world. Just two weeks previously while visiting the Portuguese pilgrimage centre at Fatima, a rebel Spanish priest had leapt at him with a bayonet. A Portuguese security official was badly slashed while protecting the Pope from his attacker. And the previous year the Pope had been lucky to survive that even more serious assassination attempt in the heart of his own St Peter's Square in Rome after the frantic Turk had opened fire on him with a revolver. Which was why a medical professor, two consultant doctors, a nursing sister and several pints of the Pope's blood type would be stationed just a few yards from the papal dais in Bellahouston Park and at Murrayfield. And so that he could be tended within seconds, accompanying the medical team there would also be an intensive care ambulance equipped for almost any health emergency should he become ill or be injured. They were confident nothing sinister would occur during his stay in Glasgow and Edinburgh. Nevertheless, they were determined to take no chances.

Scottish security chiefs had already made their initial plans. Buildings in and around any of the places the Pope would be visiting or staying were all checked out and searched. For weeks specially trained officers had been studying photographs of all known extremists, which obviously included a variety of Protestant hard-liners. They had studied their faces so long and so often they were indelibly printed on the mind of each officer. At the same time they were well aware of the fact that the most dangerous attacker would be the one whose face they didn't know and of whom there were no available photographs.

The Scotland Yard Commissioner at the time, the former Glasgow Chief Constable Sir David McNee, whose statutory duty was to protect visiting heads of state, the Pope being one, had formed a hand-picked squad of armed Special Branch detectives who would accompany the Pope throughout the tour. The Pope, of course, would also be accompanied by his own squad of protection men from Rome and, although normally armed, they would be required to hand in their guns on arrival in the UK, our rule being that if there is ever any shooting during such a visit to Britain, the shots will be fired by British officers.

One of the main figures on his protection squad would be the man who during this period never let the Pope out of his sight, and who was to accompany him everywhere in the '80s. He was Archbishop Paul Marcinkus who, it seemed, was as much a mythological figure as he was a theological one. True, he really was a Roman Catholic bishop, but it was also true they nicknamed him the Pope's Gorilla, that sobriquet being not so much for his looks as his dimensions. As colourful and controversial characters go in and around the Vatican, few have equalled the near-legendary status of this man.

Paul Casimir Marcinkus was born in 1922 in the tough Chicago suburb of Cicero, one of five children of an immigrant Lithuanian family whose dad had earned his living working as a window cleaner. The young Marcinkus's childhood years were spent in a Chicago that was torn with prohibition gang wars and where the ruling mobster was a man called Al Capone. The suburb of Cicero was one of the toughest of America's urban concrete jungles, the kind of place where survival came with a don't-mess-with-me attitude and for which the young Marcinkus was equipped and had the appropriate statistics, being six feet four inches and weighing in at around 16 stone. He had been an above-average pupil at St Anthony's Roman Catholic Grammar School, was sports mad and going on to college was to be one of their stars on the football field – American football, that is. Then he was to more than surprise classmates and friends when he opted to study for the priesthood, being ordained by the time he was 25 and, three years later, leaving Chicago for Rome in order to study canon law.

Officials in the Church's secretariat – the Vatican government – were quick to spot Marcinkus's managerial talents and he was given a temporary position in the ruling body's administration, something along the lines of being a junior civil servant. His American know-how, the confident personality and, of course, that striking physical presence, so impressed his superiors he was given a permanent position in the governing body.

After that he quickly rose through the ranks, serving as a Vatican diplomat abroad, and demonstrating that when it came to managerial and administrative prowess he had few equals. He was demonstrably the kind of man who would have made it to the main executive floor of any major American company, and with so many aspects of the Vatican just like one of these giant corporations, Marcinkus easily fitted into the top slot. He was to become the chairman of the IOR, the Vatican bank, and pro-president, or mayor, of the Vatican itself, and when they realised that early tours of the Pope had been hopelessly organised, it was Marcinkus to whom they turned to put things right.

It was to be in that capacity as boss organiser of papal visits that Marcinkus was to become the unofficial personal bodyguard to the Pope, his competence at that being put to the test when he stopped a berserk Bolivian in his tracks as he lunged with a knife at Pope Paul VI. As arrangements progressed for the UK tour, Marcinkus was to make a special trip to Britain to check on the police security arrangements, coming to Glasgow to meet with Father Dan Hart, the pair becoming firm friends in the process.

It was Archbishop Marcinkus, incidentally, who, when he bossed the Vatican bank, and as such was responsible for vital decisions in the city state's finances, one of God's bankers as it were, coined the memorable maxim, 'You can't run the Church on hail Marys'.

The mighty Marcinkus might also have said that neither can you run a Pope's tour on catechisms. For there's no business quite like the papal tour business. Putting a Pope show on the road is a big-bucks industry and with costs making the British tour a multi-million-pound project, it takes the calibre of top-flight professional moneymen to be involved somewhere along the papal progress.

While the holy route might not quite be a Hollywood production, it is one of massive proportions and requires the marketing techniques that ensure capitalising on the show and reaping as much from it as possible to cover the huge production costs in touring. Such overheads are now so high, even the top rock concerts with high-price tickets rarely make profits from tours, relying on them as promotion for the sale of tapes and discs.

Chief organiser Father Dan Hart was made fully aware of these huge on-costs right from the moment he began his 18-month job in preparing for the visit. Once it was decided that Bellahouston Park should be the location for the mammoth mass, a specialist architect was employed to create a design for the conversion of the 175-acre park as it was into a venue capable of being a safe and suitable site, adhering to all the environmental regulations for what would be the biggest crowd ever assembled in the one place at the one time in Scotland. A site which would ensure the masses would have adequate viewing locations, where specially constructed corrals would guarantee crowd control and safety, where there would be full communication facilities, with the required power and water, with the requisite marquees, a mammoth dais, and finally landscaped to make it appear it had always been like that; and then, when it was all over, that could be returned to the way it had always looked.

The plan drawn up and approved, the conversion work was then put out to tender, a variety of big construction firms lining up for the valuable £1-million project, the contract award going to one of Britain's best-known builders, Wimpey.

'Right away I was confronted with the enormity of it all,' remembers Father Hart. 'Wimpey had just started on the project when one of their engineers came to see me with the unexpected news that they would need to construct a reservoir for the huge amount of water that would be required, the existing pipes to the park being insufficient. And the news was that such a reservoir would cost around £100,000. But it was also put to me by the man that there might be the possibility of finding fresh water on the site. His [the engineer's] past experience had been that there would be a 20–1 chance of locating water if we drilled for it. And to do that would cost around £5,000 as opposed to the £100,000 reservoir. So he asked me what I thought and I said, "Go for it." It was a gamble but it was to pay off for they were to find a bountiful supply, more than enough for all the catering, washing and toilet facilities.'

It was at about the same time they were making assessments on the need for the extra water supply that another sector of the park conversion work was to throw up a challenge. Only this one wasn't to find such a simple solution as the water, at least not without it becoming the source of what was perhaps the biggest controversy of the visit of the Pope and that spectacular mass being planned for the huge crowd anticipated at Bellahouston Park. This time the opposition wasn't from any irate Orangemen, Wee Frees, varied arch-Protestants or other religionists with their objections to the coming of the man from Rome. For this protest group who were exercising the loudest of objections were lovers of trees. And they were the way only tree-lovers can be when anyone starts sharpening an axe: frenetic is one way of putting it.

The fury they were generating all began when it was revealed in a routine and fairly insignificant news story that among the varied items of preparation work going on in the park, some 200 trees would be affected. Or, to put it more brutally, many of them would have to go. And the remainder would have to be severely lopped back in order that the expected masses would not have their view of the great Church figure interrupted by the branches of trees in the full bloom of spring.

The commotion couldn't have been worse had they announced they were going to institute fox-hunting in the park. As soon as the details were released in that day's papers about what the axeman proposed to do, the switchboard at George Square was jammed with calls from irate ratepayers protesting at the plan. 'We'll chain ourselves to the threatened trees,' they vowed. 'There'll be demonstrations,' said others.

'But the trees will not be removed forever,' replied the tour organisers, giving the assurance that each tree would be put into a nursery where it would continue to grow throughout the spring and summer and then, when the park was being reconstituted, they would be replanted. And, already aware of the minefield they had unexpectedly found themselves in, they went on to stress that should any of the trees die off in the process, new ones would be planted.

Good God! Should any of the trees die off! The mere mention of the likelihood of such a catastrophic eventuality elevated the tree-lovers' tantrums to a new pitch. They were by now as much splenetic as they had been frenetic. There was to be no placating them, not even those assurances that when the visit was all over and the Pope was back in Rome the park would be restored to the way it had always looked with the same number of trees all in the same place they had been before.

No one paid the slightest attention to all the pledges, or if they did they weren't saying so, and the furore grew. Others pitched in with objections about the length of time it was now known that the park would have to be closed prior to the visit. Not good enough, said District Councillor Arthur Green, who was outraged when he heard that almost half the park would be closed for 11 weeks prior to the visit, including the sports centre being shut down for two weeks so that it could be used as a police operations centre. He was so upset at this, he said, that if possible he would take out a court order to prevent the lengthy closure.

Meanwhile, the trees controversy raged on, the protests escalating as more and more tree-lovers, or at least people who said they were tree-lovers, getting more and more upset at what they considered would be the despoliation of the woodlands in Bellahouston. 'Letters to the editor' pages had never known anything like it for years.

The tree-lovers wrote countless missives to their papers condemning those who wanted the trees removed as being 'undoubtedly shameful, sinful and bad people' and that it was 'a most destructive thing to do to God's creation', their opponents answering them for their 'sloppy sentiment and crocodile tears', while one of the indifferent, noting the damage in the park after a gale around that time, was to ask, 'Is this divine intervention?'

It was now early March and almost any day now the trees due for removal, a mixture of beech and sycamore, would start the first processes of awakening from their winter slumber, the sap flowing again and the first signs of tiny leaf buds beginning to appear along branches. They would have to be dug out before that actually happened, or else they would die in the process of transplanting, which meant they had to go – and soon. Experts had already warned that unless the trees were treated with the utmost care and attention during the sensitive uprooting operation, it would not be surprising if the success rate would be less than 90 per cent, said one leading arborialist. Which made those tree-lovers more loving and caring than ever, and by now all sorts, many of whom couldn't have told you a beech from a birch, were loudly proclaiming their arborial affection.

Urgent talks were held between officials and the District Council, city councillors and even Archbishop Winning. At one stage there seemed a possibility of the removal application being withdrawn, then it was revealed that not so many trees would have to go, perhaps around 36. Well, at least that sounded much better than 200. And there was yet another underlined assurance that their removal would merely be a temporary measure.

Nevertheless, even more tree lovers were coming out of the woods. They were to be there for the most important day of all, the sitting of the special committee of Glasgow District Council who had been nominated to decide on the removal application. Joining them in their protest at the City Chambers was the great man of protest himself, Pastor Jack Glass, more hot than ever under his dog collar and with a new-found cause about which to raise his objections. He had already labelled the plan for the trees as being 'Vatican vandalism', promising to mount guards on the threatened wood. Then together with some followers he was to air his feelings at the vital decision meeting.

'This is another carve-up between the Roman Catholic Church and the lackeys here in the council,' he shouted from the back of the committee room. Labour group leader Jean McFadden immediately jumped to her feet to tell the pastor that it was only councillors and officials who were allowed to speak at committee meetings and threatened to have him and the other protesters removed.

'You don't believe in democracy,' he shouted back as he and his supporters shuffled from the committee room. That was followed by the distinct sounds of a scuffle outside in the corridor as Pastor Jack, while being restrained by council officials, tried to return with some leaflets in his hand, but was only able to toss them into the room. The leaflets and the shouts were to make little impression on the committee, however, who by eight votes to three approved the motion for the removal of the 36 designated trees.

There had been by now so much hot air released by those who, it appeared, really couldn't see the trees for the woods, any religious objections to the forthcoming visit of the holy personage were all but forgotten. But with the council having given the plan their approval, and the Glasgow Tree Lovers Society – the ones who really *were* tree lovers – saying they were now convinced the Parks Department really would restore everything as it was, the protests fizzled out to the inevitable.

But at projected £400 per tree removal costs, adding anything between £10,000 and £40,000 to the papal visit budget depending on the number removed, and having given them the biggest kerfuffle of the show, one can but imagine what might have been heard in some confessionals! Maybe the prayers and invocations helped – and those who offered them were certainly convinced of that! – for at the end of the day only 12 mature trees, a mixture of beech and whitebeam, were eventually removed. This was done with all the care and skill of a major surgical operation to avoid root damage and they spent the summer in the park's nursery, given all the care and attention of recuperating transplant patients. When they were later replanted in their original site, it was to prove too much for only two of them, and these were replaced by younger trees. And Bellahouston Park once more looked just as it always had.

With so much money going out, the need for revenue to be flowing in was of paramount importance. The entrepreneurs were already making moves to see if there was some way in which they could cut themselves in to what promised to be a holy bonanza. It's been observed by more than one that there are few more impressive sights in the world than a Scotsman on the make. And Father Connelly was one of the first in the early stages of the preparations to be blessed with such a sight. It was on a day he had been visiting Bellahouston to see the work in progress when two men, neatly dressed and businesslike, sidled up to him and showed him a couple of objects. One was an image of the Pope, recumbent on a throne, the figure engraved on a medallion and mounted on a small marble plaque, the other a large bronze medal with the same engraving and neatly cased in a velvet-covered box, both adorned with the words that they were souvenirs of the Pope's visit to Scotland, 1982. Both were attractive mementoes, well designed and expertly turned out. 'Could we maybe do some business with these?' the men inquired. The news for them was to be, however, together with Father Connelly's apologies, that all contracts for the supervision of every description of souvenir and memento for the entire tour had already been awarded to a major company. And such was the deal that every aspect of any form of souvenir industry arising out of, during and after the tour would be completely controlled by this one company. And the company was no less than the International Management Group, one of the foremost specialists in the field of major world promotions.

IMG is the company headed by Mark McCormack, the American tycoon whose name had become coupled with the biggest of big-time events and big-time stars. And McCormack himself was no less a colourful character than the super-minder Archbishop Marcinkus and, like him, was involved in activities concerned with the Glasgow visit.

The McCormack story went back to 1955 when, after graduating from Yale Law School, he earned himself a reputation as an attorney with a keen eye for the small print in sports contracts. He teamed up not long afterwards with a young and promising golfer called Arnold Palmer, guaranteeing him personal appearances and exhibition matches in return for 25 per cent of everything Palmer earned both on and off the fairways and greens. Within two years Palmer's annual earnings had leapt from $60,000 to more than $500,000 which, even after paying that 25 per cent, left him a much richer man. Palmer was also to go on to be the US and British Open champion and one of the greatest golfers and earners of all time. It was to be the same story with a growing list of other sports and showbusiness stars who were to come under the McCormack aegis.

McCormack was the epitome of the classic American success story, the kind of guy who never takes his eye off the dollar, who can see opportunity in the blink of an eye, who doesn't know the meaning of the word problem, who talks big, acts big, and for him and his clients, makes it big. Calling the shots the way he does it, he never speaks about anything as crude as sponsorship deals, preferring instead to call them 'income opportunities'. And among the clients he has fixed income opportunities for are some of the biggest names in golf, in tennis, in classical music (Placido Domingo, José Carreras and Dame Kiri Te Kanawa) . . . and the Pope. With McCormack and his IMG company on board this papal tour and arranging all the 'income opportunities' there was certainly no room for the two Glasgow gents and their mementoes, no matter how impressive a sight these Scotsmen might have been.

As it was to turn out, all those efforts in the capitalisation of the papal visit, seeking out what the McCormack organisation termed as income opportunities, had been more than essential. Costs were to escalate considerably beyond what income sales had generated, it being discovered some six months after the event that there had been something of a shortfall in the balance. It had been anticipated that around £3,000,000 would be raised from such sources, but only half of this sum had been achieved. An IMG spokesman was to put this down to the crowds being so captivated by the 'enormity and splendour of the event' they had been reluctant to spend the time and the money at the stalls. Well, that was the nice American way of putting it. But what was a reality was the Scottish end of the tour having a £500,000 discrepancy in their anticipated budget and Archbishop Winning apologising for having to make a special appeal to congregations to raise more money to make up the discrepancy. Also to help out were the Knights of St Columba, the Catholic men's society, who spearheaded a drive to raise some of this cash by selling off unsold souvenirs at half price.

Not so happy were a group of 34 manufacturers of more than £1,000,000 worth of unsold papal scrolls, pendants, medallions and photo portraits, who wanted the Church and the IMG organisation to pay them compensation and threatened to put their claims to the Vatican if they weren't paid.

But with the big event still to take place, such fiscal matters were still over the horizon and, besides, in the light of the momentous occasion about to happen, if this were to be the worst of the afterwash, then it would be a minor detail. After all, it was only money and it would be found from somewhere, albeit with the accompaniment of the appropriate apologies. There were other matters worth considering now that the great visitor from Rome was just hours away from his historic tour, the very first Pope ever to come to Scotland. For instance, just who was this rather considerable flock of his living in this land of the Scots?

Although Catholics are a minority in Scotland, they are an identifiable, close-knit and influential minority. They are also a well-integrated minority and while it may be true that there are some areas where Catholicism might dominate, Coatbridge, Croy and Barra coming to mind, nowhere are there ghettos of Catholics.

When Robert Burns was flitting between Ayrshire, Glasgow and Edinburgh towards the end of the eighteenth century, the population of Catholics in Glasgow totalled just 50. When a census was taken in 1829 there were 25,000, and 14 years after that there were almost twice that number. Most had come from Ireland, arriving in a number of waves, due to the prevailing circumstances there, which varied between rebellions which foundered to crop harvests that failed. The biggest influx came in the mid-nineteenth century, the impoverished and starving victims of the disastrous potato famine, choosing Scotland as their new home mainly because it cost only a few pennies for a ship's steerage passage to get there, as opposed to the £4 the shippers were charging for the fare to the east coast ports of the United States. Also, should they ever be able to return to the homeland they loved most of all, it was just that little way across the water.

By 1851 the numbers of Irish-born in Scotland had risen to more than 207,000. In the year of the Pope's visit, there were varying estimates of the number of Catholics in Scotland, ranging from 700,000 to over 800,000, the figure often dependent more on enthusiasm than realism. However, a Catholic information office figure at the time put the number in Scotland at 811,540, or 14.7 per cent of the population, compared to 8.4 per cent in England and Wales, 32 per cent in Ulster and 94 per cent in Ireland. Most of the Scottish Catholic forebears came from Ireland. In Glasgow, they constitute the largest part of the varied spectrum which represents the population of the present-day city, a city that is more cosmopolitan than it has ever been, whose citizens are an agreeable amalgam with roots in a wide variety of places, ranging from Lithuania to Lombardy, the Punjab to Poland, the Gaeltacht of Ireland to our own Gaelic north, without one ingredient of which Glasgow would, undoubtedly, be an immensely poorer place.

There is the claim by some – Catholics, obviously – that the Catholics of Glasgow are under some form of threat, that they are unfairly on the receiving end of varying degrees of hostility and that bigotry is rampant. It's a view that is usually expressed by subtle attitude rather than by expressed affirmation. However, in the summer of the year leading up to the start of the new millennium, James

MacMillan, a leading Scottish composer who was to create the fanfare for the historic opening of our Scottish Parliament that year, took a much stronger stance than the normal nudges and whispers by publicly declaring at the new headquarters of the Edinburgh Festival that Scottish society was 'riddled with bigotry' and that we were an 'Ulster without the guns and bullets'. It was strong, sensational stuff and was to inspire the most profound of reactions, stimulating about as many letters to the editor as there had been about those trees. Perhaps Mr MacMillan did his fellow Catholics a favour with his outburst, clearing the air, as it were, on just how the faithful are regarded in the adopted land of most of their ancestors. Although it must also be said that at the same time it was to endorse one of the common views, that is that the problem Mr MacMillan was airing might just be confirmation of that old and rather wearied 'chip on the shoulder' allegation about Catholics.

Whatever, there was certainly an ensuing furore after his outburst, during which MacMillan was to be condemned by members of his own faith, including many leading and prominent members of the Catholic community, whose general observation seemed to be that while he might be a highly successful and talented musician, this was one score he had got completely wrong. A poll by the *Herald* newspaper on the subject was to reveal that two-thirds of those interviewed did not agree with MacMillan, the newspaper in a leader column referring to his address to the Festival as 'naïve and confused'.

Undoubtedly, bigotry does exist in Scotland. It certainly existed to a considerably worse degree in the past, intolerances being aired and exercised on both sides. In 1929 when the then *Glasgow Herald* presented a five-day series of investigative features into the immigration of the Irish into Scotland, the fear was expressed that unregulated migration could endanger 'the continued existence of Scottish nationality and civilisation'. Catholics and Protestants didn't mix, said the writer, although if it wasn't for the insistence of the Catholic Church on segregation in education and social life, the immigrants would eventually combine with the native Scot. The regulations of the Catholic Church regarding 'mixed' marriages was one of the impediments to such unity, it concluded.

Whatever view might be taken of that, the author was certainly pulling no punches. Even less in a gloomy report to the General Assembly of the Church of Scotland around the same time. It claimed that the Catholic immigrant stock 'cannot be assimilated' and absorbed into the Scottish race. 'They remain a people by themselves, segregated by reason of their race, their customs, their traditions and, above all, by their loyalty to their Church, and gradually and inevitably dividing Scotland racially, socially and ecclesiastically.' And writing in another newspaper, the convener of the committee on Church and Nation of the General Assembly was to assert that, 'wherever we turn we find the Roman Catholic Church dominated by the desire to undermine the ideals and institutions of the Scottish race . . . They are one of the potent causes of the increasingly wrong use of the Lord's Day, and in all this they are aided and abetted by the Roman Catholic priests and leaders of the Church who have set themselves to win Scotland for Rome.'

And no lesser views were considered by some Catholics. In one of their early papers, the *Glasgow Free Press*, there were regular features on the problems of mixing with the native Scot, one writer warning about the danger of such association with Protestants declaring that they could 'poison and corrupt our hearts and make us cold and indifferent about our religion and duty to God'. All of which makes it obvious why no Pope ever considered a visit to Scotland in such times.

Because they represent the largest parts of our multinational society, most bigotry in present-day Scotland is to be found in the Protestant and Catholic communities. There are Catholics who are anti-Protestant. There are Protestants who are anti-Catholic.

In the past there was widespread discrimination in the workplace – against both communities. I had my own experience of it, albeit many years ago, and one which I assume was by no means rare. The various departments of two of the newspaper firms for which I worked at the time were largely staffed – some of them entirely – with either Protestants or Catholics, the staffing being dependent on the religion of the department boss. Which didn't do much for aspiring agnostics like myself!

Despite the taunting and the flaunting of Rangers and Celtic fans when playing each other, the gross intolerances of the past have dwindled more than considerably; in most cases they have disappeared. The opposing religions still don't condone one another, but each lets the other get on with it, as it were, perhaps more due to their adherents than the actual churches themselves. Gone are the days when the General Assembly of the Church of Scotland aired such views or when the priests would preach about the dangers of intermingling with those Protestant Scots amidst their Catholic flocks. When a leader of the Scottish National Party declared in an anti-Catholic outburst nearly 20 years ago that not only would the Pope not be welcome in Scotland but that they should even turn him back at the border, the backlash was such that he had to resign.

Composer MacMillan's outburst was, in a fashion, typical of the great Protestant–Catholic divide of Glasgow and Scotland. A bit like a recurring tropical disease. For an age you neither hear nor are confronted with it and you think it has gone. Then there's an event, of sorts, and the debate is all the rage again. Often as not, it is through something or in some way connected to the greatest manifestation of that divide, the Rangers and Celtic football clubs. Their regular meetings are, of course, the ultimate paradox. Well, where else can you get around 50,000 nominal Christians in the one place at the one time – with hardly a Christian thought or expression to be heard or found among them? Where else can you witness so many minds locked in the barrack rooms of history's foibles? Where else can you watch a display of ancient attitudes, or see evidence of two tribes unable to escape their inheritance, the nightmare of history? And yet, despite the dominance of the visible and the vocal, they are not really to a man, or a woman, the way they are seen and heard. The ones who dominate tend to obscure other realities; realities that might appear to be that of the Balkans, but are not. Perhaps there are the echoes of Ulster, but not the actuality of it. There is also there another spirit, that of those who, while they may be part of all that is being manifested, are not really of it. As long as they avoid the introspection, there can be laughs with the taunts and the teasing, the barracking and the banter, and in the best of Glasgow spirit and in their true hearts, they can wish those others, whoever they are, neither harm nor evil.

MacMillan's sensational claims had followed what might have been seen as one of the most spectacular demonstrations of his views, the on-camera revelations of one of Scotland's most well-known lawyers lustily singing sectarian songs. It had been at an after-match celebration of a Rangers victory when the well-known and respected Queen's Counsel Donald Findlay, a vice-chairman of Rangers FC and regarded as the country's leading criminal defence lawyer, had been participating in what would be regarded as fairly normal practice for fans of either club in victory. And that is singing their own club songs with unbounding euphoria. Of course, such songs don't exactly contain the kind of words or sentiments heard from church choirs, men's fellowships or at children's parties. And QC Findlay was to pay dearly for his folly, resigning from his post with Rangers and some six months later having his knuckles rapped by the Faculty of Advocates who fined him £3,500 for 'professional misconduct'. The QC issued an 'unreserved apology' for his behaviour and it was interesting to note that he was also to thank the 'many hundreds' of Celtic supporters who had contacted him with their sympathies with his situation. At the same time Findlay was to fiercely contest allegations that he was a bigot, making it abundantly clear in his apology to the Faculty that he had 'never knowingly acted to the prejudice of a man or woman because of their race, colour, creed or political belief and never would'. And he was also to raise legal proceedings against a national newspaper on allegations of bigotry.

So were the MacMillan bigotry allegations accurate? Obviously, one must respect his own experiences of it, but it's difficult to conceive its widespread existence in view of the equality in the present status of both communities and the upward social mobility of Catholics. The fact that one could go through an entire lifetime in Glasgow and not suffer from bigotry doesn't mean to say that it doesn't exist.

At the same time we did have all those dire warnings and grim prognostications in years past from the men in the pulpit to both church and chapel which were never to eventuate. There may have been that considerable gulf between the social profiles of the two religions when the ranting was at its worst, but unlike so many predicted, it was not to deteriorate. According to a 1972 survey there is little meaningful difference in the social status of the two. More Catholics were obtaining university degrees than those who identified with the Church of Scotland. More than half the Catholic population now marry non-Catholics. One research shows around 50 per cent of Catholic parents even want an end to Catholic schools. Glasgow got its first Catholic Lord Provost back in 1938. During the period of the Glasgow District Council, every Lord Provost of the city was a Catholic. So then, is everything rosy in the garden between Scotland's two great religions? Of course not. But it's not as some might have it. And on the days of the Pope's visit in 1982, the events of this rather historic occasion for the city were to be ones of all-round goodwill and understanding.

If, among the prayers that were expressed on the eve of the visit, there were invocations for fine weather, someone was listening and heeding. Sweating workmen, stripped to the waist in blazing sunshine, carried out all the last-minute preparations in and around Bellahouston Park.

Had vigilant police not acted sooner, the workmen might have had an even bigger job to do. The previous night they pounced on a youth who had been preparing to burn down the special dais which had been constructed for the holy dignitary to conduct his special Glasgow mass. He was charged with 'conspiring with others' to burn down the structure.

Teams from BBC and STV spent that last night finalising the setting up of the most complex broadcast ever mounted in Scotland. It involved getting together the biggest-ever collection of outside broadcast equipment which included 41 cameras at the various sites of the visit. So big was the operation the two TV organisations had to pool their resources, borrowing equipment from BBC regions in England and Northern Ireland and from RTE Dublin. And presenting the programmes were their top-gun voices, those of Tom Fleming, David Dimbleby, the late Donnie MacLeod, together with all the papal expertise of Father Bill Anderson from the Scots College in Rome.

The 39 hours the Pope was to spend in Scotland saw him arrive at Turnhouse Airport, Edinburgh, to be greeted by Cardinal Gray, the Secretary of State for Scotland, Scottish bishops, the Lord Provost of Edinburgh and various other dignitaries. He was to greet the soil of Scotland in that hallmark fashion of his, by kneeling, after treading only a few paces from the aircraft steps, to bless with a kiss this new land he had come to visit. And that very spot where he had bestowed his papal tribute was to instantly become the most treasured souvenir of all, the hallowed sod being marked out, then solemnly cut and presented to Cardinal Gray and remaining to this day part of the lawn of the cardinal's residence in Morningside, Edinburgh.

From Turnhouse the Pope went to Murrayfield to spend an hour and a half at a special gathering of young Catholics of Scotland. And later in the evening he was to meet the Moderator of the General Assembly of the Church of Scotland, the Rt Revd John McIntyre, in the courtyard of the Assembly Hall in Edinburgh and under the gaze of history's most famous Scottish Protestant, John Knox, albeit a stern-faced statue of the man who did more than anyone to bring about the

Reformation in Scotland. One can but imagine the cogitation of the assembled reverends, knowing their ecclesiastical history as they did, on how this historic scene would have been viewed by that man looking down on them. Afterwards, Moderator McIntyre was to make his views known on the occasion, saying that if one was concerned for the unity of the Church in Scotland 'where we have a very bad record' then this had been a 'very significant event'.

The Pope's day in Glasgow began with a helicopter arrival at St Andrew's College of Education, Bearsden, and after lunch another helicopter trip, this time to a freshly landscaped and floral-bedecked Bellahouston Park, the flowerbeds beautifully sculpted in the shape of Celtic crosses. The three hours he was to spend at Bellahouston were to be the highlight occasion of the visit. The multitude who were to make up the biggest religious congregation ever assembled in Scotland had travelled from every part of the country to be there and as the Pope conducted the celebratory mass, dozens of priests stationed around the park gave communion. The priests were identified to the crowds by standing under big golf umbrellas in the Vatican gold and white colours, each adorned with the papal insignia. The story goes about the umbrellas – and it's a true one – that while a definite number of them were handed out, a totally different number were returned, their being probably the most coveted souvenir of the visit.

As well as that mass, their great leader was to tour among the crowds in the specially made Range Rover Popemobile. That particular Popemobile was to provide another story of the tour. It was one of four specially made for the British visit at around £60,000 each and paid for by the organisers. The Pope seemed to enjoy his ride in the Scottish one so much that just before his departure he was to make a comment to one of the bishops on how comfortable it had been. 'Maybe it's best we don't give his name,' said my informant. Delighted that he had been so obviously pleased with his journey in the vehicle, the bishop immediately replied to the pontiff's complimentary remark by telling him, 'Well, just have it. Take it back to Rome with you.' Which made another of the bishops take a deep gulp before whispering to his respected colleague, 'Don't you know we haven't paid for it yet, and there you are giving it away!' Nevertheless, that Popemobile was next seen in Rome. Another of these holy vehicles was to have a somewhat different destiny. It was sold to a travel firm and for years afterwards was to be seen taking tourists around the sights – in Egypt.

The promised demonstrations in Glasgow of tens of thousands of protesting Protestants were never to eventuate. The biggest demonstration, in fact, had not taken place in Scotland but in Liverpool, where there was an anti-Pope march through the city by about 2,000 in full Orange Lodge regalia, led on their four-mile trek by 40 bands. But police reported no incidents.

The Pope himself was to see some of the Liverpool demonstrators as his entourage passed through the Toxteth area of the city. Among the most vocal of these in wait for the Pope's procession had been that most recognisable of all protest figures, the Revd Ian Paisley. And when he made known his vocal dissent in the direction of the Pope, he was in turn to receive a gesture which, to him, must have been the most mortifying of experiences. For the Pope, his right hand raised in the sign of the cross, was to give him a public and papal blessing.

In Glasgow there were to be the usual brawls, of course, just as there invariably are whenever a force of Protestants and Catholics confront one another; that mostly being when their respective football teams meet. The threatened thousands who said they would demonstrate in the city were never to materialise, the biggest march, that of the Apprentice Boys of Derry together with Scottish Loyalists who were to parade from Govan to the city centre, numbered only 800 in total. There were a few brawls among the bawls and police arrested 12 at the march and around a further 50 in various incidents.

David Bryce, Grand Secretary of the Scottish Orange Order, was at pains to point out in a letter to the editor the following day that these had not, in fact, been Orange demonstrations but had been conducted by other groupings of loyalists.

The crowd at Bellahouston Park that Tuesday in June was to be by far the biggest audience seen by the Pope in Britain. At Wembley in London there had been more than 100,000; at Liverpool it was 150,000. At Bellahouston there were at least a quarter of a million, some estimates putting the huge crowd as high as 300,000. The fearful aspect of that number, however, was not to put the most militant of the protesters off, around 50 of them outside the main gates chanting anti-Christ slogans in the direction of events inside the park as they progressed towards the highlight of the whole occasion, the celebratory mass. Doubtlessly this was viewed by most as an act of impetuous indiscretion bordering on insanity more than saying something for either their conviction or their courage. However, the chance of them causing any further disruption other than merely blowing their hot air into the gentle summer breeze was more than unlikely, the two and a half score of them being surrounded by some 500 police, a senior officer warning them that if they put one foot inside the actual park itself, they would be arrested. Discretion won the day. They took the advice.

Other than that, it was to be the most memorable of occasions for the devout who had looked forward so much to welcoming the head of their Church in their own homeland. For the Church and all those who had participated in the organisation of what to them was the greatest event of their lives, it was to be all that had been planned. They had not imposed on or disrupted the nation's biggest city. There had been no anti-Catholic backlash. Not even a sign we were an Ulster without guns and bullets. And perhaps one of the most gratifying aspects to the Catholic organisers had been the overwhelming support they had received from known Church of Scotland members and others of varying faiths or with no religion, who had been determined to the utmost in making the event, particularly as it applied to Glasgow, such an outstanding success. No one was more aware of that than the chief organiser himself, Monsignor Dan Hart. 'There were so many involved who were not of our religion, whether they be police or the others helping in some way, and each and every one of them had this incredible will that everything would work . . . and it did.'

Which demonstrated more than anything that the true face of Glasgow is not what's so often seen and heard in a couple of famous soccer stadiums.

HE WAS FOR THE HIGH JUMP

Anyone who can stop a 70,000 Glasgow crowd watching a Rangers v Celtic game in order that they look at him instead has to be someone special. And that's what a tall, lanky young man from Mount Florida was when he was at the height of his athletic prowess and fame. For Alan Paterson really was someone special when it came to his particular sport. He was a high jumper, the greatest Scotland and Britain had ever known, the man who it is on record 'brought respectability to Scottish and British high jumping'. The young Glasgow man who was headline news in the immediate post-war years of the Second World War was such a star that he was put on parade alongside the greatest of news- and history-makers in that renowned hall of fame, Madame Tussaud's wax museum. And not many other Scottish sportsmen have made it there.

But, getting back to that high jump stopping a Rangers v Celtic game! Or, high jumping stopping anything! Hard to credit in the millennium years when it would appear from the rear ends of daily newspapers that there is but one sport. Although soccer has been the No. 1 sport most of this century, believe it or not there were times when it didn't dominate as a sporting attraction as it does now. And as recently as the years immediately following the Second World War you would consider yourself really fortunate if you were one of the lucky ones to get yourself a ticket for the big sports meetings held in the city. The two most prestigious of these were the Rangers Sports and the Police Sports events, which would draw capacity crowds to Ibrox and Hampden. The Rangers Sports had been a feature of the club since the early years of the century and were to be one of their most popular non-soccer attractions right up to the 1950s.

Those big Glasgow sports events were of such prominence they drew the finest athletes in the world, men and women who had been starring that season in the main arenas of the continent and America and breaking records at world and European championships. When they came to Glasgow they gave the city's contests all the flavour and appeal of a one-day Olympic Games. And, obviously, because of the calibre of stars they were, it would often as not be them who would figure in the placings. That is, until we had that world-class champion of our own, Glasgow's Alan Paterson.

It was at the Rangers Sports in early August 1947 when Paterson stopped that Rangers v Celtic game, an occurrence that only something like crowd disorder had managed to do in the past. It was a custom at the Rangers Sports that the Ibrox club and its arch-rivals would be featured in a five-a-side event as one of the side attractions of the athletics show, although, as you can imagine, whenever these two meet it tends to be no side attraction.

Their game that summer's day brought the usual big cheer from the crowd at the kick-off, but shortly afterwards there was another tremendous roar from that same crowd. But this time it wasn't cheering them on . . . it was shouting for them to stop. The players looked up puzzled and quickly appreciated what was happening, one of the Celtic men responding by stopping the game in the most effective of fashions. He simply grabbed the ball and sat on it, having realised that the crowd didn't want their football, at least not just now. For there was something else going on that they wanted to see. Something much more dramatic. It had been proceeding at one end of the park, a duel in the hot summer sun between some of the finest high jumpers in the world. But now there were just two remaining in the competition, the champion, American Bill Vessie, and the young lad from Mount Florida, still in his teens, Alan Paterson.

The bar of the jumping apparatus had gone up in stages from just below six feet, then up again, inch by inch, eliminating, as it ascended, some of the finest high jumpers in the world. When the bar had gone up to over six feet, the field quickly thinned and by the time it had got to over six and a half feet, just two remained, Vessie and Paterson.

The sight of those two men as they nervously composed themselves while they eyed the awesome height which they were now attempting to leap had the huge crowd enthralled. Never, at any track or field or any kind of sports contest held in Scotland, had a crowd been so stilled. Never had any sports meeting held here, or anywhere else in Britain, witnessed the spectacle of two men jumping at such a height. Their incredible duel in the sun had inspired the most astonishing tension, not only between the two taking part in this athletic shoot-out, but had spilled over to every part of the terracings and stands, hushed into an anticipation of absolute silence. For what they were seeing was a once-in-a-lifetime display of the highest order of athletics, and a young lad from among them was the star performer.

Silenced by the climactic tension of the occasion, there were no shouts of encouragement from the huge crowd lest it distract the concentration of the two men, the one watching as focused and engrossed on that bar as the man about to jump. Only when either one cleared the bar would there be a collective gasp and then release of their own anxiety with an almighty cheer.

The bar inched up once more, this time to 6ft 7½in or 2.2 metres. Paterson's personal best had been a sensational 6ft 6½in, having achieved that the year previously at a meeting in Antwerp, Belgium, which had made him the first Briton ever to have cleared two metres. He hadn't jumped that height since then and here he was before a capacity 72,000 home crowd faced with a bar now raised almost an inch above his record.

All other sporting activity in the huge arena had by now stopped, everyone focusing on the only event that now mattered, this incredible display of champion high jumping. Six feet seven and a half inches! Think about it, if you can. Think about getting yourself up to that incredible height. Think, too, about getting yourself down again safely. For this was in the days of jumping at its pristine purest – no freak flops, no monstrous mattresses of soft foam rubber for your welcome back to earth. And these two were up there in the stratospheric heights of their unique sport.

Paterson walked slowly up to the bar and, as was his habit, he tied a hankie to one end of the thin strip of wood, the device he, and many others, used to give them focus on just what they had to do. Vessie then approached him and they had some words together, it being revealed later the American, who had cleared this height before, was giving him some specialist advice that might help him also to do it. Different ways, different days.

There were two of the most audible gasps ever heard in any packed stadium when the two athletes finally made their bids to defy gravity at a level no one from these islands had reached before . . . but only one of them was followed by a cheer. The American made it over, but Paterson had clipped the wood with a sliver of a touch, vibrating it off its pegs. However, that didn't mean he was finished. You get three tries in such contests and on another attempt he was to make it, by the same whisper of margin as had Vessie, the bar visibly quivering in the slipstream of his passing torso, but staying in place.

The silence was over at that and the young man who was Scotland's greatest athlete of his day and had matched the American at his best got the Ibrox equivalent of the much-vaunted Hampden roar. It didn't matter that he was to be placed second in the contest by virtue of him not clearing the amazing jump at the first attempt. Alan Paterson was the crowd's winner that day and they roared for him all the more when the announcement was made that his jump had beaten all records. And what a collection they were. In that one mighty leap for Scottish mankind, Alan Paterson had broken the UK all-comers, the UK national, the Scottish all-comers and the Scottish national records.

The young man from the South Side of Glasgow had done more to put his country on the sporting map than any other single name in years.

His jumping feats before that record hurtle into unknown heights had already made him a star attraction at sports grounds throughout the country. Now he was the centre attraction for Britain at a host of championship events, ranging from the Olympics to the Empire (the original title for the Commonwealth Games) to the European championship games. He was also a centre of attraction for two other aspects of his sensational jumping career. Victoria Park, his club, was to experience one of its biggest inflows of new members, at one stage as many as 200 young hopefuls being inspired by Paterson's performances to join. At the same time, hospital casualty departments were to report a record number of lads coming to them with sprains, cuts and bruises as a result of emulating, albeit not that successfully, the man whose leaps had made him the talk of every school playground.

In an age when distance travel was severely curtailed because of the time factor in covering long journeys by ship, he nevertheless ventured to the furthest parts of the globe, displaying his talent as a world-class high jumper. And all for the pure love of being a sportsman, it still being the genuine *Chariots of Fire* days when a silver cup or shield was the only reward for the amateur competitor, the days of the shamateur still over the horizon, and of the professional much further in the distance than that.

It had been a miserable wet Saturday afternoon in June 1946, at an

241

inter-club sports meeting at Lennoxtown, that Alan Sinclair Paterson first came to the attention of the general sporting public. They had known about him, of course, in sporting circles as the man from the Victoria Park Athletic Club who was virtually impossible to beat in the high jump. The Scottish record at the time had been 6ft 0¾in, having stayed at that since 1933 when John Fraser Michie had been the first Scot to clear six feet since that height had first been jumped 29 years previously. Breaking high jump records was no weekly occurrence.

Harry Ewing, Alan's school and neighbourhood pal from Mount Florida, was with him the day he demonstrated he was destined for record heights. It was one of those horrible early spring days that you know all about if you have lived in Glasgow long enough, that kind of day that in years to come was to make fortunes for the Costas and Playas. But despite the incessant rain, Harry and Alan, two undaunted and very enthusiastic young sportsmen, made the long journey by bus and train to their field of play on the outskirts of Lennoxtown. It was an inter-club meeting, the kind of event that would normally attract only a few hundred spectators.

But that day the only spectators were the track officials. It had been too much also for some of the athletes and because the club could field only one competitor in each event, some of the athletes doubled up in other events in order to compensate for lack of numbers. High jumper Alan competed in some sprints, runner Harry contesting the high jump.

Harry remembers the day like it was yesterday. 'I was no high jumper, and certainly not on that day, for despite the weather the competition was fierce and within no time the bar was up to around six feet. And there was I running at it without spiked shoes and slipping all over the place on the wet grass and mud. It was so high on my last jump that when I jumped . . . I went right under the bar.'

The bar, in fact, had been hoisted to six feet, a rarity in such times, the Scottish record of 6ft 0¾in having stood unchallenged for 13 years. Despite the weather and the absence of a crowd, up it went again, this time to new heights, heights that Alan Paterson was to top and which had astounded officials, checking and rechecking the precise level he had reached, before confirming that, indeed, he had just performed the best-ever jump in Scotland since the '30s. He had broken the Scottish record by five-eighths of an inch. Okay, so maybe that's just a few hairsbreadths, but in the realms of this sport, just one hairsbreadth is sufficient to make you champ.

'I don't think the achievement really hit home to Alan until we returned to Glasgow on the train and there it was big news in the evening papers,' remembers his friend Harry. Paterson was just 17 years of age that day he broke the long-standing Scottish record, and as soon as the news was out, he was immediately head of the list of invites for track meetings throughout the country, assuring organisers there would be big crowds there to see him. Alan Paterson super-jumper had arrived.

Of course, long before that day at the Ibrox stadium they had known at Victoria Park they had a young athlete destined for stardom. And even before that, when he was a younger lad, sports masters had realised his sporting prowess when he was a pupil at Hutcheson's Grammar School. Sport played a big part in the school's character-building curriculum and Alan Paterson had been one of their best-remembered all-round sports champions. He had made it to their rugby 1st XV where he made his mark as being unbeatable in the lineouts, which was understandable for someone of his height and who was to eventually measure 6ft 6¾in. At cricket he was in the 1st XI as an outstanding fast bowler, even being selected to play for West of Scotland Schools against the touring West Indies cricket team captained by the legendary Sir Larry Constantine, taking four wickets in the match. And when he got into his stride in the school sports, no one could match him in the jumps and it was usually a pair of heels they saw from him in the track events.

Old classmate Allan Heath remembers a rather special story of those school events which tells a lot about this man Paterson. It was in the final years of the Second World War and they were in the last stages of the events which decided who would be the school sports champion. Heath and Paterson had been tying throughout the varied contest and then, in one of the track events, Paterson had dramatically got ahead by virtue of his main rival Heath being delayed by a false start. However, when he realised it was because of that fault he was in the lead and considering it to be an unfair advantage, he was to pull back in the following running event allowing Allan Heath to go ahead and win, thus finishing the contest with equal points. This meant the two of them were named as the school's joint sports champions.

Sport was to play a big factor in Alan Paterson's formative years, supplementing his hectic school programme of events by joining the Victoria Park Athletic Club.

This well-known sports club had been going since 1930, formed by a group of young athletic breakaways from the YMCA who wanted a purely sports-minded club. They took their name from the local park in the west of the city where they had often met and trained, although their regular training venue came to be that of the nearby Scotstoun showground. And in the years to come after their foundation, Victoria Park AC was to become one of Scotland best-known and celebrated athletic clubs, providing the British sports scene with a number of outstanding field and track champions, and littering the record books with their achievements.

Alan Paterson was living in Brownlie Street, adjacent to Hampden Park, at the time, and every Tuesday and Thursday night together with friend Harry Ewing they would take the number five bus right across the city to Scotstoun in order to train with the club. There were just two factors which were responsible for Victoria Park being the excellent club that it was – superb coaching and enthusiasm. And absolutely nothing else. After a hard day at work or college, members would find their way to that part of Scotstoun by bus and tramcar from the furthest points of the city, and many came from places even further than that, where they would meet the rest of the club athletes . . . in a corner under the stand at the showground. Although improvements were to be made over the years, Harry Ewing remembers it at the time as being merely a space under the visible structure of the stand and little else. No lockers. No baths. No toilets. Just a place to leave your clothes and get into the basics of athletic gear as they were then, the cotton vest and briefs, and then you got on with it, whether it be running, hurdling, jumping, throwing or leaping. Even the ground wasn't exclusively theirs on training nights, the Garscube Harriers also making use of it on the same nights for their workouts, each club using opposite ends of the arena. Though there was the advantage of that giving them an opportunity to watch how some of their principal rivals were doing, the usual practice of the athlete eager to know who was fit, who wasn't. When they were finished training, it was back to that spot under the stand for a rub-down with a towel and another long ride on the bus to the other side of the city before getting a decent wash at home. But there were never any complaints about that for that was the way it was if you were a sportsman then.

The ones who trained right through the winter, mainly the runners, would boast, however, that they had the best changing facilities. They used the local 'steamie' (public wash-house laundry) as their changing-rooms after the women washers had gone home. And why they boasted it was the best was because they could leave their clothes in the warming drawers where laundry was normally dried and when they returned from their training miles their gear was cosily heated and welcomely waiting.

These eager and enthusiastic amateur athletes were the purest of sportsmen. They participated in training as they did in events, with a zeal and zest that could, for instance, have them take part in something like a marathon, a serious marathon that is, where they ran their damnedest all the way, and if they won and were presented with the silver cup which was the lone and only prize, they would feel like the king of all the castles. And, in a way, they really were.

'We seemed to be competing, in one way or another, quite a lot,' said Harry Ewing. 'There were the two regular nights' training at Scotstoun and at weekends there was always a competition of some kind, whether it be inter-club or perhaps a Highland games or other event. Then there were the big sports events in Glasgow, such as the Police Sports and the Rangers Sports days. They really used to pack the crowds in because they attracted the best stars in the world.'

There was always a special appeal at these big sport carnivals in the high vaults and the various jumps. Perhaps it was the spectacle of the single contestant displaying some degree of their challenging gravity, whether it be the length of time they could stay airborne in order to cover the longest distance in a jump or, with the aid of a pole, to get right up into the heights, so high there was a real danger of injury on landing. The high jump had its own appeal to crowds, maybe with it being the simplest and purest form of defying gravity, and the chance to see all the new and varied styles of competitors in order to achieve better results.

Jumping as a sports art form has undergone all forms of changes and experimentation in its long history. They were jumping upwards long before they were kicking the soccer ball around, in an organised fashion that is. Even before Rangers and Celtic were established we had our first Scottish high jump champion. He was a Fettes schoolboy called William Finlay Methuen and after having high jumped his way to a college record of 5ft 5¼in, he went on to add another three-quarters of an inch to that height, making him the Scottish champ. Another Fettes boy, John Whitehill Parsons, jumped 5ft 11in at the Edinburgh University sports before becoming the first Scot to top the magic 6ft in 1883, something equivalent to breaking the four-minute mile barrier, although that height had first been reached in the UK by Englishman Marshall Brooks some seven years earlier.

Those early sportsmen concentrated on just one method of jumping heights. Early drawings of them show them leaping at the bar straight on, clearing the required height by simply tucking up their legs at the knees. In order to reach a reasonable elevation, their run towards the point where they would take off would be similar to the usual distance taken by contestants in the long or triple jump. Then, when they attained their maximum sprint speed, up they would go with those tucked-up legs hoping for the best. When they eventually arrived back on the ground again, the point of take-off to landing would be nearly 20 feet; a bit like doing a long jump, only with height.

There are eighteenth-century drawings of men in kilts doing it that fashion at Highland games, the artists, obviously in the interests of propriety, sketching the kilts worn by those early leaping athletes neatly in place at the knees of their folded legs. In fact, the state of the competitors' kilts in such performances would have answered, in part or in full, that perennially hackneyed question about Scotsmen and their kilts.

From those early knees-up-Mother-Brown upward leaps, the art of the high jump went through a variety of progressions over the years as participants experimented with how they could reach greater heights. New methods and techniques evolved, these being given a variety of names such as the scissors, the straddle, the western roll and the eastern cut-off, each achieving better performances for the high-aiming athletes.

Alan Paterson, like most young jumpers, would have started with the simple scissors form of jumping, that is as its title implies, one leg going over the bar first followed rapidly in a scissors action by the second. But it had its limits and when the western roll was created by young American college athletes in California – hence the western part of the title – it quickly spread across the Atlantic, Paterson being the first Scot to develop and master the technique.

The western roll was a variation of the one called the eastern cut-off – again an American college creation, this time from the Atlantic side of the States. In the eastern jump the contestant would make his thrust for the bar from his outside foot, the western from his inside foot. No matter how you jumped, however, those who took part in the sport all ended up back on earth in the same fashion, that being with an almighty thump. Even in the immediate post-war era, sports grounds were composed of the basic materials: turf and ash and, when required, sandpits for landing areas. Compare that with today's track and contest areas which can be composed of a whole range of synthetic and very competitor-friendly materials such as Tartan, Olymprene, Rubkor, Chevron 440, Resisport and Mondo. Vaulters have fibreglass poles which can almost bend double with a recoil which has the visual effect of almost rocket-launching the competitor into near space. And high jumpers, like those vaulters, can go ever upwards in any fashion they wish, safe in the knowledge those deep foam landing beds will save them from any injuries no matter how they fall.

All the new high-jump styles in Paterson's day were designed with the main factor being to give the participant a safe landing. With no cushioning on the other side of that high bar, the best that was on offer for the men whose sport involved the heights was coming down on the soft bed of sand. In big international events, they would make these bunkers with the finest of soft sand and as deep as possible. Opposed to that, in many of the lesser meetings the material in those pits could be coarse and sodden, often flattened so solid they were as inviting for the tumbling athlete as a bed of concrete.

In many of his early jumps, Alan Paterson, like other competitors, merely clattered down onto a grass pitch. In fact, it was because of his achievements in the sport that Glasgow Corporation was to dip into their funds to help the Victoria Park club build a new sandpit for the jumpers. They gave them £25.

As a result of those hard falls, Paterson, like the others who participated in similar field events, had to endure the consequences of falling from on high to inappropriate surfaces. It was something of an occupational hazard with them to be constantly being treated for various degrees of knocks, bruises, scrapes, twists and pains. Johanna, Alan's younger sister, remembers those injuries. 'It seemed he was always suffering from the results of his jumps, always being bruised or hurting his fingers when he landed. Dad, who was his trainer, used to jibe him about his complaining. But he really did suffer a lot of knocks and sprains.'

It seemed to be one top performance after another for Alan Paterson after breaking the long-standing Scottish record that wet day in 1946 at Lennoxtown. That same season he was to go up to 6ft 2½in, then 6ft 3in and then at a major meet in Belfast he shattered the British record of 6ft 5in by topping it by three-quarters of an inch and putting him in the superstar status of the sport with a series of leaps at around the six-and-a-half-feet mark. He came second in the European Championships in Oslo with a leap of 6ft 5⅛in. And for the next three years he was to perform a variety of spectacular jumps, appearing at the world's best sports gatherings from Brussels to Paris to London to New Zealand to Scandinavia.

While it had been a career adorned with so many championships, so many records, it had also been one marked with periods of great disappointment when he would fail to reach the heights not only expected of him, but which were well within his ability of achieving. At the London Olympic Games, for instance, when he could finish only equal seventh, his best jump was almost four inches below what he had jumped at pre-Olympic meetings. The same was to happen at other major events. Despite the fact that for much of his athletic career he had by his side the reassuring presence of his father, acting as his coach just like he had done all those years ago when out for walks in the park, it was his nerves which were so often to get the better of him. Harry Ewing remembers how badly they could affect him on the day of a major competition. 'He would often come to our house for me, but he couldn't sit down, just pacing up and down all the time. We would say to him, "Take a seat and relax, Alan," but he always replied that he couldn't because of his nerves working the way they did.'

Perhaps it was those same nerves working on him which made some classmates remember Paterson as being somewhat aloof with them, but they nevertheless would be in awe of him at their school's sports field at Auldhouse when he would be at practice and going over heights they never imagined anyone could attempt, let alone clear. And just as enthralled as those pupils with those schoolboy athletic performances was their rector, Tod Ritchie, who would regularly visit their playing fields with special words of encouragement for the gangly youth who seemed destined for so much.

But behind the amazing success story, that of Alan Sinclair Paterson as a champion British athlete competing on the world stage, there was another story. A story far removed from that of the man they said had 'brought respectability' to the standards of his sport. A story that says much about the bigotry which existed in the Glasgow of the period when he was the famous young champion that he was. A story of how a family became involved in that religious strife which manifested itself so much more in that era of half a century ago. A story which was to cause them untold heartache and was to be a principal factor in the champion becoming an exile from his native country. The background of the Paterson family helps in an appreciation of how the impact of this rather sad event in their lives was to affect them.

Alan Sinclair Paterson was the first child of William Sinclair Paterson and his wife Mary. He was born on 4 June 1928, when they lived in McKinlay Street, a row of old tenement buildings at the southernmost part of the Gorbals suburb. His dad, like so many young men of his day in the early part of the century, had lied about his age in order to join the army and at 16 years of age left his home town of Perth to serve with the Scots Guards in France where he remained in service for four years, being wounded several times. On demobilisation he joined the Glasgow police and worked as a turnkey in the cells at the Central police station in St Andrew's Square, not far from Glasgow Cross.

Mum, whose family had come from Bonnybridge and whose maiden name was Fraser, was a uniformed district nurse, the women who, because of that uniform, were known as the Green Ladies. Like the upright and principled Protestant family they were, they fully subscribed to the ethic that the fruits of hard work should be invested in the betterment of their young family who should live the good Christian life and be provided with the best education that could be found for them.

Their philosophy was to pay dividends, their joint earnings giving them the opportunity to improve the family circumstances before the young Alan, then three years old, was joined by a sister whom they named Johanna. They had been able to improve their living conditions by moving to a better tenement house in Cathcart Road, Govanhill, the suburb immediately south of the Gorbals, and from there another upmarket move to a house in King's Park and on from there to yet another, this time an apartment flat in a handsome red sandstone building in Brownlie Street, Mount Florida.

Schooling came very much into the equation of the hard-working William and Mary Paterson's approach to life and they were to sacrifice what savings they had to pay for both Alan and Johanna to become pupils at a private school, choosing Hutcheson's Grammar, the boys' school at the time being in Crown Street, Gorbals, the girls' school in Crosshill. Hutcheson's, founded in 1641 by two philanthropic merchant brothers, was not only one of Scotland's oldest schools but also one of its most academically prestigious.

They were happy years for William and Mary Paterson seeing the endeavours of their hard work and planning bringing its rewards, their two children happily responding to their new schools and surroundings. Even as a young lad, Alan looked like he would even outgrow the height of his six-foot-plus father, that same height giving him the initial urge for jumping, a pastime he not only enjoyed but at which he showed genuine latent talent.

'We used to go lots of walks together with dad in the nearby Linn Park,' remembers sister Johanna, who was to go on to be a distinguished singer with some of Britain's most famous opera companies before becoming a professor of music. 'I remember dad always carrying with him a long piece of string and at various places in the park he would tie one end to a tree and I would have to hold the other end and was always told to pull it hard so that it would be as straight as possible. And when it was taut enough, dad would then give Alan instructions on how to jump. He saw he was keen on jumping so tried to help him all he could. Even when he was quite young and we were living in King's Park he always seemed to be jumping and was always telling me how good he was at it. I remember him once when he had broken his arm in a fall and had just returned from hospital with it in a sling and went straight out to play and mum being horrified to see him jump over garden walls and over the gate to the house.'

But there was to be another side to those happy and carefree days of adolescence, the whole world before them. Alan was a young man of 23 years of age at the pinnacle of his athletic career, having studied hard at night classes to pass the stiff qualification exams to be a chartered accountant. The future couldn't have looked brighter or better. It was about then that he met and fell in love with a girl called Mary, the same name as his mother. Sadly, it was to be the only aspect of his girlfriend's life and background which coincided with that of his mother. For the Patersons were a Protestant family, and Alan's girl, Mary Etherson, was a Roman Catholic. When his mother discovered this, it was, as Johanna remembers, 'everything you can think of in a situation like that in those days', meaning that her parents were of a mould of Protestants more prolific in that era of half a century ago than it would thankfully appear they are today. In other words, they wished to have nothing to do with Roman Catholics.

The parents of Alan and Johanna Paterson were expressing a form of bigotry which was not an unusual one of the times, more than likely the prevailing attitude. It was none of your oafish oathings that you could hear at the football grounds. None of your ranting and raving against those of that other religion. None of your apoplectic Ballymena preacher cants. Merely a quiet and simple refusal of a Protestant family to having a Catholic as part of their family structure. But bigotry was by no means the exclusive practice of the Protestant. It was also exercised by those who were of that other religion, although they would express it in a much more insidious fashion, welcoming those who were not of their faith to their family, making them feel they were instantly one of them. But then, when the marriage would be discussed, there would be a determined and resolved insistence that they really did become one of them, and that when there were children they would most certainly be of their ways and beliefs. Intolerance has many faces.

Johanna recalls those disruptive days when the matter came to a head. 'My mother made an issue out of it and she eventually walked out of the family home because of it. It was at about the same time as I was leaving myself for London where I had secured a place in the Carl Rosa Opera Company. Mum used that as an excuse and left a letter for father telling him she would not live in the same house as him, meaning Alan, being "with that woman".'

The objections of his parents, but mainly his mother, now returned home, were to make no difference to Alan Paterson's love for his girlfriend Mary. He told his mother and father that nothing could or would change his attitude, nor would it prevent him from marrying the girl he loved, no matter what strife and problems it might cause in the family.

'So Alan left home,' Johanna went on, 'and father had the really rotten task of helping him pack and find a bedsit, mother being horrified at him moving out. And because of all this, Alan decided there was little hope of him having a happy life in Scotland, so he decided to emigrate to Canada. Because of my singing career I had gone to London abut this time and met Alan at Waterloo on his way by train to Southampton for the ship to Canada. And I'll never forget being there on that station platform waving him off and thinking how awful it all was ... how stupid for all this to be happening just because he was in love with a Roman Catholic.'

Some time after he had settled in Canada, Alan Paterson was received into the Catholic Church in a service conducted by the Bishop of Montreal and where he was also to marry Mary. 'It was in the realms of shock-horror for our parents,' Johanna recalled. 'I had a very good friend, an RC priest called Father O'Connell who we met through Alan jumping. He came to call to the house and our folks turned him away. It was awful. They just refused to acknowledge the marriage, even rejecting a suggestion by the parents of his wife Mary that it might be nice to meet. But father thought that not proper and they would have nothing to do with them. Nor would they even write to Alan.'

Alan and his sister Johanna, by now a successful mezzo in London opera circles, kept in regular contact, however, both of them to happily witness a softening of attitude by their father and mother. Time had been the kind, and only, friend of their parents in helping them to become a united and happy family once more. A son had been born to Alan and Mary and they named him William, after his grandfather. By this time Alan's father had retired from the police and he was to take the lead in restoring family relations by declaring that the episode which had brought so much strife to them had been ridiculous. Mother too then softened and letters were exchanged with the son they hadn't contacted for years.

Three years later Alan and his family visited Scotland bringing their little son with them and stayed together with his parents, the dreadful events of the past over and obviously forgotten. Years later the father was to confess to his daughter Johanna that he considered Alan's wife Mary a remarkable girl for what she had come through with them and that he would have hated it had anyone treated his own daughter in such a way.

His migration to Canada was to bring something of a premature end to the athletic career of high-jumper Alan Paterson. Because of the severe winters, he found it even more difficult to train for field events and also there was a career to think about. For all his years as a champion amateur athlete and one of the leading names to be invited to events all over the world, all there was to show for it was a roomful of silver cups, shields and enough china teasets and cutlery boxes to fill a dozen display cabinets, and nothing else. Even getting to some of those events was a hassle to these top amateur sportsmen, often having to fund some of their own expenses to do so. It had happened to Paterson more than once, like the time he was one of the likely medal contenders in the team to represent his country at the Empire Games in Auckland, New Zealand. They were to travel down under by ship, which obviously involved considerable time off work and because of that his accountant boss refused him leave. But he did make it to the games, thanks to the generosity of the Glasgow cinema magnate Sir A.B. King who paid for his return fare by air in order to compete. Paterson got through to the final of the high jump, finishing second at 6ft 5in to the Australian and Olympic champion J.A. Winter.

In 1952, by this time settled in Canada, he was chosen to represent Britain in the Olympic Games at Helsinki. However, he was badly out of form, not having competed seriously for some time and was eliminated in the early stages of the contest. That was his last appearance in any serious jumping event and thereafter he was to concentrate on his life as a chartered accountant.

But just as he had been on the sports field, Alan Paterson was to become a high-flyer in business, becoming a stockbroker and financial analyst and working as a troubleshooter for some of the world's top companies. That work was to take him and his family to live in Australia, then to London before returning to Canada, where he was to spend his latter years. Sadly, at the age of 59, he was to suffer a massive stroke from which he was never to fully recover and he died in Toronto in May 1999.

It was to be 22 years before Alan Paterson's British high jump record was beaten and, remarkably, it was to be by another Victoria Park club athlete, Crawford William Fairbrother, whose straddle technique jump took him to 6ft 8in (2.03 metres). The American Charles Dumas then broke the seven-foot barrier (2.134 metres) using the same technique.

Thereafter, the sport was to be revolutionised by a young American engineering student from Oregon called Dick Fosbury. He was to shock the sports world by making his run in the shape of the letter 'J' then leaping with his back to the bar, his shoulders going over first before landing on a deep bed of foam. Confounded sports officials were to check and recheck whether this form of jumping was legal and were to wrangle for ages over the acceptance of the style. It was eventually recognised, however, and the high jump has never been the same since, Fosbury and his radical new approach going on to shatter all records, becoming the Olympic champion in Mexico when he cleared a sensational 7ft 3in (2.24 metres).

The Fosbury Flop, as the jump was to be known, is now the universally accepted method of high jumping and in the final months of the old millennium the Scottish record stood at 7ft 6in (2.31 metres), the British record at just over 7ft 9in (2.38 metres) and the world record an incredible eight feet and almost one inch (2.45 metres). But on the way to these amazing heights, the Glasgow man Alan Paterson most certainly made his mark.

Following his death in May 1999, the ashes of Alan Paterson were kept by his family at their home near Toronto, in Canada. Exactly a year later, his widow Mary flew to Scotland and, on a glorious spring day by the banks of Loch Lomond, at a private commemorative service attended only by his family and relatives, his ashes were scattered on the site that had meant so much to him.

Selected Bibliography

Association Football and the Men Who Made It. Alfred Gibson and William Pickford (Ballantyne, Hanson and Co.; Caxton Publishing Co.).

Athletes in Action. Howard Payne (Pelham Books).

The Black 'n' White Alphabet: A Complete Who's Who of Newcastle United FC. Paul Joannou (Polar Publishing).

Edge Up: Memoirs of a Glasgow Street. John Prendergast (Prendergast Publications).

Encyclopedia of Boxing. Gilbert Odd (Hamlyn).

The Fight Game in Scotland. Brian Donald (Mainstream Publishing).

Files of: the *Daily Record/Sunday Mail*; *Glagow Herald*; *Evening Times*; *Scottish Daily Express*; *Scottish Catholic Observer*; Scottish Theatre Archives BBC scripts; *Thomson's Weekly*, Newcastle.

First for Boys: The Story of the Boys' Brigade. Donald M. McFarlan (Collins).

Flight for the Führer. Peter Padfield (Weidenfield and Nicolson).

Get Me Dowdall. Lawrence Dowdall with Alasdair Marshall (Paul Harris Publications).

Glasgow 1858. John F. McCaffrey (University of Glasgow Press).

Glasgow's Giants: 100 Years of the Old Firm. Bill Murray (Mainstream Publishing).

The Glasgow Battalion of the Boys' Brigade 1883–1983. J. Berend Shaw (Saint Andrew Press).

Heroes and Hardmen. Harry Mullan (Stanley Paul).

High Jump. Frank W. Dick (King & Jarrett).

History of Queen's Park Football Club. Richard Robinson (Hay Nisbet and Co.).

Ireland: A History. Robert Kee (Weidenfeld and Nicolson).

The Irish in the West of Scotland, 1797–1848. Martin J. Mitchell (John Donald Publishers).

I Saw Stars. R.E. Kingsley (Kemsley House).

Man of the Century, the Life and Times of Pope John Paul II. Jonathan Kwitny (Little, Brown and Co.).

Motive for a Mission. James Douglas Hamilton (Macmillan).

No Pope of Rome: Militant Protestantism in Modern Scotland. Steve Bruce (Mainstream Publishing).

The Old Firm. Bill Murray (John Donald Publishers).

On My Wavelength. Howard M. Lockhart (Impulse Books).

Old Maryhill. Guthrie Hutton (Richard Stenlake).

The People's History of Glasgow. John K. McDowell (S.R. Publishers Ltd).

Rural Eaglesham. Christina Robertson Brown (William Maclellan).

Scottish Athletics 1883–1983. John W. Keddie (SAAA).

Such Bad Company. George Forbes and Paddy Meeham (Paul Harris Publications).

Sure & Stedfast: A History of the Boys' Brigade, 1883–1983. John Springhall, Brian Fraser, Michael Hoare (Collins).

A Tale of Two Murders. Hugh Thomas (Hodder and Stoughton).

United: The First 100 Years. Paul Joannou (Polar Publishing).

The World of Damon Runyon. Tom Clark (Harper and Row).